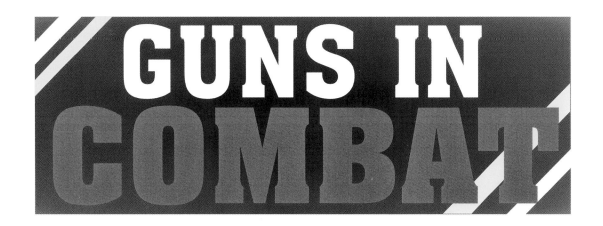

Editor: David Donald

CHARTWELL
BOOKS, INC.

Published by
CHARTWELL BOOKS, INC.
A Division of BOOK SALES, INC.
114 Northfield Avenue
Edison, New Jersey 08837

739.74
G 976

Copyright © 1998 Aerospace Publishing Ltd
Copyright © 1998 Marshall Cavendish

Some of this material has previously appeared in the
Marshall Cavendish partwork 'In Combat'.

ISBN: 0-7858-0844-2

Editorial and design by
Brown Packaging Books Ltd
Bradley's Close
74–77 White Lion Street
London N1 9PF

Printed in The Czech Republic
60280

Contents

Armalite AR-18: 'The Widowmaker'

The AR-18 is a cheap and sleazy rifle. Intended as a low-cost alternative weapon for countries that could not afford the latest Western rifles, it never achieved commercial success, but it has won a nasty reputation as a terrorist weapon, particularly in the hands of the Provisional IRA. Despite its pressed steel receiver and spot welds, it is a highly effective 5.56-mm rifle. The gun can be broken down for concealment without ruining the zeroing, so it can be pulled out of hiding and used immediately and accurately.

The AR-18 was another product of the tangled history of the Armalite company and its various partners. The full story of their employment of Eugene Stoner as designer, and the series of rifles and shotguns that they developed between 1954 and 1964, would fill many pages and be entirely confusing. The most famous gun to appear from this partnership was, of

The Armalite family. Left: the AR-10 is a 7.62-mm rotary bolt and gas-tube operated design. Next, the AR-15 is a scaled-down version of the AR-10 that became the popular M16. Unlike the AR-10 and 15, the AR-18 (second from right) was gas-piston operated, like most assault rifles. On the right is the AR-18S.

The AR-18 and AR-18S soon gained a grizzly reputation in the hands of terrorists as a very effective weapon for urban guerrilla operations. Its popularity as an assassination weapon earned the rifle the nickname 'the widowmaker' in Northern Ireland.

Inside the AR-18

The AR-18 was doomed simply because of economic and political factors, which is unfortunate as the weapon has a good deal going for it as an assault rifle – clearly demonstrated by the fact that many of its design elements were incorporated into the SA80 weapons system.

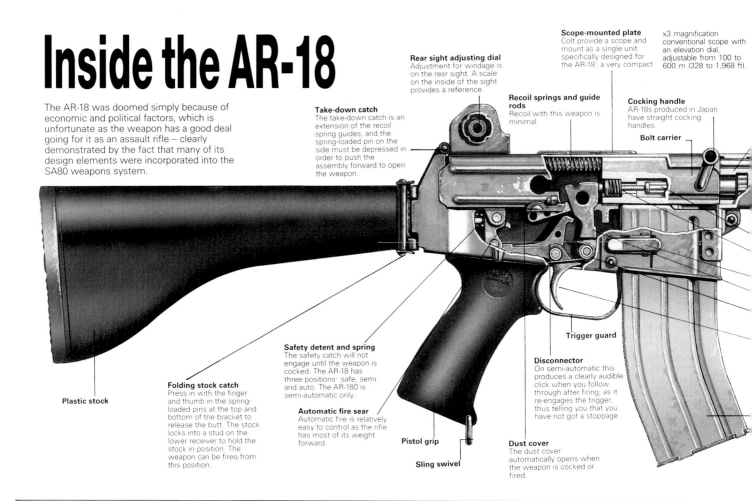

Rear sight adjusting dial
Adjustment for windage is on the rear sight. A scale on the inside of the sight provides a reference.

Scope-mounted plate
Colt provide a scope and mount as a single unit specifically designed for the AR-18: a very compact

x3 magnification conventional scope with an elevation dial, adjustable from 100 to 600 m (328 to 1,968 ft).

Take-down catch
The take-down catch is an extension of the recoil spring guides, and the spring-loaded pin on the side must be depressed in order to push the assembly forward to open the weapon.

Recoil springs and guide rods
Recoil with this weapon is minimal.

Cocking handle
AR-18s produced in Japan have straight cocking handles.

Bolt carrier

Safety detent and spring
The safety catch will not engage until the weapon is cocked. The AR-18 has three positions: safe, semi and auto. The AR-180 is semi-automatic only.

Folding stock catch
Press in with the finger and thumb in the spring-loaded pins at the top and bottom of the bracket to release the butt. The stock locks into a stud on the lower receiver to hold the stock in position. The weapon can be fired from this position.

Plastic stock

Automatic fire sear
Automatic fire is relatively easy to control as the rifle has most of its weight forward.

Pistol grip

Sling swivel

Trigger guard

Disconnector
On semi-automatic this produces a clearly audible click when you follow through after firing, as it re-engages the trigger, thus telling you that you have not got a stoppage.

Dust cover
The dust cover automatically opens when the weapon is cocked or fired.

Stripping the AR-18

1 Press in on the magazine catch and bin the magazine. Note the takedown catch located to the rear of the rear sight assembly.

2 Grasp the peculiar-shaped cocking handle on the right-hand side of the weapon and rack it back firmly with the left hand. Eyeball the chamber to make sure it is clear.

3 Leave the weapon cocked and push in the pin protruding from the take-down catch then push it forward. This releases the upper receiver from the lower receiver, which pivots on the forward body locking pin.

5 When you pull the cocking handle out, this releases the bolt and bolt carrier from the receiver and they can be drawn out backwards. The bolt can be separated from the bolt carrier, but this is not recommended in the field as the parts are small enough to be easily lost.

6 Withdrawing the recoil springs and guides at 3 automatically releases the fore-end, the top part of which lifts off, up and to the rear, to reveal the gas parts. The gas parts are made up of a three-piece piston rod and the spring and a fixed gas block.

7 Pull back on the piston rod, compressing the spring, and remove the middle piece of the piston rod. This will allow you to remove the rest of the piston forwards. This is a bit fiddly and you need to move the piston rod slightly to one side to release the connecting piece.

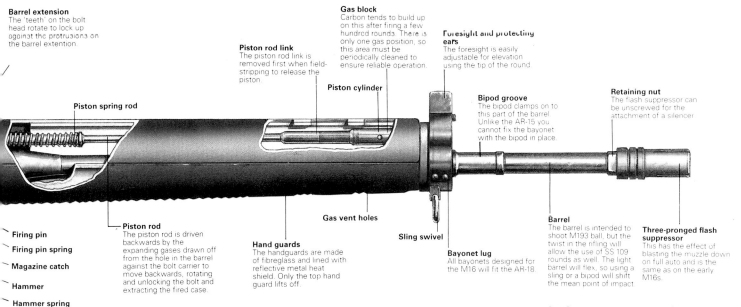

Barrel extension
The 'teeth' on the bolt head rotate to lock up against the protrusions on the barrel extention.

Piston rod link
The piston rod link is removed first when field-stripping to release the piston.

Gas block
Carbon tends to build up on this after firing a few hundred rounds. There is only one gas position, so this area must be periodically cleaned to ensure reliable operation.

Foresight and protecting ears
The foresight is easily adjustable for elevation using the tip of the round.

Piston cylinder

Bipod groove
The bipod clamps on to this part of the barrel. Unlike the AR-15 you cannot fix the bayonet with the bipod in place.

Retaining nut
The flash suppressor can be unscrewed for the attachment of a silencer.

Piston spring rod

Firing pin

Firing pin spring

Magazine catch

Hammer

Hammer spring

Trigger
Trigger pull is single stage and was a little heavy at 4 kg (8.8 lb) on the test weapon.

30-round magazine
20- and 40-round magazines are also available, but those manufactured for the M16 will need a slit cut in them for the AR-18 magazine catch.

Piston rod
The piston rod is driven backwards by the expanding gases drawn off from the hole in the barrel against the bolt carrier to move backwards, rotating and unlocking the bolt and extracting the fired case.

Hand guards
The handguards are made of fibreglass and lined with reflective metal heat shield. Only the top hand guard lifts off.

Gas vent holes

Sling swivel

Bayonet lug
All bayonets designed for the M16 will fit the AR-18.

Barrel
The barrel is intended to shoot M193 ball, but the twist in the rifling will allow the use of SS 109 rounds as well. The light barrel will flex, so using a sling or a bipod will shift the mean point of impact.

Three-pronged flash suppressor
This has the effect of blasting the muzzle down on full auto and is the same as on the early M16s.

4 Pull the recoil springs and guides to the rear and remove them. Then slide the bolt and bolt carrier back in the receiver until the cocking handle matches the hole large enough for you to remove it in the receiver.

9 The weapon fully stripped. Note the number of parts in the bolt and bolt carrier group; this is very similar to the SA80. Unlike the SLR, both foresight and rearsight are on the same piece of the weapon so the weapon can be broken down and reassembled without affecting the zero.

8 Slide the remaining part off the gas block backwards. This completes the field strip, although the weapon can be broken down further by pushing out the body locking pin to separate upper and lower receiver. The bolt can be stripped by pressing in on the back of the firing pin and tapping out the pin that holds the bolt in the bolt carrier.

course, the AR-15, which became the M16 rifle. But there are an awful lot of people who will tell you that the Armalite AR-18 was an even better weapon, and they still dream of the day somebody will put it into mass production.

In fact, the AR-18 was not a Stoner design, although it uses ideas from most of the earlier Armalite rifles. After the AR-15 had been accepted into military service and Armalite had split away from the Fairchild Engine & Aircraft Corporation, Stoner left to become a consultant to Colt. In 1959 Armalite decided that there was still a demand for a 7.62-mm rifle and they developed the AR-16, based on a much earlier design known as the AR-10.

This had failed to make much of an impression, largely due to problems with manufacturers. The object was to make a rifle that was cheap and easy to manufacture, so that it could be licensed to countries that did not have advanced industrial technology. No expensive machine tools were re-

quired. The AR-16 was simple enough to be made on lathes and milling machines.

Lightening the load

By the time the wrinkles were out of the AR-16, it was obvious that the 7.62-mm cartridge would be superseded by the emerging 5.56-mm round, and in 1963 the AR-16 was shelved in favour of a new model, the AR-18. (The AR-17, if you're interested, was a lightweight automatic shotgun that had a very brief career.) The AR-18 was basically the AR-16 scaled-down for the smaller cartridge, so it was easy to manufacture some prototypes and send 10 of them for testing to the US Army, which at that time was involved in a programme known as SAWS (Squad Automatic Weapon System).

Tests took place in 1964 and the US Army reported that the rifle had military potential, although it didn't fit its SAWS requirement. Armalite then made a few more rifles and began demonstrating them around the world, particularly in countries that might be attracted by the inexpensive manufacturing aspect of the design.

Eventually Armalite licensed production to the Howa Machinery Company of Shinkawacho, Japan, in 1967, and they began producing the military AR-18 and the civilian (semi-automatic only) AR-180 version. This didn't last long, as the Japanese government, worried by the nearness of the Vietnam War and not wishing to get involved in any way, soon forbade any traffic in arms with 'belligerent countries'. Since the USA, the prime market, was technically a belligerent in Vietnam, that was that. Howa stopped manufacture and the AR-18 went into limbo.

In 1975 it reappeared when the Sterling Armaments Company of Dagenham, famous for the Sterling submachine gun, took out a manufacturing licence and began making AR-18s and AR-180s. But this venture failed to prosper, and in 1983 Sterling sold the tooling to an unidentified foreign country. Since then nothing more has been heard of the AR-18.

So if it was as good as the enthusiasts say, why didn't it sell like hot cakes? Simple economics. Most of the countries who wanted a 5.56-mm rifle and who might have been attracted by the simple manufacture of the AR-18 were even more impressed by the price quoted for the AR-15. Colt now had that rifle in mass production and was turning them out by the tens of thousands. If the price of a complete AR-15 was a little difficult for a country to meet, it was possible to construct an assembly plant and buy the difficult bits from Colt, add a few simple things like screws, and assemble them in the country at an even lower price.

Either of these prospects was more attractive than the thought of having

to build factories, buy tools and train a workforce, no matter how simple the rifle might be. And that is why you see plenty of AR-15s and M16s but very few AR-18s or AR-180s.

How it works

The AR-18 is a gas-operated weapon, using a rotating bolt very similar to that used on the M16. The principal difference is that the AR-18 uses a conventional gas piston arrangement, though it has a slight difference: the 'cylinder' is a hollow spigot, and the 'piston' wraps around it and is blown backwards, off the spigot, by the gas pressure. The piston is a short-stroke design, which gives the bolt carrier a quick blow, sufficient to start it moving backwards.

The carrier moves back on two steel rods, compressing two return springs, and as it moves, so a cam track rotates the bolt and unlocks it. The carrier and bolt then go back, extracting the spent case, and the springs drive the assembly back again to chamber a

In addition to the protected post and aperture sights, the rifle is supplied with a scope base welded onto the top of the receiver. A quick detachable scope made by Colt or more powerful civilian scopes can be slotted on with no appreciable effect on the zero.

fresh round. The hammer is cocked during the bolt carrier movement, so that as soon as the carrier completes its forward stroke the bolt is locked and the rifle is ready to fire again.

The receiver is of pressed steel, welded together, and most of the construction is similar – pressings, pinnings, spot welds. All the furniture is plastic, but for all that the rifle feels solid and reliable, and certainly shoots well enough. The standard barrel is 464 mm (18 in) long, and the rifle is 940 mm (37 in) long with folding butt extended; with the butt folded the length is 736 mm (29 in). The standard magazine holds 20 rounds, though 30- and 40-round magazines were developed. The standard rear sight is a two-position flip aperture, for 200 and 400 m (656 and 1,312 ft), though the rear sight on civilian AR-180s actually has an adjustable aperture. There was also a compact 3× telescope sight made for the rifle, though few were sold.

A short version, the AR-18S, was developed by Armalite and a few were made by Sterling, though it does not appear to have been made in any quantity. This used the same basic mechanism but had a 257-mm barrel and a length of 765 mm (30 in) with the butt extended. The handguard was fitted with a forward pistol grip so that the rifle could be held like a submachine gun and, like the parent rifle, it had a full-auto rate of fire of 800 rounds per minute. From what few accounts there are, the AR-18S appears to have been remarkably accurate for such a short-barrelled weapon, and it had a respectable punch.

When the last round is fired the bolt locks open as shown. There is no bolt release, so after replacing the empty with a fresh mag pull back on the cocking handle to release the bolt, which will then go forward and chamber the first round ready to go.

The Beretta M92: World Beater

The Beretta 92-F beat an impressive range of rival guns in the extensive tests conducted by the US Army in the early 1980s. Accurate, reliable and with the latest safety devices to prevent accidental firing, it is a first-class weapon.

One of the more popular 'souvenirs' acquired by Allied soldiers during World War II was the Italian army's 9-mm Beretta automatic pistol, though there were many disappointed soldiers who discovered that the 9-mm cartridge which it used was the 9-mm Short and not the universal 9-mm Parabellum. The Beretta Company claims to be the oldest existing gun manufacturer in the world, but its name only came to prominence outside the specialist gun world when, in 1985, it won the contract to provide the US Army with a new pistol.

9-mm Model 34

Beretta went into the pistol business in 1915, and then only under the pressure of war; it developed a small blowback automatic in 7.65-mm calibre which was subsequently redesigned and refined to reach its zenith in the 9-mm Model 34, the wartime souvenir gun. In post-war years the Italian army decided it needed a heavier weapon, something with a locked breech which could fire the 9-mm Parabellum cartridge, and in the early 1950s Beretta duly produced the Model 951.

The Beretta 92 family of modern pistols follows on from the Model 34, which was a prized souvenir during World War II. After the war, Beretta promptly developed a new weapon chambered for 9-mm Parabellum.

Inside the Beretta 92

Resplendent in its sleek, all-black finish, the Beretta 92-F is no mere 'designer' handgun. Its large magazine capacity and rugged construction make it one of the most commercially successful pistols in recent years.

One of the most recognisable family features of Beretta pistols has always been the cutaway slide top; instead of the slide completely covering the barrel, its upper surface was cut away from just ahead of the breech block to just behind the foresight. This gave a wide and unobstructed ejection slot, but it was impossible to combine this characteristic slide shape with a locked breech dependent upon engagement between slide top and barrel as in, for example, the Colt or Browning military automatics. So for its new military Model 951 Beretta had to come up with a different method of locking the breech.

Locking breech

The system it chose is very similar to that pioneered by the Walther P38: a separate locking block beneath the barrel which is cammed into engagement with the slide as the action closes. This is more than adequately strong for the cartridge, and the gun also showed some other interesting features such as a mechanical hold-open after the last shot had been fired and a push-through cross-bolt safety catch in the frame. Many thousands of

The Italian family firm of Beretta has been making high-quality firearms for hundreds of years. The Beretta 92, in service with the US Army, is the most successful of the company's modern handgun designs.

this pistol were sold, to Italy, Israel and Egypt, among several others.

In the early 1970s Beretta began a completely new family of double-action pistols for police and sporting use. This family started with the Model 81 in 7.65-mm, and went into several variants. Then, having got the commercial designs well under way, it turned to a military model and produced the Model 92 in 1976.

Double action

The Model 92 is obviously a progression from the M951, using much the same sort of frame and slide and the same locking system, but adding a double-action trigger and making the whole pistol rather more streamlined.

Stripping the Beretta 92

1 Remove the magazine by depressing the release button located on the grip level with the trigger guard, then check that there is no round in the chamber.

2 Hold the pistol in your right hand and press the disassembling latch release button with your left hand. Rotate the latch anti-clockwise until it stops.

3 Now pull forward the slide barrel group with the locking block, recoil spring and the guide.

4 Press the recoil spring and guide in order to remove them from the barrel, and remember that they are under compression.

5 Press the locking block plunger and remove the locking group and the barrel from the slide to complete a basic field strip.

6 The Beretta 92-F field stripped: when you re-assemble it, remember to ensure that the slide is aligned with the rear end of the frame as you rotate the disassembling latch back into place.

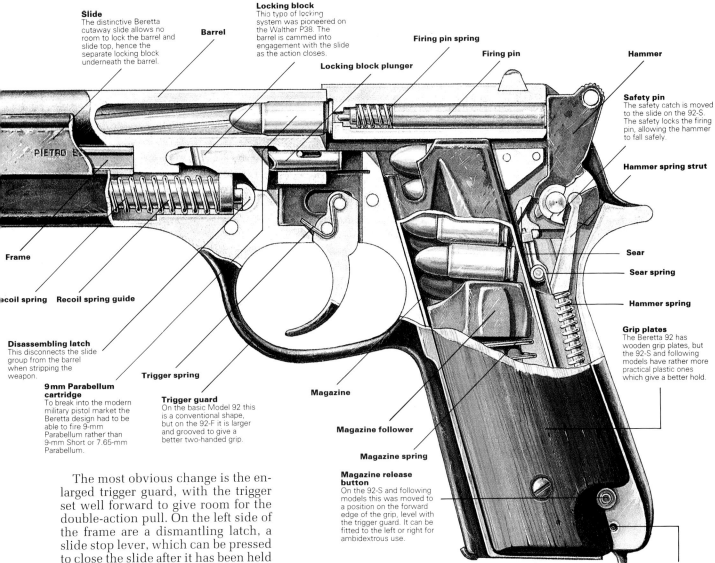

Slide
The distinctive Beretta cutaway slide allows no room to lock the barrel and slide top, hence the separate locking block underneath the barrel.

Barrel

Locking block
This typo of locking system was pioneered on the Walther P38. The barrel is cammed into engagement with the slide as the action closes.

Locking block plunger

Firing pin spring

Firing pin

Hammer

Safety pin
The safety catch is moved to the slide on the 92-S. The safety locks the firing pin, allowing the hammer to fall safely.

Hammer spring strut

Frame

Sear

Sear spring

Hammer spring

Recoil spring

Recoil spring guide

Grip plates
The Beretta 92 has wooden grip plates, but the 92-S and following models have rather more practical plastic ones which give a better hold.

Disassembling latch
This disconnects the slide group from the barrel when stripping the weapon.

9 mm Parabellum cartridge
To break into the modern military pistol market the Beretta design had to be able to fire 9-mm Parabellum rather than 9-mm Short or 7.65-mm Parabellum.

Trigger spring

Trigger guard
On the basic Model 92 this is a conventional shape, but on the 92-F it is larger and grooved to give a better two-handed grip.

Magazine

Magazine follower

Magazine spring

Magazine release button
On the 92-S and following models this was moved to a position on the forward edge of the grip, level with the trigger guard. It can be fitted to the left or right for ambidextrous use.

Hammer strut guide pin

The most obvious change is the enlarged trigger guard, with the trigger set well forward to give room for the double-action pull. On the left side of the frame are a dismantling latch, a slide stop lever, which can be pressed to close the slide after it has been held open after firing the last shot in the magazine, and a safety catch. The double-column magazine holds 15 rounds, and is slotted at the rear so that the contents can be seen and the number of rounds easily checked.

Model 92-S

Next came the Model 92-S. This removed the safety catch from the frame and placed it on the slide, interlinking it with the hammer mechanism so that applying the safety first locked the firing pin and then released the hammer to fall safely. Thus it now became possible to load the pistol, then apply the safety and drop the hammer, and then holster the pistol in a loaded but safe condition. When necessary, all that was required was to draw, release the safety and pull the trigger, so cocking and releasing the hammer.

The Model 92-SB was the Model 92-S with the safety catch on both

Shooting on the range, the Beretta proved itself to be an impressively accurate weapon with a clear sight picture. At the insistence of the US Army the weapon is designed for ambidextrous operation.

Loading the chunky, 15-round magazine of the Beretta: holes in the rear of the magazine allow you to see quickly how many shells you have left. You can drop the magazine without removing your hand from the firing position, glance at the magazine, and bang it back into place in a shorter time than it takes to read this caption.

sides of the slide, so that it could be operated by right- or left-handed shooters, and the magazine release was removed from the heel of the butt to a position on the grip frame just below the trigger grip where it could be comfortably operated by the firing hand; in case of left-handed firers, it was an easy task to remove the release button and its mechanism and mount it on the other side of the slide.

The safety system was also improved; now the safety catch positively disconnected the trigger from the hammer sear, and the firing pin was permanently locked, being unlocked only by the final movement of the trigger in the act of firing. So it was virtually impossible to fire this weapon by dropping or any blow; only correct use of the trigger could cause the weapon to fire. The Model 92-SB-C is a compact version of the SB; with an overall length of 197 mm (7.75 in) and a 135-mm (5.3-in) barrel.

By this time, the US Army had advertised for pistols to be tested for possible American adoption, and laid down some basic requirements. The weapon had to be double-action, 9-mm Parabellum calibre, and have both safety and magazine release capable of operation by either hand without adjustment. In response, Beretta built the Model 92-F. This is mechanically and dimensionally the same as the 92-SB but has the front of the trigger guard shaped for a two-handed grip, ambidextrous safety and magazine release, a curved front edge to the grip frame, new grip plates, internally chromed barrel, and the exterior finished with 'Bruniton', a type of Teflon anti-corrosive coating.

The Model 92-F came through the American tests with considerable success, particularly in the reliability field, and was duly adopted as the 'Pistol, 9-mm M9' early in 1985. A contract for some 315,000 was given, but complaints by American manufacturers that the tests were unfair and badly conducted led to a ruling by Congress that no more deliveries were to be made until a second series of trials had been conducted; these would either confirm Beretta as the selected pistol or (as the Americans hoped) replace it with an American design. In the end the Beretta was selected.

After the 92-F you might have expected Beretta to rest on its laurels for a while, but not a bit of it. Next came the Model 92-F Compact, which is a cut-down model, much the same as the SB-C but with the various Model F features. And then came the Model 92-SB-C Type M, which is simply the SB-C but with the 15-round magazine replaced by a single-column eight-shot magazine, principally intended for guard and police use.

Carabinieri use

There are also three pistols which, while not bearing the '92' number, must certainly be considered members of the family. The first of these is the Model 93-R, a most unusual weapon which has been adopted by the Italian Carabinieri. In general form it resembles the Model 92, but has an extended barrel into which slots are cut to act as a muzzle compensator.

Attached to the bottom of the butt is an ingenious folding shoulder stock and attached to the front of the frame, just ahead of the trigger guard, is a fold-down front hand grip.

All this might be thought excessive on a 9-mm pistol, until you discover that the Model 93-R can fire three-round bursts. Set to single shot it can be handled and fired just like an ordinary pistol, albeit a trifle heavier and more bulky than the Model 92; but fold out the stock, lower the hand grip, take firm hold and set the selector to burst fire, and every pressure of the trigger looses off three rounds of rapid fire. So the Model 93-R is, in effect, a small sub-machine gun or machine-pistol.

Large magazine

To fire a slightly greater reserve of ammunition the standard magazine is a 20-shot device which extends below the end of the butt grip; an ordinary 15-round magazine can also be used. It is also possible, though a trifle alarming, to fold down the front grip, leave the stock folded or even remove it, and then fire bursts in a two-handed grip.

The Model 93-R was followed by two models for people who do not require the power of the 9-mm Parabellum cartridge; the Model 98 is an SB-C but chambered for the 7.65-mm Parabellum cartridge, while the Model 99 is the SB-C Type M, also chambered for the 7.65-mm Parabellum round. And with that Beretta appears to have come to the end of its inspiration for the Model 92 family.

These Iranian women were seen being trained with a variety of pistols, including Beretta Model 92s, during Iran's long-running war with Iraq.

Beretta PM 12

The Italian army was among the first people to use sub-machine guns, and Beretta the second people to make them. The Italians devised a very light machine-gun firing 9-mm pistol ammunition in 1917, but in its original form it was somewhat impractical. So Beretta took the basic receiver, barrel and mechanism, allied it to a conventional carbine stock, and produced the Beretta M1918 sub-machine gun. With one or two subsequent modifications this remained in Italian service right through World War II, but few people realised, since it looked like just another short rifle.

The above, armed with *Beretta PM 12* sub-machine guns, 9-mm pistols and bayonets, are actually police officers of a specialist branch of the Italian *Carabinieri known as the 'Nucleo Operativo Centrale Di Sicurezze', or NOCS for short.* They are on counter-terrorist exercises in Sardinia.

Specialist accessories

A high-power illuminator grip with rechargeable battery is available for fighting through a house in darkness. Note the trigger for switching the light on at the required moment.

Night vision scopes such as third-generation image intensifiers can be fitted for night fighting: a very handy package for close target recce and other patrolling tasks.

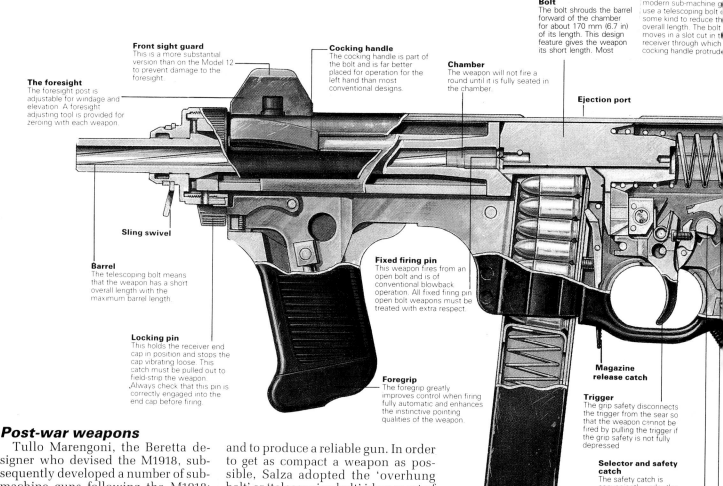

Bolt
The bolt shrouds the barrel forward of the chamber for about 170 mm (6.7 in) of its length. This design feature gives the weapon its short length. Most

modern sub-machine g[...] use a telescoping bolt [...] some kind to reduce th[...] overall length. The bolt moves in a slot cut in th[...] receiver through which [...] cocking handle protrud[...]

Front sight guard
This is a more substantial version than on the Model 12 to prevent damage to the foresight.

Cocking handle
The cocking handle is part of the bolt and is far better placed for operation for the left hand than most conventional designs.

Chamber
The weapon will not fire a round until it is fully seated in the chamber.

Ejection port

The foresight
The foresight post is adjustable for windage and elevation. A foresight adjusting tool is provided for zeroing with each weapon.

Sling swivel

Barrel
The telescoping bolt means that the weapon has a short overall length with the maximum barrel length.

Fixed firing pin
This weapon fires from an open bolt and is of conventional blowback operation. All fixed firing pin open bolt weapons must be treated with extra respect.

Locking pin
This holds the receiver end cap in position and stops the cap vibrating loose. This catch must be pulled out to field-strip the weapon. Always check that this pin is correctly engaged into the end cap before firing.

Foregrip
The foregrip greatly improves control when firing fully automatic and enhances the instinctive pointing qualities of the weapon.

Magazine release catch

Trigger
The grip safety disconnects the trigger from the sear so that the weapon cannot be fired by pulling the trigger if the grip safety is not fully depressed

Selector and safety catch
The safety catch is conveniently under the thumb and has three positions: fully back, marked 'S' in white for safe, followed by '1' in red for semi-automatic fire, and finally all the way forward, marked 'R' in red for full auto.

Sear block
This holds the bolt to the rear when the weapon is cocked and releases it wh[...] the grip safety is depress[...] and the trigger is squeeze[...] In semi-automatic mod[...] sear engages the bolt, holding it to the rear after each shot. On automatic [...] sear only engages the bol[...] when the trigger is releas[...]

Magazine
The magazine holds 32 rounds of 9-mm Parabellum. It has round holes cut in the back, marked 32, 20 and 10, so you can visually check how much ammo you have left.

Post-war weapons

Tullo Marengoni, the Beretta designer who devised the M1918, subsequently developed a number of submachine guns following the M1918; these were very successful and efficient weapons. But in the early 1950s a new designer, Domenico Salza, took a fresh look at the submachine gun idea and began putting together some experimental models. These led to the Model 12, which went into production in 1959 and was adopted by the Italian army in 1961.

The Model 12 was a very up-to-date design, employing stamped metal pressings which are spot-welded together to form the receiver, magazine housing and trigger housing. The whole design was geared to make manufacture quick, cheap and easy

and to produce a reliable gun. In order to get as compact a weapon as possible, Salza adopted the 'overhung bolt' or 'telescoping bolt' idea; most of the length of the barrel lies inside the receiver, and the cylindrical bolt is hollowed out for much of its length so that when forward it encloses the rear of the barrel. The sides of the bolt are slotted so that the cartridge can be fed and the empty case ejected, and the cocking handle is fitted to its front end, protruding through a slot in the receiver.

The advantage of this 'telescoping bolt' design is that the gun's overall length is kept short, compared with the length of the barrel. In a conventional design the front of the bolt stops at the end of the barrel; there has to be

Field stripping the Model 12S

1 Remove the magazine by pressing on the magazine release catch, which is located forward of the trigger guard.

2 Grasp the cocking handle with the forefinger and thumb and rack it back to eyeball the chamber. This weapon fires from an open bolt, so every time the bolt goes forward, if there is ammo there it will fire it.

3 Pull down the catch underneath the knurled locking receiver cap at the front of the weapon. Unscrew the ring to release the bolt and barrel assembly.

4 The bolt and barrel assembly will slide out of the weapon forwards and then separate the locking receiver cap from the barrel.

Inside the Beretta PM 12S

Rearsight
This is of conventional aperture type sight with flip-up 100- and 200-m (328- and 656-ft) apertures. The retaining catch for the rear receiver cap is fixed to the rear sight base.

Retaining catch
This secures the rear receiver cap.

Receiver end cap
The receiver cap screws onto the receiver and holds the barrel and bolt in position.

Sling swivel

Folding stock

Stock hinge pin

Return spring
When the weapon is cocked this spring is compressed. When the trigger is pulled this spring forces the bolt forward to collect chamber and fire the round. The spring acts against the force of the detonating 9-mm round controlling the rearward movement of the bolt, forcing it forward again once the rearward momentum has been overcome.

Grip safety
This feature prevents the weapon from firing if it is accidentally dropped or the firer does not have his whole hand in contact with the pistol grip. The grip must be pressed in order to release both the bolt and the trigger for firing.

Pistol grip

Butt plate release catch

Butt plate

The PM 12S is a good, solid gun with many user-friendly features that make it a very good buy as a weapon for military or police applications. It is very compact, easy to field strip and clean, and has built in safety features; it is suitably robust, and shoots very well. The only point of criticism that applies equally to all bottom-feed designs is that shooting from the prone position leaves the chest cavity a little exposed due to the length of the magazine.

A Beretta Model 12 is test-fired on the factory testing range at the Beretta plant at Gardone. This model sold very well throughout the 1950s.

Below: The telescoping bolt fits around the barrel to give the gun maximum barrel length for minimum overall length.

5 To remove the barrel from the bolt assembly, tip the barrel up and withdraw it to the rear.

6 Lift up the catch to the rear of the rear sight to release the locking receiver cap.

7 Unscrew the locking receiver cap in the same way as on the front of the weapon. Remember, this cap is under spring pressure, so take care when removing it.

8 Withdraw the recoil spring to complete the field strip. The design makes the weapon simple to strip and easy to clean, with no small pieces to lose.

a specific mass of bolt in order for the blowback system to work, and the bolt has to travel back a certain distance in the receiver to absorb the recoil and have enough room to extract, eject and reload.

Telescoping bolt

Add all these together and you finish up with a rather long weapon, which is why conventional sub-machine guns of this sort tend to have short barrels. But by telescoping the bolt around the barrel you can save length and keep a good long barrel that allows the cartridge to gain maximum velocity.

Another advantage claimed for this design is that the positioning of the

The PM 12S shoots well, and three-to five-round bursts can easily be kept on a Figure 11 target. Deliberate shooting for the standing position at 50 m (164 ft) produces a 25-cm (9.8-in) group. The gun compares very favourably with more expensive and complicated designs such as the Heckler & Koch.

Left: The Beretta's vertical foregrip, reminiscent of the 1928 Thompson, is a great help in controlling muzzle climb and producing bursts on target. The design is also a departure from current trends in not having the magazine seated in the pistol grip.

barrel and bolt make for excellent balance, and it is quite easy to fire the M12 single-handed at full automatic without very much 'climb' of the muzzle.

The M12 had a pistol grip which carried a grip safety; this has to be squeezed by the firing hand before the bolt is released, preventing accidental discharges. There was also a push-through safety catch above the grip which additionally locked the grip

safety. Another push-through button above the trigger selected single shots or automatic fire. The magazine fitted into a housing just ahead of the trigger, and a front grip gave a good holding position. There was a folding metal stock which lay alongside the receiver when folded.

Military and police use

The M12 sold well in the 1960s and was adopted by military and police forces all over the world, and in the mid-1970s the Model 12S appeared. Although this looks the same as the Model 12 there are some important improvements.

The first and most important change was in the safety and selective-fire arrangements. Instead of two separate controls, a single rotary switch lever was placed on the left side of the receiver, giving safe/single shot/automatic in one movement. The grip safety was still fitted to the pistol grip, but the rest of the selection could be done with the thumb. The foresight was made adjustable for both elevation and windage; both sights were given stronger bases and better side protection; and the catch that holds the rear body cap in place was moved from the bottom of the receiver to the top, so that it could be operated more easily when stripping, and could be inspected easily to ensure that the cap was tight. The folding stock and the internal mechanism of the trigger were improved, and the exterior of the weapon was finished with a coating of epoxy resin instead of the earlier phosphate finish.

The Model 12S has replaced the earlier M12 in the Italian army and police, and is in use with several other armies around the world. It is also made under licence in Brazil.

Although the PM 12 uses many of the modern economical manufacturing techniques, it is built and finished to the high standard expected of the Beretta company.

Bruiser from Brno The CZ75

When the war ended in 1945 the Czech army had to pick up the pieces and re-organise itself, but before it could get very far the country fell under Soviet domination and the army, like other Soviet satellites, adopted Soviet weapons. This did not suit the Czechs, who had ideas of their own, and some very good designers, so it was not long before they began developing their own weapons.

Among the most pressing needs was a pistol; their pre-war design was a horrible weapon, and anyway most had been taken by the German army.

and the current issue pistol was the elderly Soviet Tokarev. So the designers were put to work to produce a decent pistol, and the result was the CZ52, an odd design with a most complex roller-locked breech: really locked, unlike the Heckler & Koch roller system, which is only a delayed blowback. In spite of its complications, its difficult manufacture and its undoubted cost to produce, it has remained the issue Czech army pistol ever since, and it remained in production until the mid-1970s.

The CZ52 satisfied the army but it did not satisfy its makers, since it had

Above: Whacking in a fresh magazine, a shooter slaps its base to ensure it is properly seated. One weakness of the CZ75 is that it does not spit out an empty mag quite like a Colt 1911.

Above: The CZ75 shoots comfortably even with military 2z ammunition, and will happily feed semi-jacketed soft points as well as the full-metal-jacket ammunition it is designed to shoot.

The 15-shot magazine provides serious firepower and gives the pistol good instinctive pointing qualities with a grip that fills the hand. Women with very small hands may find this a problem.

Right: External dimensions of the pistol are similar to the Browning, so it will fit military holsters. Note that the earlier models have slightly shorter slides: make sure you select the long-slide version when buying.

no export potential: largely because of its complexity, but also because it was chambered for the Soviet 7.62-mm pistol cartridge, which nobody outside the Soviet bloc used. The first attempt to improve matters was the model 50, a 7.65-mm blowback more or less copied from the Walther PP. This, due to bad manufacturing technology, proved to be unpopular and unreliable, but it is still the principal pistol for Czech police and security forces.

Best shot

The next attempt was the CZ75, generally agreed to be the best pistol to come out of Czechoslovakia in the last 50 years. Here the designers turned to the best time-tested ideas, and assembled a reliable and accurate weapon. The locking system is pure Browning, using a shaped cam beneath the breech, and two ribs on top of the barrel which lock into the roof of the slide. The lockwork allows single- or

*Double tapping with the **CZ75**: a case in the air and the pistol rock steady back on target. It shoots well, and is entirely adequate for combat use. At full recoil the pistol hardly moves off target. This technique is known as the 'combat crouch'.*

Inside the CZ75

Imitation is the sincerest form of flattery, and the CZ75 has been copied more frequently than any other modern pistol. The Italians have made a bargain-basement copy, the TA 90; the Swiss have an up-market copy and a cut-down police version. The design also formed the basis for the excellent but ill-fated Bren 10 pistol. The pistol is now available in a product improved version, the CZ85, with ambidextrous controls and better finish.

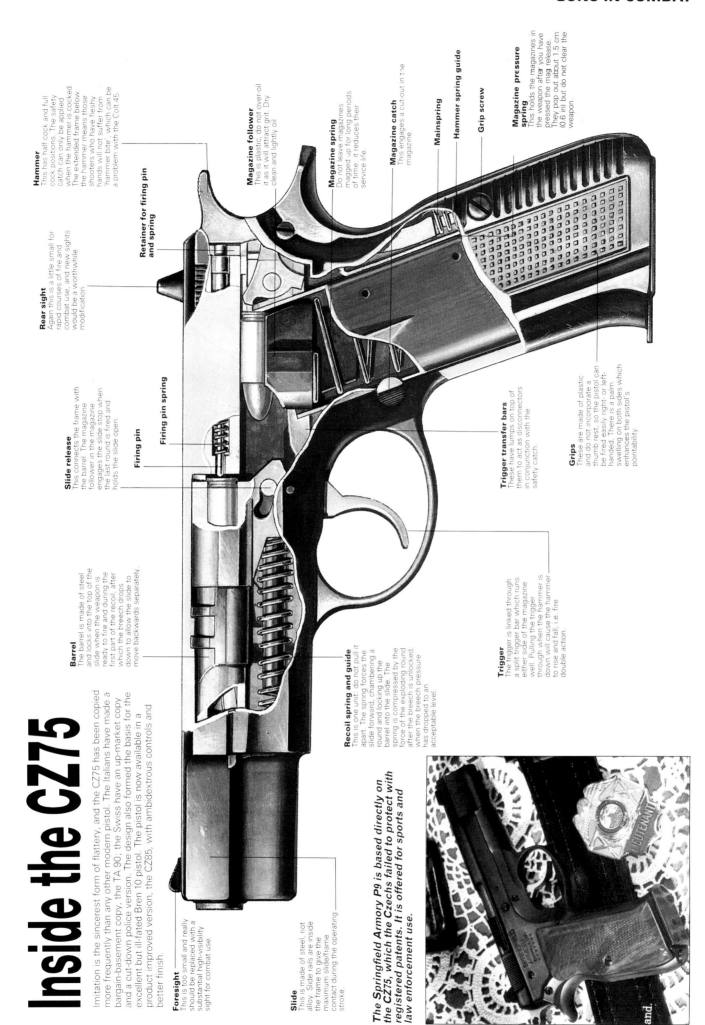

Hammer
This has half cock and full cock positions. The safety catch can only be applied when the hammer is cocked. The extended frame below the hammer means those fleshy shooters who have fleshy hands will not suffer from 'hammer bite', which can be a problem with the Colt 45.

Magazine follower
This is plastic, do not over-oil it as it will attract grit. Dry clean and lightly oil.

Magazine spring
Do not leave magazines magged up for long periods of time, it reduces their service life.

Magazine catch
This engages a cut-out in the magazine.

Mainspring

Hammer spring guide

Grip screw

Magazine pressure spring
This holds the magazines in the weapon after you have pressed the mag release. They pop out about 1.5 cm (0.6 in) but do not clear the weapon.

Rear sight
Again this is a little small for rapid courses of fire and combat use, and new sights would be a worthwhile modification.

Retainer for firing pin and spring

Slide release
This connects the frame with the barrel. The magazine follower in the magazine engages the slide stop when the last round is fired and holds the slide open.

Firing pin spring

Firing pin

Foresight
This is too small and really should be replaced with a substantial high-visibility sight for combat use.

Slide
This is made of steel, not alloy. Slide rails are inside the frame to give the maximum slide/frame contact during the operating stroke.

Barrel
The barrel is made of steel and locks into the top of the slide when the weapon is ready to fire and during the first part of the recoil, after which the breech drops down to allow the slide to move backwards separately.

Recoil spring and guide
This is one unit, do not pull it apart. The spring forces the slide forward, chambering a round and locking up the barrel into the slide. The spring is compressed by the force of the exploding round after the breech is unlocked, when the breech pressure has dropped to an acceptable level.

Trigger
The trigger is linked through a split trigger bar which runs either side of the magazine well. Pulling the trigger through when the hammer is down will cause the hammer to rise and fall, i.e. fire double action.

Trigger transfer bars
These have lumps on top of them to act as disconnectors in conjunction with the safety catch.

Grips
These are made of plastic and do not incorporate a thumb rest, so the pistol can be fired easily right- or left-handed. There is a palm swelling on both sides which enhances the pistol's pointability.

The Springfield Armory P9 is based directly on the CZ75, which the Czechs failed to protect with registered patents. It is offered for sports and law enforcement use.

The pistol out of the box is sighted in for a target at 25 m (82 ft). The sights are perhaps a shortcoming, as they are a little too small for a really clear sight picture. However, for slow fire work the sights are usable.

double-action firing. The magazine holds 15 rounds of 9-mm Parabellum, and the pistol is well-proportioned and sits comfortably in the hand.

The first models were carefully and slowly made by machining solid steel billets to make the frame and slide, but this was too expensive so they used investment casting. This was beyond Czech technology at the time, and the first cast components were imported from Spain. Eventually the Czech factory perfected the casting technique, and the pistols were made entirely in Czechoslovakia. Early machined pistols have a slightly different frame contour to the cast models, and they are also identifiable by having the front face of the trigger grooved.

In the endeavour to reduce production costs, some bureaucrat ordered that the half-cock notch on the hammer be removed, since he could see no purpose for it. After loads of reports from Germany of accidental discharges, the half-cock notch was rapidly restored to the design.

The quality of manufacture and finish on the CZ75 is well ahead of any other pistol produced in post-war Czechoslovakia, and after its introduction in 1976 it sold well in Germany and other European countries. It shoots well, is robust and reliable, and the cost is attractive when compared with Western products.

Copies of the CZ75

An additional income has been the licensing of manufacture outside Czechoslovakia. One such licensed copy is the Swiss AT84. However, the Swiss have made some minor but important modifications; the AT84

safety catch works whether the gun is cocked or uncocked, whereas the CZ only renders the pistol safe when it is cocked. The Swiss design has adopted a custom-made German Peters-Stahl barrel of exceptional hardness and accuracy. The finish is of the highest order, better than the CZ product.

New developments

However, the Czechs were not content to sit on their design, and recently they introduced the CZ85 model. This is the 75 brought up to date by incorporating an ambidextrous safety catch and slide stop. The top of the slide has been ribbed to cut down reflection and give a clearer sight picture, and some minor changes in the lockwork have resulted in a smoother trigger-pull. The finish of this pistol is really first-class, and it remains to be seen how well it will do in the commercial market.

Strange as it may seem, the CZ75 has not been adopted by the Czech army or police forces; it is entirely for export, to gain much-needed hard currency. Also there may be sufficient CZ52 and 83 models (the 83 replaced the 50, and is no more than a slight improvement on it), to satisfy military and police needs. Certainly the 75 and 85 could not be adopted before 1989, since the 9-mm Parabellum is a Capitalist cartridge, not to be tolerated in a good socialist state; but it should not be beyond the capability of the Czechs to remodel the 75/85 into 7.62-mm if they really wanted.

Springfield P9

P9 Standard Model

P9C Compact Model

**P9 LSP Model
(Long Slide Ported)**

Springfield Armory's P9 range includes the standard model double-action CZ75 derivative; the P9C compact designed for home defence and concealed carry; and the LSP competition pistol which includes adjustable sights, extended thumb safety and rubber grips.

The Browning High Power

When you pick up a Browning High Power, the bulky size of the butt grip is instantly obvious. Inside is a double-row magazine containing 13 rounds, just one short of twice the magazine capacity of the famous Colt .45 M1911. The Browning was the first pistol to have such a large magazine, and this has been one of the main reasons for its success as a military weapon and for its popularity with soldiers.

Safe and reliable

John Browning began the gun that bears his name shortly after he had designed the Colt M1911. The High Power was of simpler construction, but retains the reliability and safety of the Colt. Three major design changes were made, of which the most significant was the adoption of a cam system to lock the breech. A forged lump was positioned underneath the chamber and a shaped cam path cut into it. This engaged with a cross pin in the pistol frame, so that as the slide and barrel recoiled after firing, the cam, riding on the cross pin, drew the rear end of the barrel down and freed it from the slide. This is more linear than the curving movement involved in the 'swinging link' system used in the Colt.

The second major change was the replacement of the stirrup that connected the trigger with the hammer with a connecting bar that was mounted in the slide, and so doubled as a disconnector. Only when the slide was properly forward and the breech securely locked was the trigger connected to the striker. In his original design for the High Power, Browning replaced the external hammer of the Colt with an internal firing pin driven by a spring.

The menacing picture of a Browning High Power in the grip of a trooper from Britain's elite **SAS** is a testimony to the handgun's reliability, since the **SAS** know their weapons as well as anyone in the world.

The basic High Power has not changed for over half a century, although the example shown here has had some cosmetic changes, with a red dot sight and Pachmayr non-slip grips having been added.

giving (for those days) the unprecedented ammunition capacity of 13 shots. In this respect, Browning's 'transfer bar' trigger connection was most fortunate, because it would never have worked with the stirrup connection. Saive's other good idea was to remove the internal striker and fit an external hammer, which makes it instantly obvious whether your pistol is cocked.

'Grand Puissance'

The name 'High Power' conjures up an image of a pistol of awesome strength but the Browning is not a monstrous magnum automatic. The title is a translation of 'Grand Puissance', the name given to it by the Belgian army, which adopted it in 1935. It was simply much more powerful than anything the Belgians had used before. Its official designation was 'Model 35' pistol'.

Both sides used the Browning during World War II. Some 56,000 weapons had been produced prior to the German occupation of Belgium, and the Germans manufactured 329,000 under the designation 'Pistole 640(b)'.

However, Saive and some of his design staff escaped from Belgium and settled in Britain, where they were

Perhaps the most remarkable change was in calibre. Long before anyone had really studied the matter, Browning had realised that 9-mm Parabellum was going to be the most important pistol cartridge of the future, and he designed his new gun around it. Today, this cartridge is universally employed and manufactured all over the world.

Belgian development

Browning took his pistol design to Fabrique Nationale in Belgium in 1923, and continued to work on it until his death in November 1926. Thereafter, development was in the hands of Dieudonné Saive, FN's chief designer, and much of the final form of the pistol is due to him rather than to Browning. One of his first moves was to develop the double-row magazine,

Above: People have been predicting the demise of the military pistol for many years, but it is still of great use when you expect to be fighting at short ranges in enclosed spaces.

Right: The Browning was the first of the modern high-magazine capacity pistols, and its 13-round magazine as well as its reliability was one of the factors which made the SAS choose the pistol as a back-up weapon.

The Browning High Power is one of the world's most widely used service pistols, being used from the Arctic to the tropics. It is in service with military and police forces of more than 50 nations.

soon employed at the Royal Small-Arms Factory, Enfield. The British were interested in the High Power and, although the records are vague, there seems little doubt that a small number of pistols were made in Enfield in 1941: there is a record of a 'Pistol, Browning (FN) Automatic Mark 1 (UK)', formal approval for which was officially cancelled in April 1945.

Chinese model

In 1942 the Chinese army, now allied with Britain against Japan, wanted to be supplied with the High Power. The British passed their request to a Canadian gun manufacturer, John Inglis of Toronto. But unfortunately the original drawings of the pistol vanished during the attempt to smuggle them across Occupied France and out to England, so the Inglis design office had to obtain six pistols from China and 'reverse engineer' them, producing drawings from the dismantled pistols.

The Chinese design incorporated a rather optimistic adjustable tangent sight graduated to 500 metres, and the rear of the grip was slotted to take a detachable butt-stock. It was officially known as the 'Pistol, 9-mm Automatic (FN) No. Mark 1'. The British/Canadian model used simple fixed sights and was not able to take the butt-stock, and was adopted as the 'Pistol, 9-mm, Automatic (FN) No. 2 Mark 1'. After a short production run some small changes were made in the design of the extractor and ejector and in some components of the trigger mechanism in order to ensure complete interchangeability, and the pistols were then 'Mark 1*'. Inglis produced 151,816 pistols before ceasing manufacture in September 1945.

Back to Belgium

After the war FN began production at Liège in Belgium once again, calling the pistol the 'Model 1946' for military sales and the 'High Power' for commercial sales. After their wartime experience the British, Australian and Canadian armies adopted it as their standard service pistol, and their example was rapidly followed by other armies, so that it is now in military service in some 55 countries. It has also been manufactured under licence in Argentina and Indonesia, and an identical copy is made in Hungary.

Getting old

In the 1990s, it must be admitted, the High Power is feeling its age, and apart from the 13-shot magazine has very little in common with the more modern pistols that now challenge its position in the market. But the fact that it has been in service for so long proves its reliability as a military weapon. It is accurate, easy to master, and, apart from a somewhat 'sticky' trigger pull, has no vices. It is now manufactured in the 'Mark 2' version which has slightly different grip plates and an ambidextrous safety catch.

With a magazine capacity of 13 rounds, the High Power makes a fine personal gun. But it remains a short-range weapon: if you need a detachable buttstock to hit the target then maybe you should be using a sub-machine gun!

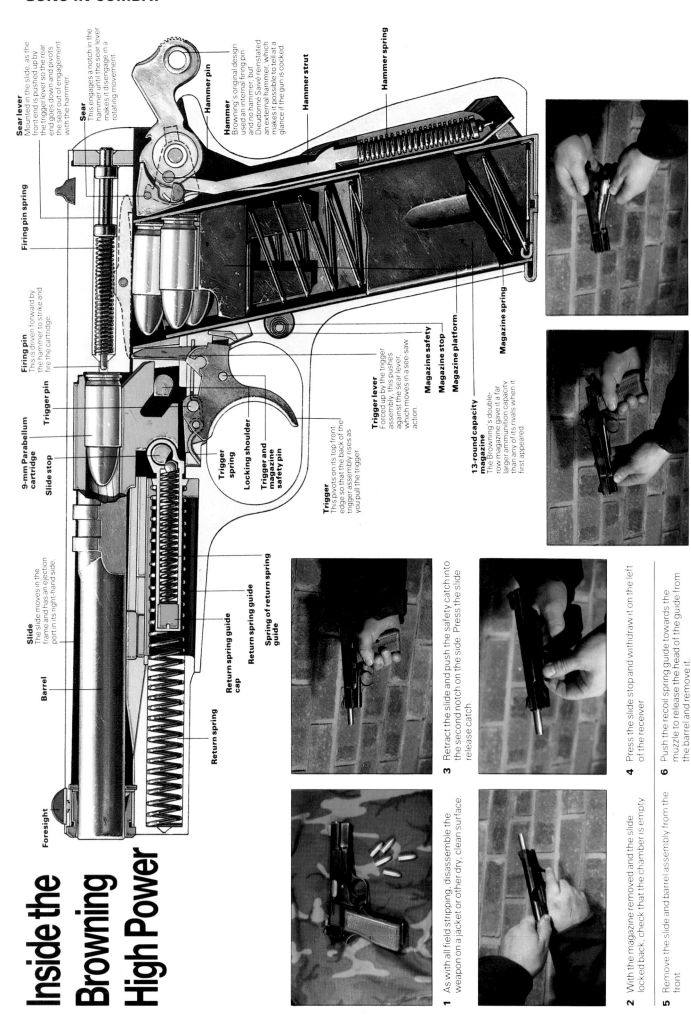

Inside the Browning High Power

Sear lever
Mounted in the slide, as the front end is pushed up by the trigger lever so the rear end goes down and pivots the sear out of engagement with the hammer.

Sear
This engages a notch in the hammer until the sear lever makes it disengage in a rotating movement.

Hammer pin

Hammer
Browning's original design used an internal firing pin and no hammer, but Dieudonné Save reinstated an external hammer, which makes it possible to tell at a glance if the gun is cocked.

Hammer strut

Hammer spring

Firing pin spring

Firing pin
This is driven forward by the hammer to strike and fire the cartridge.

Trigger pin

9-mm Parabellum cartridge

Slide stop

Slide
The slide moves in the frame and has an ejection port in its right-hand side.

Barrel

Foresight

Return spring

Return spring guide

Return spring guide cap

Spring of return spring guide

Trigger spring

Locking shoulder

Trigger and magazine safety pin

Trigger
This pivots on its top front edge so that the back of the trigger assembly rises as you pull the trigger.

Trigger lever
Forced up by the trigger assembly, this pushes against the sear lever, which moves in a see-saw action.

Magazine safety

Magazine stop

Magazine platform

Magazine spring

13-round capacity magazine
The Browning's double-row magazine gave it a far larger ammunition capacity than any of its rivals when it first appeared

1 As with all field stripping, disassemble the weapon on a jacket or other dry, clean surface.

2 With the magazine removed and the slide locked back, check that the chamber is empty

3 Retract the slide and push the safety catch into the second notch on the side. Press the slide release catch.

4 Press the slide stop and withdraw it on the left of the receiver

5 Remove the slide and barrel assembly from the front

6 Push the recoil spring guide towards the muzzle to release the head of the guide from the barrel and remove it.

MIXING IT WITH THE M16

The American infantry who fought in Operation Desert Storm were armed with the M16A2 rifle. This is a modified version of the rifle used in Vietnam and supplied to armies all over the world. Many British units have used the M16, from the jungles of Borneo to the Falklands and Northern Ireland. Wherever soldiers needed a lightweight but accurate weapon, the M16 has been a natural choice.

The M16 was developed from the AR-10, a revolutionary weapon built with extensive use of plastics and alloys. The designers modified the AR-10 at the Army's request, and the result was the AR-15. Firing a new 5.56-mm cartridge, it was a far cry from the US Army's existing weapons. But in 1959 the Army lost interest and turned instead to a new development programme, the 6-mm SPIW (Special Purpose Individual Weapon).

Airfield defence

That might have been the end of the story but for the US Air Force, who were looking for a small and handy short-range weapon with which to arm airfield guards. They looked at the AR-15, liked it, and ordered 8,000 in 1962. Shortly after this it was issued to guards in Vietnam. The ARVN

Left: Iraqi POWs are covered with an M16A2 during the Gulf war. US troops have used the M16 for nearly 30 years.

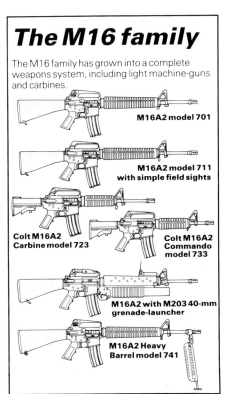

The M16 family

The M16 family has grown into a complete weapons system, including light machine-guns and carbines.

M16A2 model 701

M16A2 model 711 with simple field sights

Colt M16A2 Carbine model 723

Colt M16A2 Commando model 733

M16A2 with M203 40-mm grenade-launcher

M16A2 Heavy Barrel model 741

The M16 of this US Marine in Saudi Arabia is fitted with the M203 40-mm grenade launcher. This can fire HE or smoke grenades through a window from 150 m (492 ft), and is a useful weapon when fighting in built-up areas. US troops in the Gulf used the M16A2 version, which fires three-round bursts rather than fully automatic.

Inside the M16

The M16 is gas-operated, but whereas most such weapons use the gases produced on firing to move a piston which in turn moves the bolt, the gases in the M16 act directly on the bolt. This is a simpler system, but it won't work properly unless the weapon is regularly cleaned.

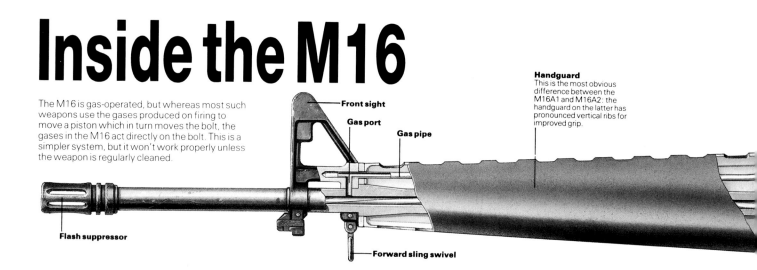

Front sight

Gas port

Gas pipe

Handguard
This is the most obvious difference between the M16A1 and M16A2: the handguard on the latter has pronounced vertical ribs for improved grip.

Flash suppressor

Forward sling swivel

An M16 rests on an American 'Tiger Stripe' camouflage jacket, a favourite uniform of the US Special Forces in Vietnam. Professional troops had few troubles with the M16 in Vietnam, but freshly-drafted conscripts who didn't clean their rifles had endless stoppages.

(Army of the Republic of Vietnam) saw them, thought that they would be ideal for their small-statured men, and asked for some to be supplied by the USA. One thousand were sent out in 1962, and it became highly popular.

New interest

The US Army decided to get in on the act; the 6-mm SPIW programme was a failure, and interest returned to the AR-15. In 1963 85,000 rifles were ordered for the Army and another 19,000 for the Air Force.

Before the Army could standardise the weapon, they insisted on some small modifications; of these, the most important was the addition of a 'bolt closing device'. Occasionally a dirty cartridge or a dirty chamber caused the breech to stick before being fully

Stripping the M16

1 Push in the takedown pin with a bullet after locking the bolt open, placing the fire selector on safe and checking that the receiver and chamber are clear.

2 Pivot the upper receiver from the lower receiver. These can be separated by pushing the receiver pivot pin forward of the magazine housing, but this is not necessary for a basic strip.

3 Pull back the charging handle and the bolt carrier.

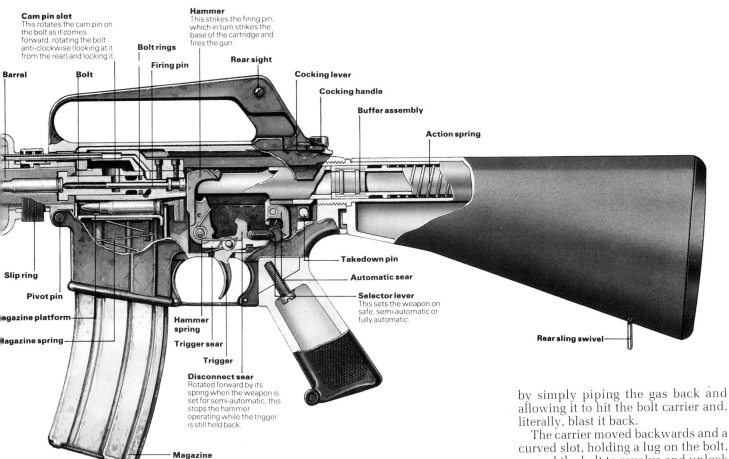

Cam pin slot
This rotates the cam pin on the bolt as it comes forward, rotating the bolt anti-clockwise (looking at it from the rear) and locking it.

Hammer
This strikes the firing pin, which in turn strikes the base of the cartridge and fires the gun.

Bolt rings

Firing pin

Rear sight

Barrel

Bolt

Cocking lever

Cocking handle

Buffer assembly

Action spring

Slip ring

Pivot pin

Magazine platform

Magazine spring

Hammer spring

Trigger sear

Trigger

Disconnect sear
Rotated forward by its spring when the weapon is set for semi-automatic, this stops the hammer operating while the trigger is still held back.

Magazine

Takedown pin

Automatic sear

Selector lever
This sets the weapon on safe, semi-automatic or fully automatic.

Rear sling swivel

closed, and a positive closing plunger was added on the right hand side of the receiver. With this, the rifle now became the M16A1 and received official blessing.

It got a semi-official cursing in Vietnam, acquiring a terrible reputation for stoppages and jams in action; this was because the US ammunition factories changed the propellant powder without troubling to tell anyone. The new propellant caused much more

fouling, compounded by idleness on the part of soldiers who didn't bother to clean the rifle.

Piping the gas

The reason the powder caused problems was tied in with the peculiar method of operation of the M16. Most gas-operated weapons tap gas from the barrel into a cylinder, where it drives a piston backwards to operate the bolt. But the M16 simplified things

by simply piping the gas back and allowing it to hit the bolt carrier and, literally, blast it back.

The carrier moved backwards and a curved slot, holding a lug on the bolt, caused the bolt to revolve and unlock from the chamber, after which the carrier pulled the bolt back and ejected the spent case. Two springs then propelled the bolt forward again to collect a new round from the magazine and re-load.

Foul gas

During the backward stroke a hammer had been cocked, and a fresh pull on the trigger now fired the next round. Automatic fire was achieved by the bolt carrier tripping the sear as the bolt finally closed, and so squirting the bolt carrier full of fouling-

4 Remove the bolt carrier and the bolt. If the weapon is very dirty, remove the extractor pin and the extractor for cleaning.

5 The cleaning kit lives in the hollow butt. Because of the way that the gas operates directly on the bolt, it is especially important to keep the M16 clean.

6 When cleaning the bolt, check it for any cracks or fractures, particularly around the cam pin area. Replace the bolt if it is pitted near the firing pin hole.

Left: The M16 was an immediate success with the small-statured soldiers of the South Vietnamese army.

With practically no recoil, the M16 is a very comfortable weapon to shoot; you can keep the sights on the target even when shooting rapidly.

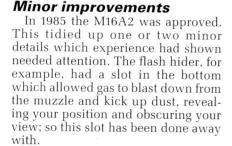

Above: US troops in Vietnam praised the M16 for its light weight and automatic firepower. This soldier is armed with the M16A1 with a 20-round magazine.

You cock the M16 by pulling back the charging handle, located just behind the carrying handle. If the magazine is empty the bolt carrier will be held to the rear.

laden gas was bound to cause problems. Some education of the troops, prolific issue of cleaning kit, and modification to the propellant cleared up that problem, and since then the M16 has been trouble-free.

Minor improvements

In 1985 the M16A2 was approved. This tidied up one or two minor details which experience had shown needed attention. The flash hider, for example, had a slot in the bottom which allowed gas to blast down from the muzzle and kick up dust, revealing your position and obscuring your view; so this slot has been done away with.

The US Army started by trying to find a weapon which would do the job without needing any skill from the man holding it; they asked the wrong question. What they have finished up with is an accurate and reliable rifle which is virtually the world standard in its calibre; they got the right answer.

A US Army Ranger carries the Colt Commander. This was a cut-down M16 developed during the Vietnam War for close-quarter fighting. Barrel length is halved, which forces you to fit a large suppressor or produce horrendous muzzle flash.

Colt .45 Combat Classic

American servicemen have fought with the Colt M1911 .45 pistol from World War I to the Gulf War. More than 80 years after its introduction, this classic handgun is still widely regarded as one of the best combat pistols in the business.

The venerable Colt was recently replaced in US service by a version of the Beretta 92 9-mm pistol. But this new weapon, designated M9, has been dogged by problems, and deliveries were so far behind schedule that the Colt went to war once again in Operation Desert Storm.

The story behind the American love affair with the Colt .45 began with John Browning, who took out a number of patents covering possible methods of operating automatic pistols in 1897. Within a year he and the Colt company to whom he had licensed all the patents were demonstrating a .38 calibre automatic to the US Army.

When the Army fought fanatical tribesmen in the Philippines, American soldiers demanded a very powerful pistol cartridge which would be guaranteed to disable the most ferocious spearman. .38s were not considered sufficiently powerful and in 1904 a series of tests was con-

ducted by firing a variety of different weapons against live animals and human corpses. The Army concluded that only .45 calibre would do and Colt re-worked the design to accommodate this larger round.

Army tests in 1907 recommended that the Colt and a design by Savage should be given more extensive trials. These were completed in 1909 and both pistols sent back for some modifi-

US soldiers still use the Colt M1911 because deliveries of its replacement are behind schedule, and many soldiers prefer this old but powerful weapon.

cations. In fact Browning more or less completely redesigned the Colt, and by the spring of 1910 this new model was submitted. Army tests throughout 1910 caused the Savage to be eliminated, and more detail work to be

A US Marine officer at Khe Sanh fires a few defiant rounds from his .45 during the North Vietnamese attacks on the base.

done on the Colt, with the final result that on 29 March 1911 the Colt design was formally approved as the 'U.S. Pistol, Automatic, Caliber .45, Model 1911'.

Browning locking system

The Browning design is of classic simplicity, so classic and so simple that it is still appearing on new pistol designs to this day. The pistol consists of three major components, the frame, the barrel and the slide. The slide moves back and forth on rails in the frame, and the rear half of the slide is the breech block, carrying the firing pin and extractor.

The frame consists of the butt, holding the magazine, the trigger, the hammer, and a grip safety device which prevents the hammer going forward unless the butt is properly held and the grip compressed. The barrel is attached to the frame by a short link pinned underneath the barrel at its upper end and anchored to the frame by a cross-pin at its lower end; this acts as a sort of hinge around which

Right: A GI armed with a Colt M1911 covers the doorway as American soldiers search a house in Germany at the end of World War II.

Below: The M1911 drives its .45 bullet clean through car doors. Only the engine block provides any cover.

the rear of the barrel can swing. The top of the barrel has two ribs machined on it, and these match two grooves in the inner surface of the slide top.

To fire the pistol you insert a magazine into the butt, pull back the slide against a spring which lies beneath the barrel, and release it. The slide runs forward and the edge of the breech block collects a cartridge and pushes it into the chamber of the barrel forward, and the 'swinging link'

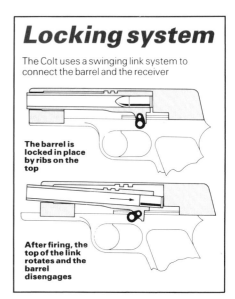

Locking system

The Colt uses a swinging link system to connect the barrel and the receiver

The barrel is locked in place by ribs on the top

After firing, the top of the link rotates and the barrel disengages

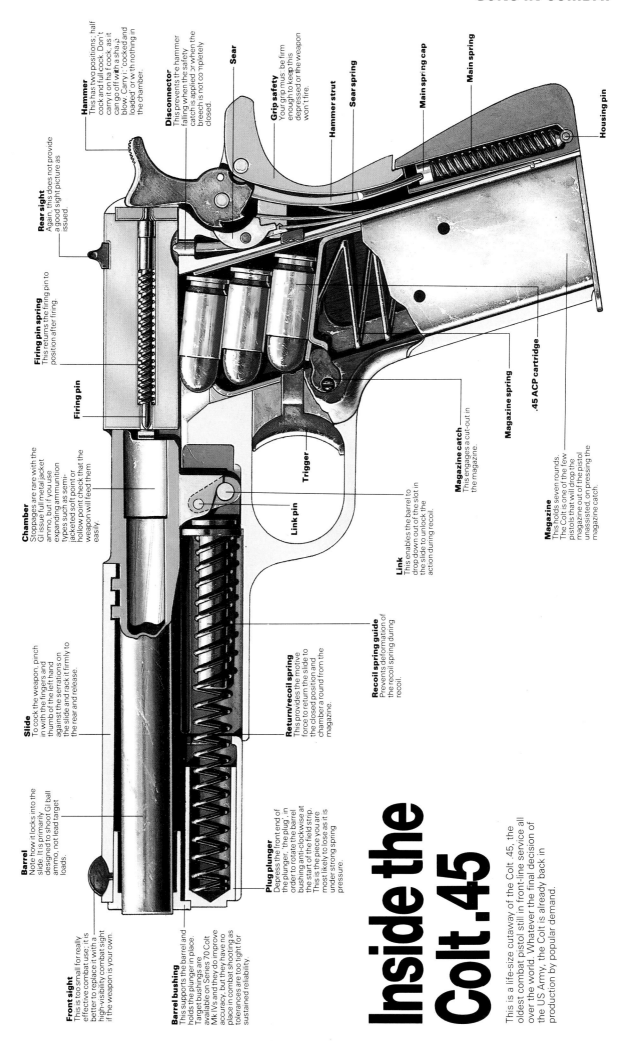

Hammer
This has two positions; half cock and full cock. Don't carry it on half cock as it can go off with a sharp blow. Carry it cocked and loaded or with nothing in the chamber.

Disconnector
This prevents the hammer falling when the safety catch is applied or when the breech is not completely closed.

Sear

Grip safety
Your grip must be firm enough to keep this depressed or the weapon won't fire.

Sear spring

Hammer strut

Main spring cap

Main spring

Housing pin

Rear sight
Again, this does not provide a good sight picture as issued.

Firing pin spring
This returns the firing pin to position after firing.

Firing pin

Chamber
Stoppages are rare with the GI issue full metal jacket ammo, but if you use expanding ammunition types such as semi-jacketed soft point or hollow point check that the weapon will feed them easily.

Trigger

Link pin

Link
This enables the barrel to drop down out of the slot in the slide to unlock the action during recoil.

Magazine catch
This engages a cut-out in the magazine.

Magazine spring

.45 ACP cartridge

Magazine
This holds seven rounds. The Colt is one of the few pistols that will drop the magazine out of the pistol unassisted, on pressing the magazine catch.

Slide
To cock the weapon, pinch in with the fingers and thumb of the left hand against the serrations on the slide and rack it firmly to the rear and release.

Return/recoil spring
This provides the motive force to return the slide to the closed position and chamber a round from the magazine.

Recoil spring guide
Prevents deformation of the recoil spring during recoil.

Barrel
Note how it locks into the slide. It is primarily designed to shoot GI ball ammo, not lead target loads.

Barrel bushing
This supports the barrel and holds the plunger in place. Target bushings are available on Series 70 Colt Mk IVs and they do improve accuracy, but they have no place in combat shooting as tolerances are too tight for sustained reliability.

Plug plunger
Depress the front end of the plunger, 'the plug', in order to rotate the barrel bushing anti-clockwise at the start of the field strip. This is the piece you are most likely to lose as it is under strong spring pressure.

Front sight
This is too small for really effective combat use; it is better to replace it with a high-visibility combat sight if the weapon is your own.

Inside the Colt .45

This is a life-size cutaway of the Colt .45, the oldest combat pistol still in front-line service all over the world. Whatever the final decision of the US Army, the Colt is already back in production by popular demand.

underneath it causes it to pivot forward and up. As it does so, the lugs on top move into place in the grooves inside the slide top and the barrel and slide are locked together.

Pull the trigger and the hammer drops, hits the firing pin, and fires the cartridge. The bullet goes down the barrel and the barrel recoils. In doing so it makes the slide recoil as well, since the two are locked together, so the breech stays firmly closed until the bullet has left the muzzle and the powder pressure inside the barrel has dropped to a level where it is safe to begin opening the breech.

As the barrel moves back it pivots around the link until the lugs are pulled free from the slide recesses. At this point the barrel stops moving, but the slide has been given sufficient momentum, by the recoil, to continue back, extracting the empty case and ejecting it and cocking the hammer by

A Colt M1911A1 as carried during the Vietnam War. Note the chunky .45 rounds in stripper clips next to the loaded magazine.

EYEWITNESS

.45 at the ready

"**S**uddenly movement in the dried vegetation towards the front of the gun pit got my attention. I turned cautiously around and waited, holding a cocked .45 automatic pistol at the ready. The rustling movements drew closer. My heart pounded. It was definitely not one of Peleliu's numerous land crabs that scuttled over the ground all night, every night. It must be a Japanese trying to slip in as close as possible, stopping frequently to avoid detection. He had probably seen the muzzle flash when I fired the mortar. Crouching low so as to see better any silhouette against the sky above me, I flipped off the thumb safety on the big pistol. A helmeted figure loomed up against the night sky in front of the gun pit. I couldn't tell whether the helmet was US or Japanese. Aiming the automatic at the centre of the head, I pressed the grip safety as I also squeezed the trigger slightly to take up the slack.

'What's the pass word?' I said in a low voice.

No answer.

'Pass word!' I demanded as my finger tightened on the trigger. The big pistol would fire and buck with recoil in a moment, but to hurry and jerk the trigger would mean a miss for sure.

'Sle-Sledgehammer!' stammered the figure.

I eased up on the trigger.

'It's de l'Eau, Jay de l'Eau. You got any water?'

'Jay, why didn't you give the pass word? I nearly shot you!' I gasped. He saw the pistol and moaned, 'Oh, Jesus,' as he realised what had nearly happened. 'I thought you knew it was me,' he said weakly."

Eugene B. Sledge
3rd Battalion/5th Marine Regiment 1944

simply rolling over it. Recoil stops, the spring forces the slide back, the pistol reloads and the barrel and slide lock together again.

After experience with the pistol during World War I the US Army requested some small changes that improved the handling without changing the significant features, and the pistol then became known as the M1911A1 in 1926. No further improvements were made throughout its service life, and today Colt still manufacture to the same pattern for commercial sale.

Man's cartridge

Firing the Colt .45 is not a pastime for dilettantes; it has a powerful cartridge and when you pull the trigger you are left in no doubt that you have just touched off a .45. Because of this it takes a good deal of time and a good deal of ammunition before you reach a competent level of skill and a lot more of both before you become really expert. As a combat pistol it is highly regarded simply because of its reliability and its awesome stopping power; hit somebody with a .45 and he immediately loses interest in the argument.

The Colt does have its drawbacks, especially in the 1990s when large magazine capacities are all the rage. The magazine only holds seven rounds; it is a single action gun, which means that either you carry it unloaded and have to pull back the slide before going into action, or you load it,

leave the hammer cocked and put on the safety. Some experts frown on both these concepts today; it's heavy; and the sights are scarcely up to target standards.

Add that to the training problem and you see why the US Army is trying to adopt a modern double-action 9-mm pistol with a 15-shot magazine. But there are an awful lot of people in America who feel that a 9-mm bullet isn't going to stop arguments with anything as certain as the finality of a .45 slug.

The M1911 is still made today for sports shooters. Here the hammer is cocked and the shooter is releasing the safety.

The Enfield No. 2/ Webley Mk 4

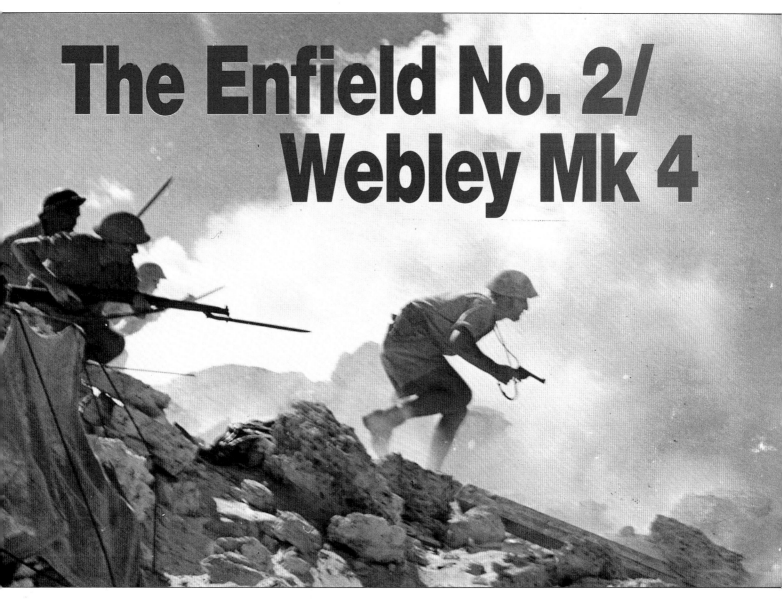

Above: A British officer leads his platoon forward in the grand old manner, drawn revolver clearly marking him out to any Afrika Korps riflemen present.

A British officer in a snow camouflage suit photographed leading a patrol near the German Frontier in January 1945. The jacketed heads of the bullets in the cylinder can just be seen.

During World War I the standard British service revolver was one variant or other of the Webley .455 pistol. These were very effec- tive pistols, but their weight and bulk made them very difficult to handle correctly without a great deal of train- ing and constant practice, two com- modities that were in short supply at the time. After 1919 the British Army decided that a smaller pistol firing a heavy .38-cal bullet would be just as effective as the larger-calibre weapon but would be easier to handle and would require less training. So Webley and Scott, which up to that time had been pistol manufacturers of a virtually official status for the British armed forces, took its .455 revolver, scaled it down and offered the result to the military.

Webley design

To the chagrin of Webley and Scott, the military simply took the design, made a few minor alterations and then placed the result in production as an 'official' government design to be pro- duced at the Royal Small Arms Fac- tory at Enfield Lock in Middlesex. This procedure took time, for Webley and Scott offered its design in 1923 and Enfield Lock took over the design in 1926. Webley and Scott was somewhat nonplussed at the course of events but proceeded to make its .38 revolver, known as the Webley Mk 4, all over the world with limited success.

The Enfield Lock product became the Pistol, Revolver, No. 2 Mk 1, and was duly issued for service. Once in service it proved sound and effective enough, but mechanical progress meant that large numbers of these pistols were issued to tank crews and other mechanised personnel, who made the unfortunate discovery that the long hammer spur had a tendency to catch on to the many internal fittings of tanks and other vehicles with what could be nasty results. This led to a redesign in which the Enfield pistol had the hammer spur removed altogether and the trigger mechanism lightened to enable the weapon to be fired double-action only. This revolver became the No. 2 Mk 1*, and existing Mk 1s were modified to the new standard. The double action made the pistol very difficult to use accurately at all except minimal range, but that did not seem to matter too much at the time.

Accuracy in service pistols has often been a matter of luck. The Enfield No. 2 had few pretensions as a target weapon: it was designed for self-defence at 23 m (25 yd) or less. By 1942

with British forces at full stretch in the North African desert and in the Far East, the volume of weapon production was more important than the quality. To accelerate the manufacture of No. 2 pistols, several features were dropped including the hammer safety stop. The resulting No. 2 Mk 1** was quicker and cheaper to make but was essentially a dangerous weapon. If dropped on a hard surface with a round in the chamber, the pistol was liable to go off. If this seems a foolhardy decision, it is important to remember that British factories were then churning out tens of thousands of Sten guns which were even more prone to accidental discharges. The Mk 1**s were recalled after the end of World War II and safety stops were added before their return to service.

Bullet sizes

The British 200-grain .38 cartridge fired by the Enfield revolver was very different to the 9-mm Luger round favoured by the German forces. Roughly speaking, it fired a bullet twice the size but at half the speed. The black art of terminal ballistics was then in its infancy and this diametrically opposite approach had little to do with the respective bullet's behaviour when they struck a target. The Germans simply had the most power-

Above: Smith & Wesson revolvers are unwrapped after delivery from America. British factories could not meet the demand for pistols at the start of WW II.

ful round that was practical for an early 20th century automatic. The British had begun with the .455 Webley cartridge and wanted to

Below: The Royal Armoured Corps disliked the spurred hammer on the Enfield Mk 1, since it could snag on the many awkward corners inside an AFV.

Inside the Enfield revolver

The Enfield .38 revolver was closely based on a Webley and Scott design and was very similar to the pistols carried by British troops during World War I. The change to a lighter calibre was called for to make training easier.

Sights
The blade foresight and 'V' rear sight are good enough for combat shooting at 20 m (65.5 ft) or less. They are designed to take the hard knocks of service life without breaking, and the weapon is solid enough to double as a club in extremes.

380/200 service cartridge
This was the British designation for the .38 Smith & Wesson round fired by the Enfield revolver. The Army regarded its 200-grain jacketed bullet as having almost as much stopping power as the old .455 round

Hammer
The spurred hammer of the Mk 1 allowed the weapon to be cocked manually and fired single action. This seems to have been the preferred technique judging by the training pictures shown on pages 34 and 36.

Tip-up action
The revolver was loaded and emptied by depressing the release catch to the left of the cylinder (see photograph on this page). The pistol swung open and the ejector star pushed upwards to dump the empty cases.

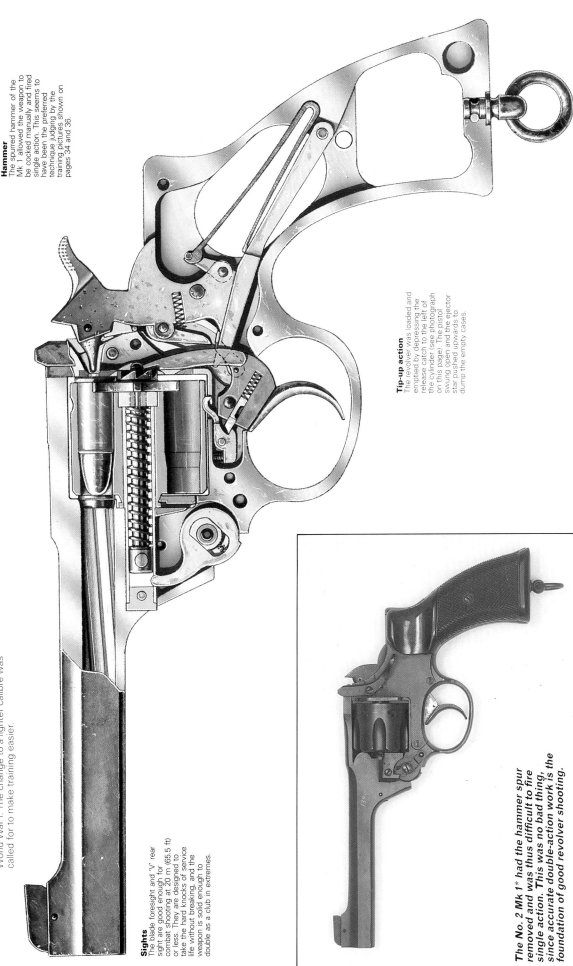

The No. 2 Mk 1* had the hammer spur removed and was thus difficult to fire single action. This was no bad thing, since accurate double-action work is the foundation of good revolver shooting.

lighten it to give inexperienced shooters a better chance of hitting the target.

Webley and Scott re-entered the scene during World War II, when supplies of the Enfield pistols were too slow to meet the ever-expanding demand. Thus the Webley Mk 4 was ordered to eke out supplies, and Webley and Scott went on to supply thousands of its design to the British Army after all. Unfortunately, although the two pistols were virtually identical in appearance, there were enough minor differences between them to prevent interchangeability of parts.

Wartime service

Both pistols saw extensive use between 1939 and 1945, and although the Enfield revolvers (there was a No. 2 Mk 1** which embodied wartime production expedients) were the official standard pistols, the Webley Mk 4 was just as widely used among British and Commonwealth armed forces. Both remained in service until the 1960s and both are still to be encountered as service pistols in various parts of the world.

Above: More 'duelling stance' revolver shooting; this time from the RAF. These men are firing Webley revolvers from which the Enfield design was developed.

Below: An officer from the Parachute Regiment armed with an Enfield revolver during the ill-fated attack on Arnhem during 1944.

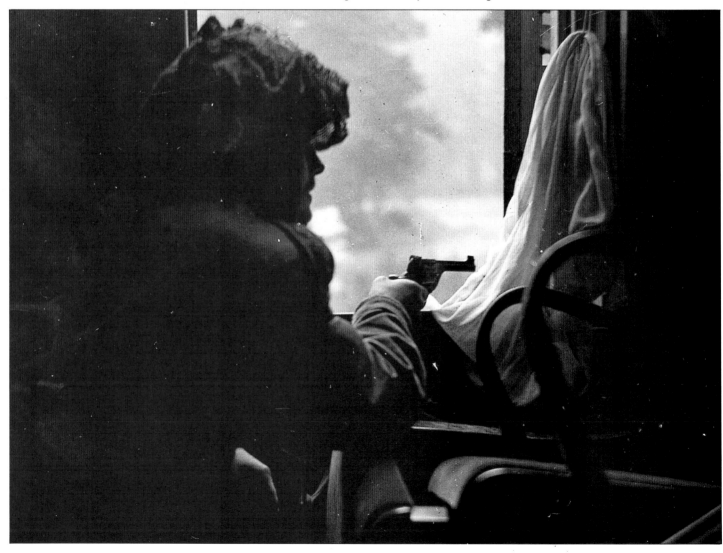

Maschinen Pistole 40

It is one of the most famous weapons in the world. Star of countless war movies of the 1950s and 1960s, the Schmeisser machine pistol seemed to be the favoured weapon of every German soldier, from prison camp guards through Gestapo agents to the hapless troops fighting the weather and the Russians on the Eastern Front.

Unfortunately that picture, like so many emanating from Hollywood, is false. Hugo Schmeisser had nothing to do with the design of the sub-machine gun; designated as the MP38, it was manufactured by the Erfurter Maschinenfabrik, otherwise known as Erma-Werke. Although it was made in large numbers, its issue was largely restricted to specific front-line units. Far from being popular with everyone, it was often ditched on the Russian Front in favour of captured Soviet PPSh-41s, which though crudely made were far more reliable. Even so, the MP38 and the product-improved MP40 which followed were very important and influential weapons.

The sub-machine gun was a result of the trench warfare of World War I. Infantrymen in most armies were equipped with high-powered rifles: long, unwieldy, but accurate to ranges of 1,000 m (3,280 ft) or more. But a long weapon was a definite handicap in the close-quarter fighting of the trenches, and long-range capability was wasted when combat usually took place at ranges of tens of metres or less.

German first

A number of armies experimented with new weapons, but it was the Germans who have some claim to having produced the first true sub-machine gun or machine pistol. The MP18 introduced most of the basic attributes of the sub-machine gun. It was short and handy, employed a simple operating system known as blowback to produce automatic fire, and used a low-powered pistol round which was sufficient for short-range accuracy but which made the weapon much more easy to control than if full-power cartridges were used.

Blowback is very simple. The gun is cocked by pulling back the breech block. Pulling the trigger releases the

Right: The light weight of the sub-machine gun meant that a weapon like the MP40 was ideal equipment for troops like this mountain soldier, who might be expected to operate for long periods without any transport but himself.

Below: By the end of World War II, many of the million or so MP38s and MP40s that had been made were in the hands of Germany's last ditch defence: the old men and young boys of the Volkssturm.

Inside the MP40

Muzzle
The muzzle has a steel jacket housing the muzzle cap and the foresight. The resting bar beneath the barrel protects the metal when the weapon is fired from the rest. The bulge at the front of the bar prevents the gun from slipping back when fired.

The MP38 and MP40 machine pistols developed and built by the Erfurter Maschinenfabrik concern were among the first weapons of their type to incorporate plastic and sheet metal in their construction. They were not true mass production weapons, however, in spite of appearances. The MP38 still required extensive use of expensively machined parts, and although the MP40 was simplified for ease of production, it was nowhere near as economical to produce as the British Sten or the American M3 'Grease Gun'.

Barrel
The MP38 and the MP40 used the same barrel. It was 25 cm (9.8 in) long, with six grooves in a right-hand spiral, 9-mm Parabellum ammunition produced a muzzle velocity of about 380 m/sec (1,246 ft/sec), and the M38 and its developments had an effective range of 100 m (328 ft) or more.

Action
The MP38 was a simple blowback weapon. It was not very safe when carried with a loaded magazine. If it received a jolt, the bolt could bounce back far enough to pick up a round from the magazine. With no other safety, the telescoping recoil spring would force the bolt forward, firing the weapon.

Magazine
German sub-machine guns of World War II usually fed from magazines in which 9-mm Parabellum rounds were stored in a single row. This meant that magazines tended to be long and slightly unwieldy, and also prone to misfeed.

block, which is activated by a powerful spring. As it moves forward, the breech block picks up a round from the magazine feed, automatically inserting it into the chamber. As the block continues to move forwards, the firing pin ignites the cartridge. The recoil forces so produced are balanced by the forward movement of the breech block, which is brought to a halt and 'locks' in place as the bullet is fired. As the recoil forces continue to mount, the breech block is forced back, extracting and ejecting the spent case. If the trigger is held back, the action repeats automatically.

The essence of the sub-machine gun is its simplicity. The operating mechanism should be basic and light, and the low power of pistol rounds means that the weapon does not need to be too strongly constructed. This fact escaped the notice of gunmakers

Wehrmacht soldiers break into a peasant's hut during Germany's invasion of Russia. The handy compactness of the MP40 was a definite asset in the confined spaces of urban and house-to-house combat.

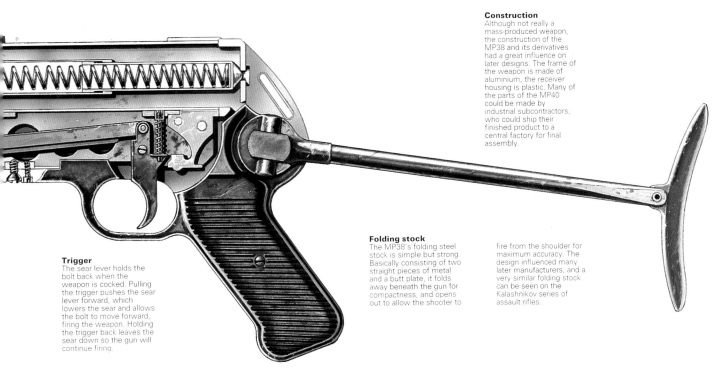

Construction
Although not really a mass-produced weapon, the construction of the MP38 and its derivatives had a great influence on later designs. The frame of the weapon is made of aluminium, the receiver housing is plastic. Many of the parts of the MP40 could be made by industrial subcontractors, who could ship their finished product to a central factory for final assembly.

Trigger
The sear lever holds the bolt back when the weapon is cocked. Pulling the trigger pushes the sear lever forward, which lowers the sear and allows the bolt to move forward, firing the weapon. Holding the trigger back leaves the sear down so the gun will continue firing.

Folding stock
The MP38's folding steel stock is simple but strong. Basically consisting of two straight pieces of metal and a butt plate, it folds away beneath the gun for compactness, and opens out to allow the shooter to fire from the shoulder for maximum accuracy. The design influenced many later manufacturers, and a very similar folding stock can be seen on the Kalashnikov series of assault rifles.

in the post-World War I years, and most sub-machine guns of the 1920s and early 1930s had much care and attention lavished on their construction. Built to high standards, using largely machined metal and best quality wood, sub-machine guns of the period were far from cheap.

German army request

The MP38 changed all that. For a long time, the Wehrmacht considered the sub-machine gun to be primarily a police weapon, with some limited military value in trench warfare. However, in the late 1930s the German army changed its opinion, perhaps as a result of the lessons learned during the Spanish Civil War. It asked the Erma company to produce a simple, easy to manufacture weapon, intended to arm the Wehrmacht's newly formed Panzer forces and the Luftwaffe's Fallschirmjäger, or any other troops who might have to fight in confined spaces.

It was the first sub-machine gun to be completely manufactured from metal and plastic parts, and the first with a folding stock. The folding metal stock was influential, a similar design being used by the Soviets on the postwar Kalashnikov assault rifle. It somehow looked cheaper and more military than previous designs, although

French volunteers in the Wehrmacht pose for the cameras of Germany's wartime propaganda magazine 'Signal'. Wehrmacht and the Waffen SS units fighting on the Eastern Front included troops from almost all European nations.

that cheapness was illusory, since the working parts were made in the traditional manner, expensively machined from solid steel.

The MP38 was fairly conventional. It had a blowback bolt, with a vertical magazine below the receiver feeding 9-mm Parabellum rounds into an equally conventional feed system. The cocking handle on the left of the receiver operated in an open slot, but although dirt and foreign matter could enter the working parts they were sufficiently robust to continue working even when severely fouled.

In action, some problems came to light with the MP38. If the gun was cocked, the bolt could be dislodged by a jar or a knock, firing the weapon without a touch on the trigger. A number of casualties were caused before a cross-bolt safety pin was fitted. This enabled the weapon to be carried cocked. The single-column magazine, inherited from the original MP18, was also a problem. It was inefficient and prone to jamming, and the length of the 32-round box projecting downwards meant that it was difficult to use from prone positions or from behind low cover. It was these characteristics which led many soldiers on the Eastern Front to swap their own machine pistols for the tough and reliable Soviet PPSh-41.

In 1940, the MP40 appeared. This was virtually identical to the MP38, with minor changes to the receiver, the magazine release catch and the ejector. Where it differed was in the materials and manufacturing techniques used in its production. Non-essential parts were made from pressed metal and plastic using mass production techniques. Many of the parts could be turned out by non-specialist metal workshops. Sub-assemblies could be put together by contractors all over Germany. All joints were spot welded, and use of expensively machined high-quality steel was kept to a minimum.

Although the modifications made it possible to manufacture the MP40 in large numbers – about a million MP38/40 series weapons were produced between 1938 and 1945 – this compares unfavourably with 4,000,000 British Stens made in half the time. Production of the MP40 was undertaken by the original manufacturers at Erma, with a second production centre at Haenel Waffenfabrik.

The Schmeisser

In spite of its reliability problems, captured MP40s were quite popular with Allied troops, who knew it as the Schmeisser. It was probably a faulty intelligence report which led to the name of Haenel's chief designer being credited with the weapon's design. Hugo Schmeisser was a gifted engineer, and might have had something to do with the modification of the MP38 into the MP40, but the basic design was a product of an engineer named Vollmer, who worked for Erma.

After Germany invaded Russia in 1941, it was found that the Soviet PPSh-41 with its 71-round drum magazine had much greater firepower than the MP40. In an attempt to match the crude but reliable Soviet weapon, the MP40/II had two 32-round magazines clipped side by side. Once one magazine was emptied the new one could be slid into place immediately, and the empty magazine could be changed. In theory this was a good idea, but in practice it messed up the machine pistol's balance. A bigger handicap was the uncovered top of the unused magazine. Open as it was to the mud, dust or snow (depending on the season) that Germans encountered in Russia, it led to many life-threatening jams.

Although manufacture of the MP40 stopped in 1945, large numbers of machine pistols were exported or smuggled out of a defeated Germany. Many found their way into the hands of guerrilla groups around the world. As it is a 9-mm Parabellum calibre weapon, finding ammunition for the MP40 has been no problem. It is a tribute to the basic soundness of the design that after 50 years the MP40 can still be encountered in use in various parts of the world.

Panzer grenadiers crouch in a shell hole as they encounter fierce Soviet resistance in the early stages of the battle for Stalingrad. It can be seen that the MP40's long magazine could be awkward when firing over such cover.

FN Battle Rifle
Falklands Warrior

Royal Marine Commandos armed with L1A1 self-loading rifles stand guard on a desolate Falkland hillside, during the successful British campaign to wrest the islands from their Argentine invaders.

The FN FAL was the first rifle issued to the British Army that had not been designed in Britain. When it first appeared, such things as pistol grips, plastic fore-ends and self-loading were something of a novelty, and many British soldiers swore they could never shoot as well with the FAL as they could with the Lee-Enfield. But with practice and increased familiarity the FAL soon became respected as a reliable and accurate weapon, and generations of soldiers who have known no other rifle have been unable to find serious faults in it. Now, with the advent of the new

The British Army has used its FAL derivative for many years, and it became a familiar sight on the sectarian strife-torn streets of Northern Ireland.

The Australian army used its own versions of the FN, and many Australians used them in combat in Vietnam. Some removed the flash suppressor and modified their rifles to fire fully automatic.

Inside the FN FAL

Fabrique Nationale's light automatic rifle, the right arm of the free world, has earned a reputation as one of the most successful assault rifle designs of the post-war years. The FAL is gas piston-operated and is chambered for the heavyweight 7.62-mm NATO cartridge. The result is an extremely robust, almost 'soldier-proof' piece of kit.

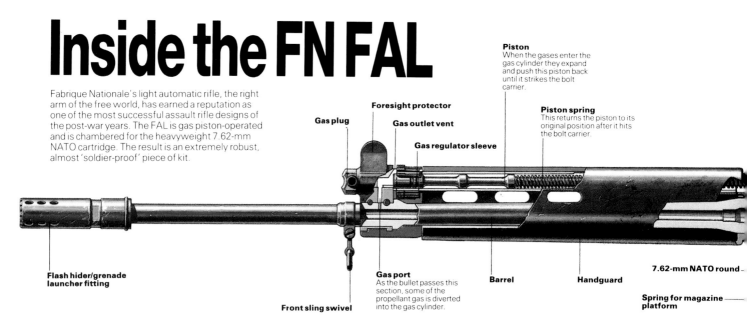

Piston
When the gases enter the gas cylinder they expand and push this piston back until it strikes the bolt carrier.

Piston spring
This returns the piston to its original position after it hits the bolt carrier.

Foresight protector

Gas plug

Gas outlet vent

Gas regulator sleeve

Flash hider/grenade launcher fitting

Gas port
As the bullet passes this section, some of the propellant gas is diverted into the gas cylinder.

Front sling swivel

Barrel

Handguard

7.62-mm NATO round

Spring for magazine platform

5.56-mm SA80 rifle, the traditionalists are bemoaning the passing of the FAL, just as we lamented over the Lee-Enfield.

The search for a reliable semi-automatic military rifle had begun a good deal further back than you might imagine; some armies tested self-loading rifles before World War I. In 1939 Fabrique Nationale of Belgium had almost got it right when war broke out and their design team fled to Britain. They kept on with their design work, and after the war produced a rifle in the traditional form, with full-length wooden stock, called the M49.

This was adopted by a number of countries, and the company then

FNs come in a variety of sizes as each country modified the design slightly. Apart from the Heavy Barrel LMG model, the British SLR is the largest of all the FN FAL rifle versions.

Stripping the FN FAL

1 Remove the magazine, pull back the bolt and check that the feedway and chamber are clear. Let the bolt forward and rotate the take-down lever anti-clockwise to open the rifle.

2 Pull the bolt cover to the rear and remove it from the receiver. Do not press the trigger while the rifle is open.

3 Pull back the rod on the slide and place your fingers under the breech block as it is withdrawn from the body of the rifle.

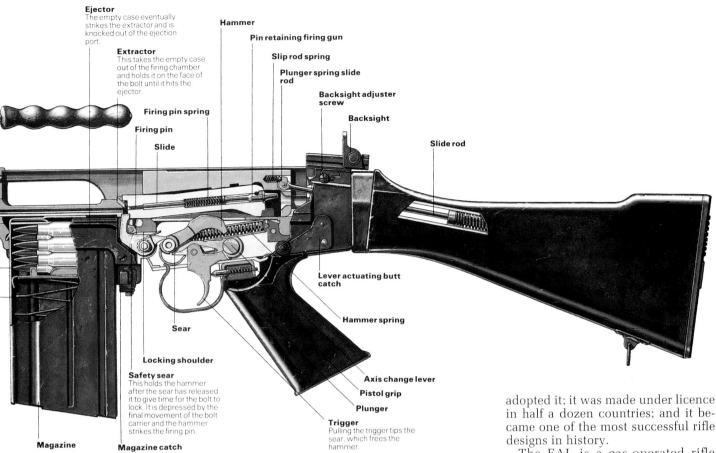

Ejector
The empty case eventually strikes the extractor and is knocked out of the ejection port.

Extractor
This takes the empty case out of the firing chamber and holds it on the face of the bolt until it hits the ejector.

Hammer

Pin retaining firing gun

Slip rod spring

Plunger spring slide rod

Backsight adjuster screw

Backsight

Slide rod

Firing pin spring

Firing pin

Slide

Lever actuating butt catch

Hammer spring

Sear

Locking shoulder

Axis change lever

Safety sear
This holds the hammer after the sear has released it to give time for the bolt to lock. It is depressed by the final movement of the bolt carrier and the hammer strikes the firing pin.

Pistol grip

Plunger

Trigger
Pulling the trigger tips the sear, which frees the hammer.

Magazine

Magazine catch

decided to try something more modern in appearance, using the same mechanism. At about this time the NATO countries were disputing the size and shape of the future standard cartridge. FN could see that, whatever the outcome, some of the armies were going to be losers and would need a new rifle quickly, so they began designing around the various potential cartridges which were being suggested.

When the 7.62×51-mm was standardised, FN had a design ready, and since the British had gambled on their own 7-mm rifle and lost, they turned to FN to provide them with a new military rifle.

Light automatic

FN called it the Fusil Automatique Leger (light automatic rifle), or 'FAL'; the British called it the Self-Loading Rifle or 'SLR'. About 92 other armies adopted it; it was made under licence in half a dozen countries; and it became one of the most successful rifle designs in history.

The FAL is a gas-operated rifle which, in its original form, can be fired single-shot or automatic. The British, Canadian, Dutch and Indian armies preferred not to risk soldiers blasting ammunition off faster than the supply services could truck it up to them, so their rifles do not have the automatic feature. The gas cylinder is above the barrel and carries a short-stroke piston, the rear end of which faces a bolt carrier which holds the bolt. On firing, some of the gas behind the bullet passes through a gas port and drives

4 Lift out the breech block by its front end. The firing pin and its retaining pin are then removed along with the lower part of the extractor

5 Next you remove the gas parts: use a round to push in the wide end of the plunger, turn the plug a quarter-circle downwards and remove it and the piston.

6 Remove the piston and piston spring, which completes the basic strip. Pay particular attention to the gas plug when cleaning the weapon.

the piston back; it strikes the bolt carrier a sharp blow, then a spring returns the piston.

The carrier has had sufficient impulse to drive it all the way back in the receiver and, as it moves back, shaped ramps inside the carrier lift the rear of the bolt out of engagement with a locking face in the floor of the receiver.

Ejection

The continued movement of the carrier now pulls the bolt back, ejecting the spent case, until a return spring sends the bolt forward again. On the forward stroke it pushes a cartridge from the box magazine into the chamber, the bolt closes on the base of the cartridge and the bolt carrier continues forward. As it does so, more ramps inside the carrier thrust the rear end of the bolt down to lock against the prepared face.

On its way back the bolt rolled over a hammer and cocked it. When the trigger is pressed this hammer is released and flies forward to strike the firing pin in the bolt and fire the cartridge, starting the whole cycle off again. When firing on automatic, the final movement of the bolt carrier trips a release which frees the hammer, so provided the trigger is kept pressed the rifle will continue to fire.

The sights vary slightly between different countries, since many armies have their own preferences, but generally speaking the sight is an aperture fitted so that it can be slid along a ramp to give the required elevation. The foresight is a blade set between two prominent protectors at the front of the gas cylinder.

British differences

The British model varies from the standard FAL in some minor details, largely to suit British manufacturing methods but also in having prominent oblique cuts in the bolt carrier which are intended to scour away any dust or dirt inside the receiver and eject it through the ejection opening as the bolt moves back and forth. The Australian army devised a slightly shorter version than standard, by modifying the barrel and flash hider; they also use the heavy-barrel model as a light machine-gun substitute for units other than infantry.

The Canadian army version had an aperture in the receiver cover through which the magazine could be replenished by stripping chargers of five rounds down past the open bolt. Brazil has begun making a more or less full-sized FAL but chambered for the 5.56-mm cartridge. The number of variations is legion, but all are matters of detail; the basic FAL remains the same, whatever the national preferences might be.

A British corporal shows off the newly arrived FN, which his battalion evaluated under combat conditions in Malaya during the early 1950s.

One of the most enduring images of the British Army is the SLR held in a 'non-threatening' position by soldiers on the streets of Northern Ireland.

Changing magazines: like most 7.62-mm NATO rifles the FN's magazine holds 20 rounds, as opposed to the 30 rounds in Kalashnikov rifles.

Above: The magazine catch in close-up. When loading, the front part of the magazine should be inserted first and the back rotated upwards.

Below: Royal Marines in a patrol base near Mount Kent check their rifles. In the Falklands both sides used their own versions of the FN FAL.

Glock's Plastic Pistol

The Glock pistol is a remarkable weapon. This ugly, black pistol broke all the rules: largely made of plastic, its design makes no concessions to the popular view of what a pistol should look like. It has no safety catch or de-cocking lever. The dull matt finish of the steel slide completes the picture. This is a brutally functional killing machine.

When it first appeared there were widespread press reports about this sinister plastic pistol. Why plastic? Was it deliberately designed to be smuggled through security checkpoints at airports – was the Glock intended as the latest weapon in the terrorist arsenal? In fact the Glock is firmly on the side of law and order. The slide, barrel and trigger group are all metal, so it is not X-ray proof. And the Glock is now in widespread service with police forces worldwide. No fewer than 40 per cent of American law enforcement agencies that use automatic pistols have adopted the Glock.

Can stand the heat

The Glock's receiver is made of a type of plastic that will only melt in temperatures over 200°C (392°F). But this very tough material is exceptionally light; a fully loaded Glock is lighter than most comparable metal pistols

Below: Glock was one of the first gunmakers to offer its pistols chambered for the new .40 Smith & Wesson cartridge. The Model 22 was announced in January 1991.

With no safety catch or de-cocking lever to manipulate, the Glock is as easy to shoot as a revolver. Internal safety devices prevent it from firing unless the trigger is pulled.

when they are empty. For any soldier or police officer who has to wear a pistol on their hip all day long, this is an important consideration.

The old military adage of 'Keep It Simple' has been rigorously applied in the design of the Glock. It has only 33 parts, and can be stripped in a mat-

Above: The Glock's metal parts are finished with a non-glare matt Tenifer process that protects them from corrosion in tropical climates. Left: Glock pistols have been tested in temperatures ranging from -40°C (-40°F) to 200°C (392°F): the gun keeps working long after its human operator can!

ter of seconds. Best of all, it has no external safety catch to release – nothing to remember in the stress of action. Unlike almost all pistols in military service, the Glock is ready to fire from the moment it leaves your holster. Draw and fire: that is all you need to do. A group of internal safety mechanisms keeps the weapon in a safe condition until the trigger is pulled.

There are several methods of carrying conventional automatic pistols ready for action. Since the introduction of the Walther P38 by the German army, double-action pistols have been popular with the military. The pistol is carried with a round in the chamber and the hammer down. It cannot fire unless the trigger is pulled, and the relatively heavy pull required to both cock and fire the gun practically guarantees against an accidental discharge.

Safe carry technique

Single-action pistols like the famous Colt M1911 or the British Army's Browning High Power are more problematic. They can be carried 'cocked and locked': hammer cocked but held by a safety catch. However, this may be satisfactory in the hands of a well-trained pistol shot. But it is a recipe for disaster otherwise. Safeties can be knocked or brush against clothing – and if accidentally released the trigger needs only a light touch to fire the gun.

Double-action pistols have been adopted by most armies as the safer alternative. But they are open to two main criticisms – the first shot requires a heavy trigger pull. It does not matter if the gun carries a 15-round

*In 1990 a **Glock 17** fired 10,140 rounds in three hours and 47 minutes. The weapon was assembled from 20 pistols with the parts mixed together, so witnesses saw it was not a specially selected pistol.*

magazine; it is often the first shot that matters most. Secondly, double-action weapons like the Beretta 92 have external safety catches as well. There are enough recorded instances of police officers drawing such guns and forgetting to release the safety to give cause for concern. Poor training? Perhaps. But this is a particularly important point about pistols in general. As a service weapon they are issued to

many personnel as a last-ditch defensive weapon. Tank or vehicle crew, gunners, officers, medics – men and women whose jobs leave little time for pistol practice.

Unfortunately, it takes training and regular practice to maintain a reasonable standard of pistolcraft. However brilliantly a pistol performs in the hands of elite special forces units fighting behind the lines, the true test

Inside the Glock

The secret of the Glock's success is its simplicity. With only 33 different components in each pistol, maintenance is quick and cheap. The Glock is equally simple to operate, with no safeties or de-cocking levers: it is as easy to shoot as a revolver.

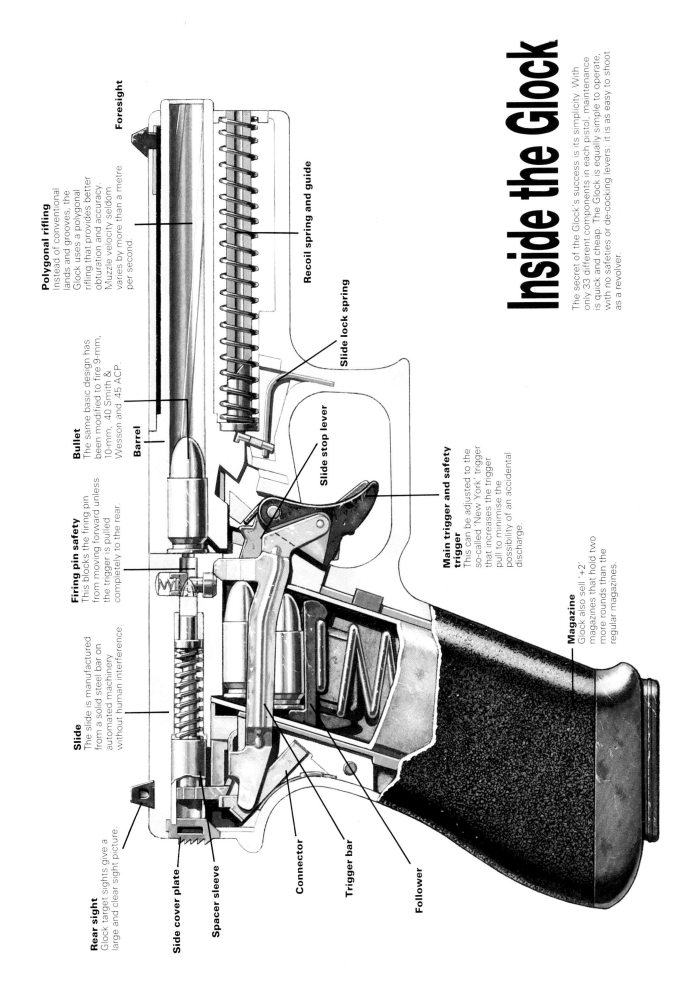

Foresight

Polygonal rifling
Instead of conventional lands and grooves, the Glock uses a polygonal rifling that provides better obturation and accuracy. Muzzle velocity seldom varies by more than a metre per second.

Bullet
The same basic design has been modified to fire 9-mm, 10-mm, .40 Smith & Wesson and .45 ACP.

Barrel

Firing pin safety
This blocks the firing pin from moving forward unless the trigger is pulled completely to the rear.

Slide
The slide is manufactured from a solid steel bar on automated machinery without human interference.

Recoil spring and guide

Slide lock spring

Slide stop lever

Main trigger and safety trigger
This can be adjusted to the so-called 'New York' trigger that increases the trigger pull to minimise the possibility of an accidental discharge.

Magazine
Glock also sell '+2' magazines that hold two more rounds than the regular magazines.

Rear sight
Glock target sights give a large and clear sight picture.

Side cover plate

Spacer sleeve

Connector

Trigger bar

Follower

of a military handgun is at the other end of the battlefront. How does it perform in the hands of a cook or a typist when enemy commandos arrive unannounced at your headquarters?

The Glock is not a true double-action weapon; its actual operation defies the standard categories and is called 'Safe Action' by the manufacturers, who know a good advertising slogan when they hear one. The trigger is in two parts: pulling it back disengages the trigger safety and fully cocks the striker. As you continue to pull on the trigger the firing-pin lock is released and eventually the gun fires. When the trigger is released, the striker goes to half-cock but remains secure and the other safety devices all re-engage.

It feels like a single-action trigger with a lot of take-up. Because it does not demand the heavy trigger pressure of most double-action autos, the Glock is more accurate in the hands of an average shooter. The trigger pull can be adjusted. Some police agencies in the USA prefer the so-called 'New York' trigger – a heavier trigger pull adopted for added safety. Tense hands near the Glock's relatively light trigger have led to black jokes along the lines of 'Stop! Or I'll accidentally shoot you'. Police departments were sued, libel suits flew thick and fast, and the armourers got to work. Never-

theless, the Glock's simplicity and durability have made it many friends, and its success has made it the envy of many other manufacturers.

The Glock 17 9-mm is the most widely used Glock pistol. Adopted by the Austrian army and various special forces units, it is an outstanding handgun. Military men and law enforcement personnel who have to shoot it out with well-armed drug dealers, all value its exceptional magazine capacity. The standard 17-round magazine is now supplemented by an extended version holding 20 rounds.

The Glock is now available in several other calibres. Glock were one of the first manufacturers to launch a 10-mm pistol. One more step in search of the ultimate pistol cartridge, the 10-mm is a far more lethal round than the standard 9-mm Parabellum used by most armies. Most commercial ammunition for the 10-mm is extremely powerful and only suitable for well-trained shooters whose handgun is their primary weapon. The FBI has been experimenting with the 10-mm cartridge for several years.

In 1990 a new pistol cartridge was introduced in the USA. The .40 Smith & Wesson looks increasingly like the ideal combination of weight, muzzle velocity and controllability. A version of the Glock chambered for the .40 S&W appeared within a matter of

months, and Glock's quick-draw manufacturing stands to win major orders. The rush to launch the Glock Model 20 delayed the arrival of a Glock in .45 ACP, but the latter is now in production. With the addition of the .45, there is a version of the Glock in all significant pistol calibres. A model of functional design, the Glock may have offended traditionalists but its performance speaks for itself.

Above: Glocks have no trouble feeding Silvertip hollow points or other specialist ammunition which some guns have problems with.

Below: The Glock Model 20 fires the very powerful 10-mm cartridge recently adopted by the FBI.

M3 'Grease Gun'

A Korean War vintage M3A1 is put through its paces. A heavy sub-machine gun firing .45 ACP, the M3 remained in US service for many years after World War II, particularly in the hands of tank crew. It fired the same ammunition as the then service pistol, the Colt M1911.

Although by the beginning of 1941 the United States was not yet directly involved in World War II, the American economy was getting onto a war footing. The authorities had taken note of combat-inspired weapon developments in Europe, and new products were being planned or manufactured.

As with most armed forces in the inter-war years, the US War Department had taken little note of the sub-machine gun, deeming it little more than a specialist short-range device for use in trench warfare. However, it rapidly became clear from the war in Europe that the sub-machine gun was in fact a very useful weapon.

The Americans already had the Thompson in production, but although tough and reliable it was a complex weapon involving a considerable investment in manufacturing resource, and it could not be produced in anything like the numbers required.

Study the Sten

The British Sten and the German MP40 indicated to the War Department what a simple, mass-produced sub-machine gun of the future should be like. Using an imported Sten, the US Army Ordnance Board initiated a design study to produce an American Sten-type weapon.

The study was handed over to a team of specialists which included George Hyde, who was responsible for a number of simplified Thompson-like sub-machine gun designs in the previous decade. The team also included engineers from General Motors, who would be responsible for the mass-production of the resulting weapon. Progress was rapid, and in a very short time prototypes were ready for trials.

The first development guns were handed over just before the Japanese attack on Pearl Harbor brought the United States into the war. The massive expansion of the United States armed forces thus made new weapons a priority, and it was not to be long before the first examples of the new sub-machine gun were designated M3 and issued to the troops.

The M3 was a far cry from high-quality products of the gunmaker's art such as the Thompson. Construction was all-metal, with most parts being simple steel stampings spot-welded into place. Only the barrel, the breech block and part of the trigger mechanism required any machining.

Simple blowback

The M3 is an extremely simple blowback weapon. There is no safety fitted and the weapon only fires fully automatically. This is no real handicap, however, since the cyclic rate of fire is relatively low. It fires the standard .45 ACP pistol cartridge. There was provision in the original design for conversion to 9-mm Parabellum. This involved changing the barrel, breech block and magazine, all of which could be done without tools. A small number of weapons so converted appeared in Europe, but the vast majority of the 700,000 US-made M3s were in .45 calibre.

The receiver is of tubular pressed steel, with a straight 30-round, single-column box magazine projecting downwards. The somewhat flimsy cocking handle is awkwardly located just forward of the trigger on the right-hand side. The bolt travels on guided rods within the receiver, doing away with the need for finishing the interior to any great extent. The cartridge ejection port has a hinged cover. The barrel screws directly into the receiver,

Below: A US Marine fires an M3A1 at North Korean positions during the battle for Seoul.

This side view shows the massive bolt and the guide rod group. Unlike the British Sten gun and the German MP 40, where the bolt slides back and forth supported by the receiver tube, the M3's bolt runs on the two guide rods, so the inside diameter of the M3's receiver is far more resistant to jams.

and sights are rudimentary. There are no luxuries such as sling swivels, and the telescoping butt is simply a bent piece of wire.

Rushed into production early in 1942, it became clear that in spite of its simplicity the M3 had some design faults. The faults could be put down to the fact that manufacture was being undertaken by factories more used to making car and truck components. The cocking handles broke off, the wire stocks bent too easily and some important parts of the trigger mechanism broke because the metal they were made from was too soft. However, these could be lived with, and in service the weapon showed itself to be reasonably effective.

Poor impression

The M3 was not wildly popular with the troops. For a start, its somewhat industrial appearance was against it. Almost instantly nicknamed the 'Grease Gun', in Europe it would often be ditched in favour of the Thompson or captured MP40s. This was somewhat unfair since, in general, the M3 was a simple, robust weapon with adequate performance. More importantly, at least in terms of the war effort, it cost less than one-tenth the amount that it took to produce the Thompson. In the Pacific, where there were no alternatives ready to hand, the M3 gained at least grudging acceptance.

Simple as the gun was to produce, it was decided in 1944 to make production even simpler. The M3A1 followed the same general pattern as the M3,

Right: A tank crewman from a US Army M60 on exercise in Germany during 1987. In the same way that British tank crew have obsolete Sterling SMGs for personal defence, the M3 survived as an emergency weapon.

Inside the M3

The M3 was the US equivalent of the British Sten gun: a simple sub-machine gun designed above all else for cheap manufacture. Easy to fire and to maintain, it is an archetypal 'soldier-proof' weapon.

Bolt guide rods
Visible here above the top 45 cartridge, the rods are what the bolt rides on. It does not run along the sides of the receiver as on the Sten or MP40, and thus is less liable to stoppages caused by dirt inside.

Magazine
Like all SMGs with a single-column feed, the M3 is vulnerable to stoppages if the magazine is dirty. Plastic covers were issued from 1944 to keep the magazines clean. The magazine lips are made of heavier steel so they are less likely to get dented.

Bolt
The massive bolt of the M3 disturbs your aim as it slams forward to chamber and fire each cartridge. However, with a little practice you can hit a man-sized target at 100 m (328 ft), which is quite respectable for a World War II SMG.

Retractable stock
This simply yanks out to the extended position and it is relatively sturdy by comparison with other wire stocks. Retracting it is slower for the unitiated – the lock button is rather fiddly. Use of the stock is essential unless the target is in the same (small) room.

Right: A 1950s vintage infra-red sight fitted to an M3. This Heath-Robinson device was actually based on the wartime German 'Vampir' system.

Since it looked more at home in a garage than a battlefield, the M3 was soon nicknamed the 'Grease Gun'. Note its compact dimensions if the wire stock is retracted and the magazine is removed.

A US Army Ranger on patrol with an M3A1. The cocking handle of the old M3, which was prone to breakage, has been deleted in favour of the finger-slot system used on the A1 version.

use of some parts as tools to strip other parts.

The biggest fault with the M3 was a result of its single-column magazine. As with the German MP40, this was prone to stoppages. A plastic cover managed to keep some of the dirt out of the magazine, but it was never totally satisfactory. Nevertheless, it worked well enough, and its cheapness and simplicity meant that it was the M3 rather than the Thompson which became the standard post-war US Army sub-machine gun.

South East Asian combat

M3s were used in Korea and Vietnam. The sub-machine gun's compact size made it easy to handle in confined spaces, and US Army tank crewmen could still be found armed with M3s right into the 1980s. The weapon was also built under licence or copied in a number of Latin American countries.

but with one quite substantial change introduced as a result of combat experience: the ejection port was enlarged and exposed the full travel of the breech block. Cocking was simply a matter of placing the finger into a recess in the block and pulling it back, thus doing away with the easily broken cocking handle. A flash hider was added, together with a number of minor changes. The weapon could be easily disassembled by the ingenious

Field stripping the M3 sub-machine gun

1 Remove the magazine, clear the weapon and then ease the bolt forward by putting your finger in the cocking slot and pulling the trigger.

2 Press the stock latch in and withdraw the stock completely from the receiver.

3 Use the stock as a wrench to unscrew the barrel counter-clockwise, while depressing the barrel ratchet spring with your thumb.

4 Remove the barrel. Note the interrupted threads in the barrel collar of the receiver that allow the guide rod locating plate to index properly at the chamber.

5 Pull the bolt and the guide rod group through the front of the receiver.

6 Use the end of the stock extension as a tool to unseat the retaining clip from the front of the bolt assembly.

7 Remove the retaining clip and lift off the guide rod retaining plate.

8 Use the stock to lever the trigger guard out of its slot in the pistol grip.

9 Withdraw the trigger housing assembly from the receiver. This is as far as you need to go. Note the hammer-shaped ejector protruding from the housing.

Heckler & Koch rifles
Worldwide Warriors

Cases fly from a Heckler & Koch G3 as a burst of fire is sent down range. The G3 is capable of fully automatic fire, at a rate of 500 to 600 rounds per minute.

"If it's good enough for the German army, it must be good enough for us," is the cry sounded by over 50 countries for the Heckler & Koch G3 rifle, and at the last count 14 countries were manufacturing it under licence. Add to that the G3 SG/1, the PSG 1, the HK 33E, the G8 and the G41 and it becomes apparent that Heckler & Koch has a good design on its hands.

War's end

A good design takes time to develop, and the history of the Heckler & Koch rifles goes back a long way. It began in 1945 when Mauser were developing a new rifle for the German army, but the war ended before they got beyond a prototype and the various engineers were scattered. Some of them arrived in Spain and began working for CETME, the Spanish weapons development agency; they took with them the drawings of the Mauser rifle and continued with the development until in 1956 they had a serviceable rifle.

Inherited design

In an endeavour to sell it, the Spaniards gave a licence to NWM of Holland. And just at that time the newly-constituted Bundeswehr was looking for a rifle. It tested the NWM-CETME rifle, approved of some parts but disliked others, and gave the design to Heckler & Koch to improve.

Heckler & Koch was a post-war firm which, by coincidence, was at that time operating from one of the old Mauser factories, so that the rifle had come full circle and back to its birthplace. After three years of further development the rifle was adopted by the Bundeswehr as the Gewehr 3 (G3) in 7.62-mm calibre, and H&K then went to work to develop some variations.

The G3 is slightly unusual in using the delayed blowback system of operation, rarely seen in weapons firing such a powerful cartridge. The secret lies in the bolt; this is in two parts, a light front piece and a heavy rear unit, with two rollers lying between the two

Heckler & Koch have sold the G3 to many armies around the world. It was used by several forces in the Gulf War, including the Saudis.

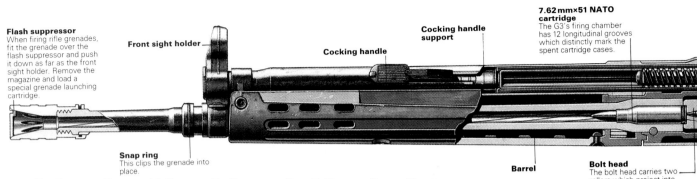

Flash suppressor
When firing rifle grenades, fit the grenade over the flash suppressor and push it down as far as the front sight holder. Remove the magazine and load a special grenade launching cartridge.

Front sight holder

Cocking handle

Cocking handle support

7.62 mm×51 NATO cartridge
The G3's firing chamber has 12 longitudinal grooves which distinctly mark the spent cartridge cases.

Snap ring
This clips the grenade into place.

Barrel

Bolt head
The bolt head carries two rollers which project into recesses in the barrel extension. These retard the rearward movement of the bolt head, so that this moves at a quarter of the speed of the bolt carrier.

Follower and spring

Magazine
The G3 uses a 20-round magazine like the SLR, but the heavy-barrelled G8 can be belt fed or use a 50-round drum.

Inside the Heckler & Koch G3

The G3 was the great rival of the FN FAL in the 7.62-mm market during the 1960s, and it was adopted all over the world. By offering a scaled-down version able to fire 5.56-mm ammunition, H & K are cashing in on the excellent reputation of the G3, which has proved to be a rugged and accurate rifle.

The G41 has been developed specifically for the 5.56-mm NATO round and follows NATO specifications throughout. It includes a bolt-closing device, a bolt catch to hold the bolt open after the magazine has been emptied, and takes NATO standard 30-round magazines. It is built to sustain a service life of 20,000 rounds and, as seen here, can be fitted with a bipod. This is the Italian version, built under licence by Franchi to enter in the Italian army competition.

parts. As the bolt moves forward to chamber a round, the two halves of the bolt are kept apart by the rollers, which ride on the interior of the gun body.

As the cartridge is chambered, the front half of the bolt is stopped; but the rear half is still moving, driven by a spring. The front end of this half is sloped, so that as it moves forward it can force the rollers outwards and into recesses machined in the side of the gun body. Everything now stops moving and the rifle is ready to fire.

Firing process

Pulling the trigger releases a hammer and drives a firing pin forward to fire the cartridge. The explosion pressure pushes the cartridge backwards, and it pushes on the front half of the bolt. This cannot move back because the two rollers, lodged in the walls, prevent it moving, and the rollers cannot move because the front part of the rear half of the bolt is still in place, forcing them outward.

Stripping the G3

1 Check that the chamber is empty and remove the magazine.

2 Depress the pin that holds the butt and receiver together.

3 Remove the pin from the other side of the weapon: make sure that the bolt is closed when you do this.

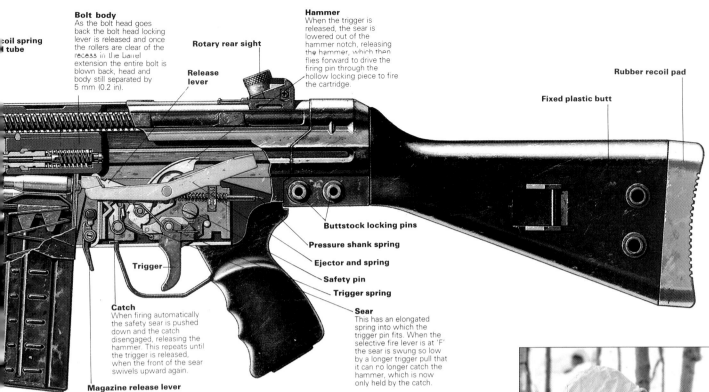

Bolt body
As the bolt head goes back the bolt head locking lever is released and once the rollers are clear of the recess in the barrel extension the entire bolt is blown back, head and body still separated by 5 mm (0.2 in).

coil spring tube

Rotary rear sight

Release lever

Hammer
When the trigger is released, the sear is lowered out of the hammer notch, releasing the hammer, which then flies forward to drive the firing pin through the hollow locking piece to fire the cartridge.

Rubber recoil pad

Fixed plastic butt

Buttstock locking pins

Pressure shank spring

Ejector and spring

Safety pin

Trigger spring

Trigger

Catch
When firing automatically the safety sear is pushed down and the catch disengaged, releasing the hammer. This repeats until the trigger is released, when the front of the sear swivels upward again.

Magazine release lever

Sear
This has an elongated spring into which the trigger pin fits. When the selective fire lever is at 'F' the sear is swung so low by a longer trigger pull that it can no longer catch the hammer, which is now only held by the catch.

This Norwegian soldier is on exercise with British forces in northern Norway. Norway is one of 14 countries to manufacture the G3 rifle under licence.

But the recesses in which the rollers lie have been very carefully designed so that under pressure the rollers can roll back and be squeezed inwards; as they do so, they squeeze the shaped front end of the bolt's rear half and begin to force it back as well. Slowly, the whole bolt begins to move, all at different speeds, until the rollers gradually squeeze the rear part of the bolt backwards sufficiently to allow them to roll clear of the recesses. And as soon as they do that, everything clicks into place. The bolt becomes a one-piece assembly once more, and is driven smartly back against its spring, extracting the spent case and cocking the hammer. When it runs back the whole cycle begins again.

The first thing to come from the G3 was the G3 SG/1, since the German army wanted a sniping rifle. This is no more than a G3 which has, during its factory testing, shown itself to be particularly accurate.

Police use

A step up from the G3 SG/1 is the PSG 1; this is the same action mechanism but allied to a heavy barrel and a very sensitive trigger.

The last of the 7.62-mm members of the family is the G8 rifle, previously called the HK 11E. This has been specially designed for use by police and anti-terrorist forces.

When the 5.56-mm cartridge began to make its presence felt in the 1960s, H&K soon developed a suitable rifle, simply a scaled-down G3 using exactly the same system of delayed blowback. This has gone through several minor changes and is now known as the HK 33 rifle.

When NATO adopted the 5.56-mm cartridge as standard, it did so with a new and heavier bullet than the American M193. This meant that weapons like the HK 33, which were rifled to suit the M193, did not per-

4 The top receiver now comes away from the lower receiver.

5 Pull the bolt assembly out of the upper receiver.

6 Here the two-part bolt is removed from the weapon, ready for cleaning.

Portuguese paratroopers patrol the streets of Lisbon, armed with G3 rifles made in Portugal, during Left Wing demonstrations in the early 1970s. Portuguese troops used G3s in the colonial wars in Angola and Mozambique.

G11 caseless rifle

A remarkable weapon, it can fire single shots, automatic, or three-round bursts at the phenomenal rate of 2,300 rounds per minute – in effect, one pull of the trigger produces a prolonged roar and three shots have gone before you feel the recoil.

Unfortunately, Heckler & Koch's investment in the G11 was to prove the company's downfall. When the German government indicated that it was no longer interested in the revolutionary new rifle, H&K's financial problems became overwhelming, and it only survived by being taken over by Britain's Royal Ordnance.

form well enough with the new cartridge. H&K has therefore developed the G41, rifled to suit the NATO bullet and generally the same as the HK 33 but having the addition of a three-round burst mechanism.

It would be unfair to leave H&K without mentioning its revolutionary G11 rifle. This is totally different to any other H&K rifle, or any other rifle anywhere for that matter, since it is 4.7-mm calibre and fires a caseless cartridge. This has been under development for several years and was due to go into service with the Bundeswehr in 1990. It was also one of four advanced designs undergoing trials with the US Army, which was looking for a service rifle to replace the M16. However, it was rejected.

The Heckler & Koch family

G3 with silencer (above)
All H & K rifles will take their standard silencer, which reduces noise levels on firing ranges.

HK33SG1 sniper rifle (right)
The G3 and HK33 both provide the basis for sniper rifles. Weapons which prove very accurate during proof testing at the factory are fitted with a special trigger group and a Zeiss telescopic sight.

G3 with collapsible butt (left)
With the butt retracted the G3 is only 840 mm (33 in) long. A hollow plastic pistol grip is fitted.

G41 (left)
This is follows every NATO specification for 5.56-mm rifles and is aimed squarely at those NATO armies yet to adopt a 5.56-mm rifle.

Left: Firing the HK 33, which is a scaled down version of the G3, chambered for 5.56-mm ammunition. It has a more robust feel than an M16 but shooting characteristics are similar.

Right and above right: The HK 33's 25-round box magazine is loaded. The magazine is a sturdy piece of kit, unlike the tinny American M16 magazines currently being used with the British SA80 rifle. The G41 gives you an extra five rounds magazine capacity.

MP5

Members of an American police SWAT team move in on a crack house, MP5 sub-machine guns at the ready. Note the two magazines clipped together: 60 rounds ready to go.

Strong Arm of the Law

Sub-machine gun design tends towards two extremes: the cheap and cheerful, like the Sten gun and the Soviet wartime designs — crude weapons which can kill you just as well as more expensive guns — or the complex and costly, like the Swiss MP41. But there is a middle area where quality and cost sometimes come together to produce something which gives the best of both worlds, and one of the most outstanding examples of this is the Heckler & Koch MP5 design.

Heckler & Koch have applied the same basic breech mechanism to a variety of rifle designs, machine-guns and their famous sub-machine gun. This was something of a gamble, because very few sub-machine guns with a complicated mechanism have ever prospered. But the H&K weapon has one supreme advantage over most other sub-machine guns: it fires from a closed breech.

Most SMGs are prepared for firing by pulling back the breech block and holding it there; when ready, the firer presses the trigger and the block is driven forward by a spring to chamber the round, fire it, and be blown back by the force of the explosion acting on the empty case.

Closed bolt system

The H&K design, on the other hand, cocks the gun by pulling back the breech block and cocking a hammer, then allowing the block to go forward, load a cartridge and close the breech without firing. When the trigger is pressed the hammer falls, strikes a firing pin, and the gun fires.

What this means in practice is that when you pull the trigger of an average SMG there is a perceptible shift in weight and balance as the heavy bolt flies forward and slams into the chamber, and accurate firing under these circumstances is pot luck. With the H&K design the minimal movement of the hammer doesn't affect the balance or the aim, and thus you have a far higher chance of hitting the target with the first shot.

The MP5 uses a pressed-steel body

Below: Unlike some sub-machine guns, the MP5 will cycle hollow point ammunition without trouble. This SWAT MP5 is loaded with 9-mm Silvertip, which expands on impact with the target.

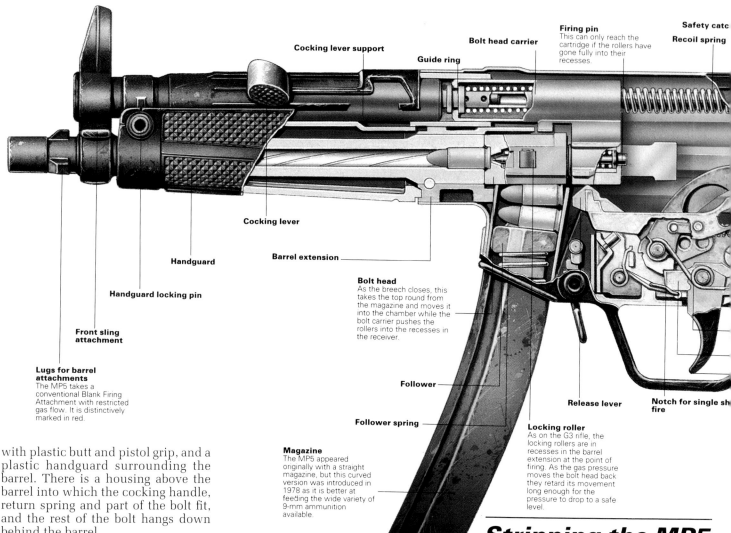

Cocking lever support

Bolt head carrier

Guide ring

Firing pin
This can only reach the cartridge if the rollers have gone fully into their recesses.

Safety catc

Recoil spring

Cocking lever

Handguard

Barrel extension

Handguard locking pin

Front sling attachment

Bolt head
As the breech closes, this takes the top round from the magazine and moves it into the chamber while the bolt carrier pushes the rollers into the recesses in the receiver.

Lugs for barrel attachments
The MP5 takes a conventional Blank Firing Attachment with restricted gas flow. It is distinctively marked in red.

Follower

Follower spring

Release lever

Notch for single sh fire

Locking roller
As on the G3 rifle, the locking rollers are in recesses in the barrel extension at the point of firing. As the gas pressure moves the bolt head back they retard its movement long enough for the pressure to drop to a safe level.

Magazine
The MP5 appeared originally with a straight magazine, but this curved version was introduced in 1978 as it is better at feeding the wide variety of 9-mm ammunition available.

with plastic butt and pistol grip, and a plastic handguard surrounding the barrel. There is a housing above the barrel into which the cocking handle, return spring and part of the bolt fit, and the rest of the bolt hangs down behind the barrel.

The bolt is divided into two parts, a light front section and a heavier rear section, and the two are connected by a pair of rollers and the firing pin. As the breech closes, so the forepart of the bolt thrusts a cartridge from the box magazine into the chamber and stops. The rear part of the bolt, riding along behind, squeezes the two roll-

Captured Iranians aboard USS Guadalcanal are escorted to helicopters by US Special Forces personnel armed with a mixture of M16s and H&K MP5A3s.

ers, which are between the two parts of the bolt, outwards into recesses in the receiver. Unless these rollers are fully out and fitting their recesses, there is insufficient space between them to permit the firing pin to pass, so that it is impossible to fire the weapon unless the bolt has functioned properly.

Roller operation

When the trigger is pressed, a hammer is released to strike the firing pin and fire the cartridge. The explosion pressure then forces the cartridge backwards and tries to force the breech block back as well. The front part moves very slightly, but is then stopped by the rollers, which interfere with the rearward movement.

To obtain any more movement the forepart of the bolt has to drive the rollers out of their recess, and this recess is carefully angled so that in order for the rollers to move they must push back the rear part of the bolt, which is heavy, at a mechanical disadvantage. This slows down the rearward

Stripping the MP5

1 Remove the magazine and pull back the cocking handle. Look in the breech to check that there is no round in the chamber.

4 The pistol grip can now hinge down.

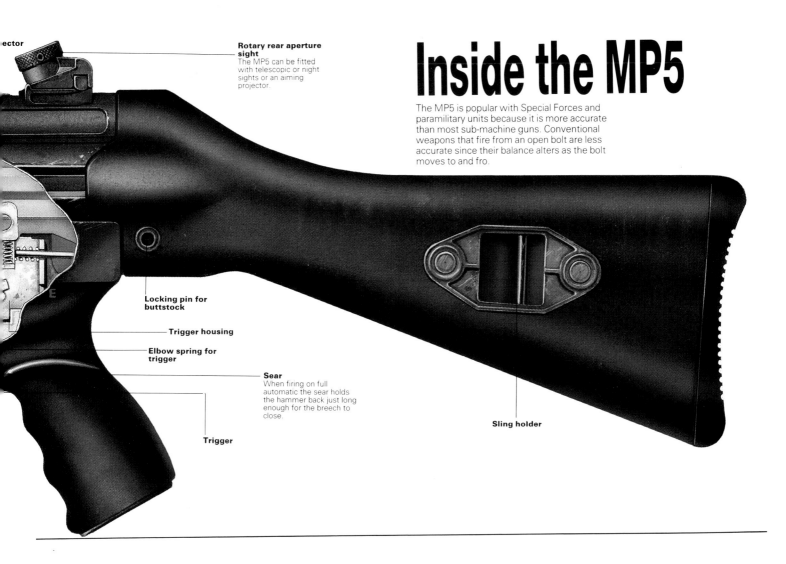

ector

Rotary rear aperture sight
The MP5 can be fitted with telescopic or night sights or an aiming projector.

Inside the MP5

The MP5 is popular with Special Forces and paramilitary units because it is more accurate than most sub-machine guns. Conventional weapons that fire from an open bolt are less accurate since their balance alters as the bolt moves to and fro.

Locking pin for buttstock

Trigger housing

Elbow spring for trigger

Sear
When firing on full automatic the sear holds the hammer back just long enough for the breech to close.

Trigger

Sling holder

2 Pull out the locking pin behind the pistol grip.

3 Remove the butt.

5 Pull back the cocking lever to permit the bolt and return spring to come out of the rear of the receiver.

6 By turning the bolt head through 90° it can be taken out of the bolt body and the firing pin can be removed.

7 The field strip of the MP5 completed: further dismantling is not necessary for routine maintenance. Most SMGs with complex mechanisms have proved to be failures, but the MP5 is an exception.

underneath a jacket or fitted into a briefcase and fired by a trigger contained in the handle, for inconspicuous carriage by bodyguards.

A list of the forces using the MP5 and its variants, if one could be acquired, would be a long and interesting one. It is in extensive use by military and police forces throughout the world and is now being manufactured under licence in Greece, Portugal and Turkey.

It received a great deal of publicity in Britain after being seen in the hands of the SAS during the Iranian Embassy affair, and is carried by police at the major British airports. Its utter reliability and superlative accuracy give it an edge, for certain applications, over most other contenders.

Left: The MP5 is exceptionally accurate when firing a short burst. This MP5 is fitted with a suppressor which reduces the sound to about that of a .22 rifle.

movement and allows the bullet to leave the barrel and the pressure inside the chamber to drop to a safe level before the rollers come free and the entire bolt unit begins to move back, extracting and ejecting the empty case. The bolt then moves back freely, cocking the hammer and loading a return spring; it stops, then begins moving forward again to repeat the cycle.

The gun can be set to fire single shots, in which case the hammer is held by the trigger, or it can be set to fire automatic, in which case the hammer is held by a sear until the breech has closed, whereupon the sear is automatically released to fire the next round. In automatic mode the MP5 fires at about 800 rpm.

Variants in service

There are a number of variant models of the MP5. The current models are the MP5A2 with fixed butt and the MP5A3 with sliding metal butt. The MP5SD is the silenced version; this has the barrel enclosed in a silencing shroud and there are some 30 holes in the barrel which allow the propelling gas to be leaked into the silencer, so reducing the noise made by the exit of gases from the muzzle.

The final model of the MP5 family is the MP5K, designed for use by police and anti-terrorist squads who wanted the most compact weapon possible. It uses exactly the same mechanism but is much shorter, has a forward hand grip and no butt of any sort, and uses a 15-shot magazine as standard. The 30-shot magazine can be used, but this rather destroys the compactness of the design. The MP5K can be carried

Taking aim with the MP5 set to fire three-round bursts. The torch provides a little extra weight at the front to reduce muzzle climb. The FBI and US Special Forces are currently experimenting with an MP5 chambered for the new 10-mm cartridge.

The Galil is an effective assault rifle, based on the supremely reliable Kalashnikov design. It is made in a variety of forms, from a short 5.56-mm calibre para rifle, to the highly accurate 7.62-mm calibre Galil Sniper seen here.

Galil

Israeli Defender

When the Israeli army came into being it was armed with a ragbag of rifles collected from all over the world, and supplying them all with the correct ammunition must have been a quartermaster's nightmare. In the 1950s some order was imposed, the wartime relics were discarded, and the FN FAL in 7.62-mm calibre became the standard, backed up with the heavy-barrel version as the squad automatic weapon.

During the Six Day War of 1967 Israel reached the conclusion that the FN FAL was too cumbersome and that the 7.62-mm cartridge was too powerful for the type of warfare the desert produced. At that time the US Army in Vietnam was beginning to use the M16 rifle and the 5.56-mm cartridge. A number of other 5.56-mm designs had appeared, and so the decision was taken to develop a new rifle based on

the 5.56-mm cartridge.

After a period of discussion and assessment of various proposals, a series of tests was carried out on a selection of weapons. The M16, the Heckler & Koch HK 33, the Stoner 63

(an American design), the Soviet Kalashnikov, a rifle designed by Lieutenant-Colonel Uziel Gal (the designer of the Uzi sub-machine gun), and another designed by Israel Galil were all put through strenuous trials.

The 5.56-mm Galil has been adopted by the South African Defence Force. It is slightly larger than the Israeli version, to allow for the greater average size of South African soldiers.

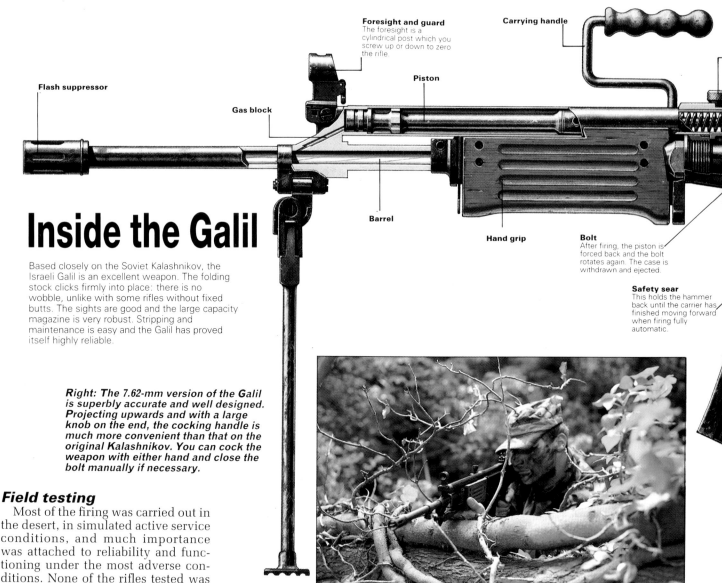

Flash suppressor

Gas block

Foresight and guard
The foresight is a cylindrical post which you screw up or down to zero the rifle.

Piston

Carrying handle

Barrel

Hand grip

Bolt
After firing, the piston is forced back and the bolt rotates again. The case is withdrawn and ejected.

Safety sear
This holds the hammer back until the carrier has finished moving forward when firing fully automatic.

Inside the Galil

Based closely on the Soviet Kalashnikov, the Israeli Galil is an excellent weapon. The folding stock clicks firmly into place: there is no wobble, unlike with some rifles without fixed butts. The sights are good and the large capacity magazine is very robust. Stripping and maintenance is easy and the Galil has proved itself highly reliable.

Right: The 7.62-mm version of the Galil is superbly accurate and well designed. Projecting upwards and with a large knob on the end, the cocking handle is much more convenient than that on the original Kalashnikov. You can cock the weapon with either hand and close the bolt manually if necessary.

Field testing

Most of the firing was carried out in the desert, in simulated active service conditions, and much importance was attached to reliability and functioning under the most adverse conditions. None of the rifles tested was considered to be perfect, but the design submitted by Galil came closest to what the army wanted. It was selected for further development and was eventually approved for service in 1972.

Not to put too fine a point on it, the Galil is basically an improved Kalashnikov, though some critics claim that it was copied from the Finnish Valmet

and that the first 1,000 rifles were built with receivers bought from Finland – which amounts to the same thing.

However you choose to look at it, the mechanism is just the same; a top-mounted gas cylinder containing a piston attached to the bolt carrier, inside which is a rotating bolt, locked

and unlocked by a cam on the bolt working in a curved cam path in the carrier.

American inspiration

The firing mechanism is much the same as that in the American Garand, which has been the inspiration for

Stripping the Galil

The Galil in 7.62mm or 5.56mm field-strips for normal daily cleaning in exactly the same way as the Kalashnikov, to which it bears more than a passing resemblance.

1 Check the safety, remove the magazine, release the safety and cock the weapon to eyeball the chamber. Release it, but do not fire off the action.

2 Press in on the take-down catch on the rear of the receiver and remove the receiver cover by lifting up and to the rear.

3 Pull the recoil spring assembly backwards out of the bolt carrier, and remove it.

cking handle
hen this is pulled back
d released, the bolt
rrier is driven forward
d the top round in the
agazine is pushed into
e chamber.

Bolt carrier
The carrier continues
moving forward after the
bolt stops and a cam pin
engaged in a slot in the
carrier makes the bolt
rotate.

Rear sight
The sights allow aimed fire
to 600 m (1,968 ft). The rear
sight is a flip aperture set
for either 0-300 m (0-984 ft)
or 300-500 m (984-1,640 ft).

Trigger sear
This rotates forward and
downwards when the
trigger is pulled, releasing
the hammer. If the carrier
is fully forward, the
hammer will strike the
firing pin.

eturn spring

Change lever

Folding stock

Selector lever
If set to 'safe' this locks
the trigger extension,
which prevents either sear
being depressed.

Trigger

Auxiliary sear
When firing semi-
automatic the auxiliary
sear holds the hammer
back; the bolt goes
forward but the weapon
cannot fire until the trigger
has been released. This

moves the trigger
extension up and to the
rear, releasing the hammer
from the auxiliary sear
where it is caught by the
main sear and is now
ready to fire again.

Hammer
As in the Kalashnikov
rifles, the Galil's trigger
has two bents and the
trigger extension has two
sears. The recoiling carrier
re-cocks the hammer
when the gun is firing
semi-automatic; on full
auto, the hammer is only
controlled by the safety
sear.

**Magazine
catch**

Magazine
Illustrated here is the
standard 35-round
magazine.

*Right: The South African Army uses a
modified version of the 5.56-mm Galil.
Designated R4, it is strengthened to cope
with the rough and tumble of bush
warfare and has a longer butt, since
South African soldiers tend to be bigger
than Israelis.*

drawn and the hammer goes down to
fire the next shot.

Automatic firing

On automatic fire the hammer is
rocked back as before and is held by
the safety sear. The bolt closes, and as
it does so the safety sear is released so
that the hammer goes down and fires
once more, the firer having kept the
trigger pressed all the time. This continues as long as the trigger is held
down; as soon as it is released, the
hammer is caught once more.

The first Galil rifles were issued
with bipods, and the press made
much of the fact that the bipod could

many designers. This uses a hammer
with two bents and a trigger unit with
two sears. In single-shot mode, pulling the trigger releases the hammer to
strike the firing pin. As the bolt carrier
comes back, under the pressure of the
gas piston, it rotates the hammer back
until it is caught on the second bent
and auxiliary sear.

The bolt then goes back and reloads,
but since the firer is still holding the
trigger pressed, nothing happens.
When the firer releases the trigger and
re-pulls it, the auxiliary sear is with-

4 Slide the bolt and bolt carrier to the rear of
the receiver and then lift it out.

5 Rotate the bolt to separate it from the bolt
carrier. The bolt carrier is fixed to the piston rod,
where most of the carbon is deposited during
firing.

6 The gas piston tube slides off the body
backwards, allowing you to clean out the gas
block.

The Galil has been manufactured in 7.62-mm calibre in the same variants as the smaller calibre models. This is the Galil ARM, with a long barrel and a permanently attached bipod.

be used for cutting barbed wire and for opening beer bottles, though in truth there was nothing new about either of those ideas. Very soon, though, three distinct patterns of Galil appeared, to be used as appropriate by different types of troops.

The standard rifle is the ARM. This has a 460-mm barrel, a bipod, and a folding tubular stock. Next comes the AR Assault Rifle with 460-mm barrel and folding stock, but no bipod. And for airborne and commando troops there is the SAR (Short Assault Rifle) with 332-mm (13-in) barrel, folding stock and no bipod.

Magazine capacity

The standard magazine contains 32 rounds, but a 50-round magazine may be used with the ARM in the light machine-gun role. The muzzle is shaped into a flash hider and is of the standard 22-mm (0.8 in) external diameter, so that rifle grenades may be fired from the AR and ARM models.

Right: Galils can fire the wide range of anti-personnel and anti-armour grenades produced by Israel Military Industries. Disposable plastic sights which fit over the rifle's foresight are provided with each grenade.

Below: The 7.62-mm ARM displays the folding stock common to all versions of the Galil. That of the Galil Sniper is made of wood, while the other variants have the tubular metal stock shown.

Once the Galil had been issued to the Israeli Defence Force, the manufacturers (Israel Military Industries) began looking at the export market. It was sold to Bolivia, Guatemala and Nicaragua, and the South African Army adopted a slightly modified version as its 'R4'.

It appeared that there were armies still looking for a good 7.62-mm rifle, and so the design was now modified to 7.62-mm NATO calibre in the same three versions, the ARM and AR with 535-mm (21-in) barrels and the SAR with a 400-mm (15-in) barrel. So far as we are aware, only small numbers of these have been sold and they are not in service in any quantity.

The last design

The last of the Galil designs appeared in the early 1980s as the 'Galil Sniper'. The 7.62-mm SAR had been tried as a sniping rifle, but the Israeli army felt that it was not good enough and made some suggestions for improvement which IMI followed up. The result was a recognisably Galil weapon but with a much heavier barrel, a muzzle brake to reduce recoil, a more solid (though still folding) butt, a bipod attached to the receiver, and a sturdy mount for an optical sight. The positioning of the bipod gives a stable weapon without placing any stress on the barrel, and it is close enough so that the firer can reach out and adjust it without undue movement.

The sight bracket allows the telescope sight to be mounted and dismounted rapidly without affecting the zero of the weapon. There is also a two-stage trigger which gives an almost hair-trigger release, and there is no provision for automatic fire. The barrel is 508-mm (20-in) long, and there is a special 20-shot magazine. The Galil Sniper has been in use with the Israeli forces for some years, but has not yet been exported in any numbers.

'Uzi'

Short, easy to handle, and above all reliable, the Uzi sub-machine gun is one of the weapons most often chosen by hostage rescue units, counter-revolutionary warfare teams and special operations troops.

Brutally simple and easy to operate, the Uzi sub-machine gun has established a powerful reputation in the last 30 years. In Israel it is practically a national symbol, armies in every continent have now adopted it, and it is used by US Special Forces.

When John Hinkley tried to assassinate President Reagan in 1981 he quickly found himself on the wrong end of an Uzi held by a US Secret Service agent.

The Uzi is a very well-balanced weapon, which makes it comfortable to shoot both from the hip and the shoulder. Its stability helps make it accurate when firing in the single-shot mode and ensures that it is easy to control when firing on full auto. Another reason for the Uzi's popularity is its reputation as a very dependable weapon. Uzis have been dropped in water, buried in sand and bounced down cliffs, yet they faithfully continue to function.

The Uzi is named after its inventor, Lieutenant Uziel Gal of the Israeli army. When it was formally organised in 1948 the Israeli army was using a huge variety of weapons including German MP38s and MP40s, British

When President Reagan was wounded by an unbalanced gunman in Washington, Uzi sub-machine guns appeared in the hands of the President's bodyguard the instant the shots were fired.

65

Sten guns and Italian Berettas. Weapons training, maintenance and the supply of spare parts were a nightmare, and Gal settled down to design a new gun altogether. He studied every sub-machine gun he could get his hands on, comparing their strengths and weaknesses. He wanted, and the Israelis desperately needed, a gun that was reliable, compact and simple to manufacture.

When it appeared the Uzi was revolutionary. It was quickly recognised as a masterpiece of gun design and orders flooded in from armies around the world, keen to examine it for themselves. There were several reasons for this, but the most obvious was the convenient stubbiness of the Uzi. The German MP40 sub-machine gun, often (but incorrectly) called the 'Schmeisser', was a first-class gun, 68 cm (26 in) long, with a 25-cm (10-in) barrel. Gal's Uzi was 47 cm (18.5 cm) long but had a 26-cm (10-in) barrel.

The size of the MP40 was governed by the size of the bolt and the distance it recoiled against the spring. A bolt had to be 10-12 cm (4-4.7 in) long, recoiling for 15 cm (6 in); from the rear of the barrel the gun body had to be at least 27 cm (10.6 in) long.

'Wrap-around bolt'

Uziel Gal didn't like this. He wanted a short and handy gun which would be more convenient for Israeli tank crew, easily stowed in vehicles and ideal for Special Forces operations. One of the sub-machine guns he examined was the Czech Model 23 which had an unusual feature called the 'wrap-around bolt'. This was the answer: a rather longer bolt than usual, of which the forward two-thirds was hollow.

The barrel was fitted into the gun body so that it was unsupported inside the body, and thus when the bolt ran forward the hollow part 'wrapped around' the rear of the barrel until the bolt face met the chamber. Slots in the hollowed-out portion of the bolt allowed for feed from the magazine and ejection of the empty case.

The gun now consisted of a barrel which was largely inside the gun body; a long bolt of which only one-third was behind the breech at the moment of firing; and only sufficient space inside the gun body to allow the solid section of the bolt to move far enough back to permit extraction and feed through the slots.

Uziel Gal adopted another idea from the Czech design: that of placing the magazine inside the pistol grip. Most sub-machine guns had their magazines well forward, where they were often useful as a second hand-grip, but putting the magazine in the pistol grip became necessary due to

The Uzi's cocking handle is located on the top of the receiver. It has a notch cut out to allow the gunner to see through the foresight.

There are no frills to the Uzi's manufacture. It is largely made of cheap plastics and pressed steel parts.

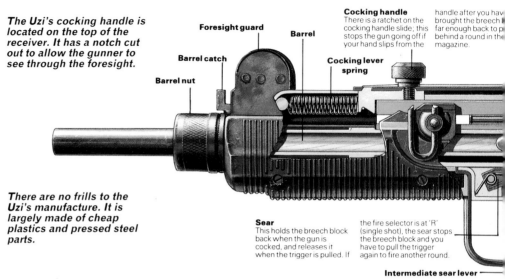

Cocking handle There is a ratchet on the cocking handle slide; this stops the gun going off if your hand slips from the handle after you have brought the breech far enough back to p behind a round in the magazine.

Foresight guard

Barrel

Barrel catch

Cocking lever spring

Barrel nut

Sear This holds the breech block back when the gun is cocked, and releases it when the trigger is pulled. If the fire selector is at 'R' (single shot), the sear stops the breech block and you have to pull the trigger again to fire another round.

Intermediate sear lever

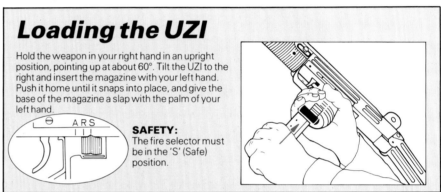

Loading the UZI

Hold the weapon in your right hand in an upright position, pointing up at about 60°. Tilt the UZI to the right and insert the magazine with your left hand. Push it home until it snaps into place, and give the base of the magazine a slap with the palm of your left hand.

SAFETY: The fire selector must be in the 'S' (Safe) position.

Field stripping the UZI

In keeping with its simplicity, the UZI is an easy weapon to field strip. Only five parts need to be handled, and no tools are required. Strip the gun on a clean surface; in the field, use a jacket, for example. To make re-assembly easy, place each part on the jacket in the order it was removed. Re-assembly is done in reverse order.

1 Remove the top cover by depressing the catch, which is in the forward end of the rearsight seating.

2 Lift the rear part of the cover and pull it upwards and backwards to remove it from the gun.

4 Remove the breechblock and return spring assembly by bringing it forwards over the front sight.

5 Press the barrel catch in the front part of the foresight seating, and unscrew the barrel nut.

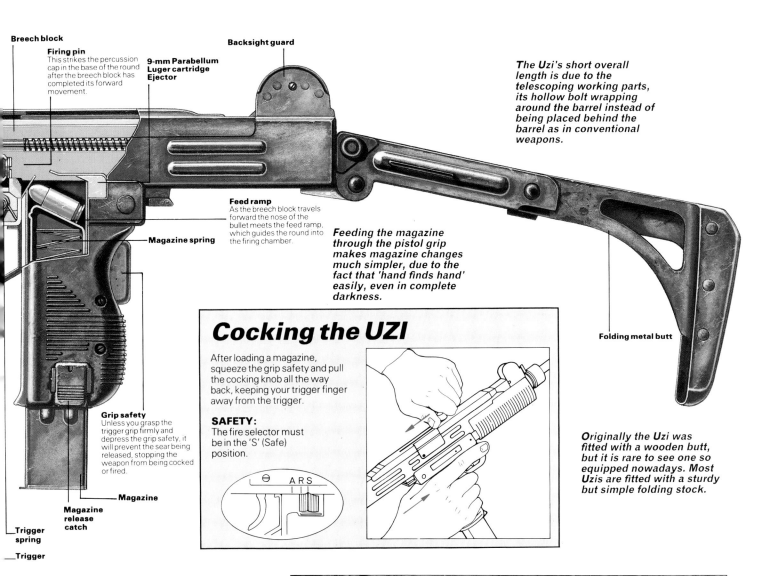

Breech block

Firing pin
This strikes the percussion cap in the base of the round after the breech block has completed its forward movement.

9-mm Parabellum Luger cartridge

Ejector

Backsight guard

The Uzi's short overall length is due to the telescoping working parts, its hollow bolt wrapping around the barrel instead of being placed behind the barrel as in conventional weapons.

Feed ramp
As the breech block travels forward the nose of the bullet meets the feed ramp, which guides the round into the firing chamber.

Magazine spring

Feeding the magazine through the pistol grip makes magazine changes much simpler, due to the fact that 'hand finds hand' easily, even in complete darkness.

Folding metal butt

Cocking the UZI

After loading a magazine, squeeze the grip safety and pull the cocking knob all the way back, keeping your trigger finger away from the trigger.

SAFETY:
The fire selector must be in the 'S' (Safe) position.

A R S

Grip safety
Unless you grasp the trigger grip firmly and depress the grip safety, it will prevent the sear being released, stopping the weapon from being cocked or fired.

Originally the Uzi was fitted with a wooden butt, but it is rare to see one so equipped nowadays. Most Uzis are fitted with a sturdy but simple folding stock.

Magazine

Magazine release catch

Trigger spring

Trigger

3 Raise the breechblock until its front is clear of the gun body.

6 Pulling the barrel out completes the basic field strip.

This UZI is field stripped and ready for basic maintenance. Most malfunctions in sub-machine guns are caused by negligence: failure to clean the working parts or spot barrel bulging or problems with the extractor. Before oiling, the bore must be so clean that you can pass a piece of white flannel along it without it getting dirty.

the short bolt movement, and it also made changing magazines in the dark very much easier because you don't need to see to put your hands together.

To make manufacture easy, the body of the gun was made from heavy steel stampings welded and pinned together – this replaced the older system of machining gun bodies from solid steel, and made manufacture both cheaper and quicker. A wooden but was fitted to the rear of the gun body, and a plastic fore-end, beneath the front of the gun body, gave the firer's second hand something to grasp when controlling the weapon.

The result, the Uzi sub-machine gun, went into production in 1951. It was an immediate success and was soon standard issue throughout the Israeli army.

The Uzi was rapidly taken into service by the Federal German Army, the Netherlands army, and the armies of Ireland, Belgium, Thailand and many other countries. It has also been widely used by police and security agencies throughout the world.

Mini-Uzi

By the early 1980s smaller SMGs were all the rage, and the Israelis produced the Mini-Uzi. This uses exactly the same mechanism but is reduced in all dimensions so that the gun, with stock folded, is only 360 mm (14 in) long, with a 197-mm (7.7-in) barrel. Instead of the folding stock, the Mini-Uzi has a steel wire stock with shoulder-pad which folds sideways and acts as a forward handgrip. The whole gun when empty, weighs only 2.7 kg (6 lb), and a special short 20-round

magazine is used instead of the 25-round or 32-round magazines of the original Uzi design.

As if this were not enough, in 1985 the company produced the 'Micro-

Shotgun- and Uzi-armed policemen leave the scene of a siege in Oklahoma city. The Uzi is a popular weapon with police special units, as well as with the criminals they are combatting.

Uzi'. This has been shrunk even more, to a length of only 250 mm (9.8 in) with the wire stock folded, weighs 1.95 kg (4.3 lb) empty, and uses the same 20-round magazine as the Mini-Uzi.

The technical drawback to small sub-machine guns is that as the size goes down, so does the mass of the bolt. This is going to be blown back very much faster, and the gun is thus going to have a very high rate of fire, making the weapon less easy to control. The original Uzi fired at 600 rounds per minute; the Mini-Uzi fires at 950 rounds per minute.

Weight increase

Something had to be done to the bolt of the Micro-Uzi or it would be so fast as to be uncontrollable, so the designer placed a heavy tungsten insert into the bolt to beef up the weight, keeping the rate of fire down to a mere 1,250 rounds per minute. This means that an incautious squeeze of the trigger can empty the magazine in 0.95 of a second!

New machine-guns have frequently appeared over the years, but the Uzi family continues to hold its own. Its crude strength and reliability are proven, and the basic Uzi design can boast over 30 years of success in combat.

The Uzi seen here has a spare magazine clipped to the base of the one in use. Such an arrangement is useful to the Uzi gunner: if the magazine not being used is pointing forwards it is full, while if it points to the rear it is empty. In addition, this Uzi has a red-spot laser sight attached beneath the barrel.

AK-47 The Guerrilla Gun

Look where you like in the trouble spots of the world today and you will see the Kalashnikov rifle. It will never win prizes for grace, beauty or elegant engineering, but it certainly wins them for reliability, toughness and simplicity. Pick it up – it doesn't balance particularly well – and snap the magazine into place. Pull back the cocking handle and release it, and the rifle is loaded.

Push up the combined fire selector and safety catch – a long spring-loaded arm on the right side of the receiver to make the weapon safe. This locks the trigger, but it is still possible to pull back the bolt far enough to check if there is a round in the chamber.

Then press the selector down one notch for automatic fire, or to its lowest position for single shots. But be careful; the selector tends to be noisy, and more than one operator of a Kalashnikov has attracted unwelcome attention from the opposition by allowing the selector to announce his

Egyptian infantry taking part in Operation Desert Storm used Soviet-supplied AKM assault rifles and RPD light machine-guns. The AK-47 series is the most widely manufactured of all military rifles. Simple to operate and extremely reliable, it is an outstanding weapon.

presence. Moreover, it's almost impossible to operate if you are wearing heavy gloves. But that's a minor defect.

Take aim across the rear sight notch and the foresight blade and, if the light isn't too good, notice the luminous spots on each sight which give you some assistance. Squeeze the trigger and fire. The recoil is easily controlled, although at automatic fire the rifle soon climbs away from the point of aim if you insist on too long a burst.

Up to 300 m (984 ft) range you could hit a man-sized target, but beyond that the Kalashnikov is no prize-winner; the general standard of manufacture and the loose tolerances make the accuracy poor in comparison to most Western rifles. But it

The AK rifles

Finnish M76T automatic rifle

East German MPiKM with studded plastic stock

Polish PMK-DGN-60 rifle fitted for LON-1 rifle grenade

AK-74 5.54-mm assault rifle

Romanian AK-47 with forward pistol grip

Chinese Type 56-1 assault rifle with folding stock

Hungarian AMD-65 assault rifle with stock folded

Inside the AK-47

The AK-47 is the most successful military rifle since World War II, and probably the most widely manufactured rifle of all time. This is a cutaway of the Chinese Type 56, a direct copy of the later version of the Soviet AK-47.

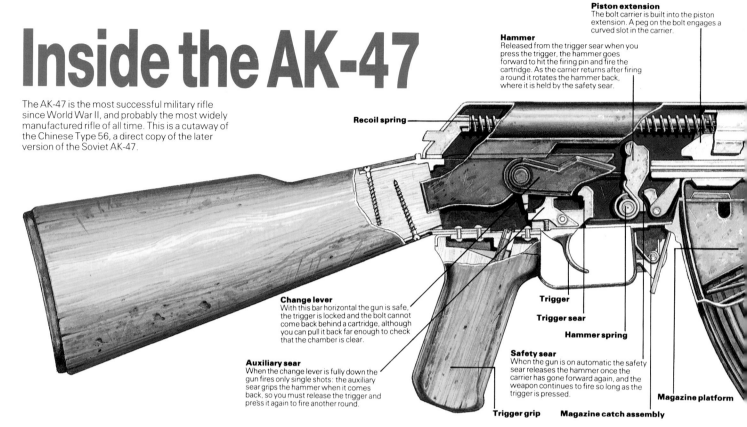

Piston extension
The bolt carrier is built into the piston extension. A peg on the bolt engages a curved slot in the carrier.

Hammer
Released from the trigger sear when you press the trigger, the hammer goes forward to hit the firing pin and fire the cartridge. As the carrier returns after firing a round it rotates the hammer back, where it is held by the safety sear.

Recoil spring

Change lever
With this bar horizontal the gun is safe, the trigger is locked and the bolt cannot come back behind a cartridge, although you can pull it back far enough to check that the chamber is clear.

Auxiliary sear
When the change lever is fully down the gun fires only single shots: the auxiliary sear grips the hammer when it comes back, so you must release the trigger and press it again to fire another round.

Trigger

Trigger sear

Hammer spring

Safety sear
When the gun is on automatic the safety sear releases the hammer once the carrier has gone forward again, and the weapon continues to fire so long as the trigger is pressed.

Trigger grip

Magazine catch assembly

Magazine platform

works, and works, and goes on working after many more expensive weapons will have given up the struggle.

The origin of the Kalashnikov is shrouded in mystery: officially the Soviets developed a short 7.62-mm round, and in 1944 Mikhail Kalashnikov began development of a carbine to fire it. This came to nothing, and he then sat down and designed the rifle which became the AK-47.

We know that the Soviets had been experimenting with small-calibre cartridges before 1939, and the appearance of the German 7.92-mm *kurz* cartridge with the MP44 assault rifle probably led them to draw on their researches and develop the 7.62×39-mm M1943 round.

Their first weapon chambered for this was a Simonov rifle, which appeared in the late 1940s. But the Kalashnikov design was simpler and

easier to manufacture; moreover, it was in the 'assault rifle' style, whereas the Simonov was a fully-stocked weapon which was more in the style of the old-time bolt-action weapons. The Kalashnikov, being smaller and more handy to operate, allowed the Soviet army to get rid of its vast stock of sub-machine guns and settle on a standard weapon which performed the roles of rifle, sub-machine gun and light automatic all in one package.

Gas operation

The AK-47 is a gas-operated weapon, using a rotating bolt inside a bolt carrier. Over the barrel lies the gas cylinder, with a loose piston rod. When the rifle is fired, some of the gas behind the bullet enters the gas cylinder and drives the piston backwards. The rear end of the piston emerges over the top of the chamber and strikes the heavy bolt carrier,

knocking it back.

The bolt, lying inside the carrier, has a peg which protrudes into a curved slot in the carrier, so that as the carrier moves back it drags this slot across the peg, causing the entire bolt to rotate. This unlocks the lugs on the bolt from corresponding recesses in the back end of the barrel and, as the carrier continues backwards under the impetus given by the piston, it pulls the unlocked bolt back, extracting the empty cartridge case and ejecting it.

As the carrier and bolt go back, they compress a return spring, and at the end of their movement the spring drives carrier and bolt back. The bolt face collects a fresh cartridge from the magazine, rams it into the chamber and stops. The carrier, still moving forward, causes the bolt to rotate so that the lugs lock into the barrel and the rifle is then ready to fire the next

Stripping the AK-47

1 Press the magazine release catch forward to remove the magazine and check that the chamber and feedway are clear.

2 Using your thumb, press the end of the return spring guide into the end of the receiver.

3 This allows you to lift off the top of the receiver on all AKs except the Polish PMK-DGN-60, which has a lock-on return spring guide which you must push down.

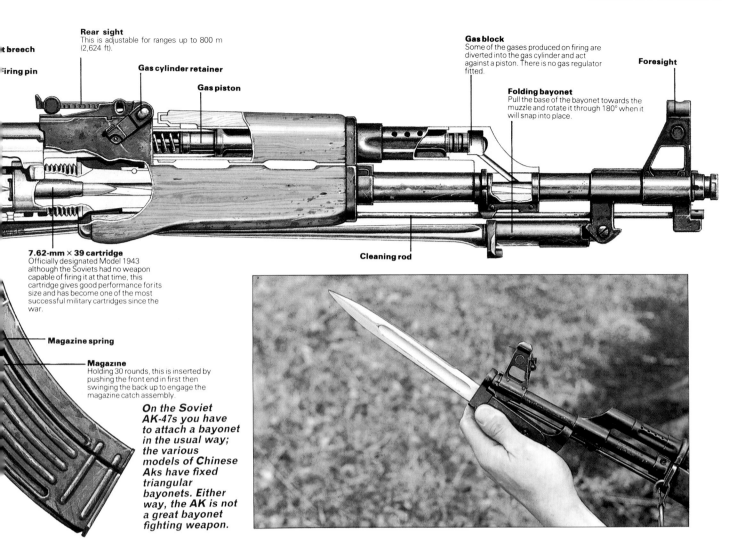

breech

firing pin

Rear sight
This is adjustable for ranges up to 800 m (2,624 ft).

Gas cylinder retainer

Gas piston

Gas block
Some of the gases produced on firing are diverted into the gas cylinder and act against a piston. There is no gas regulator fitted.

Foresight

Folding bayonet
Pull the base of the bayonet towards the muzzle and rotate it through 180° when it will snap into place.

7.62-mm × 39 cartridge
Officially designated Model 1943 although the Soviets had no weapon capable of firing it at that time, this cartridge gives good performance for its size and has become one of the most successful military cartridges since the war.

Cleaning rod

Magazine spring

Magazine
Holding 30 rounds, this is inserted by pushing the front end in first then swinging the back up to engage the magazine catch assembly.

On the Soviet AK-47s you have to attach a bayonet in the usual way; the various models of Chinese Aks have fixed triangular bayonets. Either way, the AK is not a great bayonet fighting weapon.

shot. As the carrier went back it cocked an internal hammer; this can now be released by pressing the trigger, so that it flies up and strikes the firing pin in the bolt.

Selective fire

The AK-47 can be set for single shots or for automatic fire. In the latter case, as the bolt carrier makes its final closing movement it trips a release which frees the hammer to come up and strike the firing pin. This automatic action continues as long as there is ammunition and the trigger is kept pressed.

The first issues of the AK-47 used a stamped steel receiver which did not prove to be robust enough for active service, and in about 1951 this was replaced by a machined steel receiver. This required a more complicated manufacturing process, and the Soviets worked on the design for several years, finally perfecting a much better stamped steel receiver in 1959. This version became known as the AKM (M for Modernised) and the principal advantages were a reduced weight and cheaper manufacture.

In the 1960s the Western military world began looking seriously at the 5.56-mm cartridge, and in the 1970s the adoption of this smaller calibre became widespread. The Soviets watched this with interest and in the late 1970s introduced a new version of the Kalashnikov, the AK-47, chambered for a new 5.45-mm cartridge. This is again mechanically the same, merely adopting a new barrel and bolt, and adding a muzzle compensator which helps keep the weapon under control when firing at automatic.

Estimates vary, but it seems safe to assume that something close to 50 million Kalashnikov rifles of one sort

4 Push the return spring forward to clear the end of its housing and remove it to the rear.

5 Now pull the cocking handle to the rear and remove the bolt carrier and bolt. You can now separate the bolt and the carrier.

6 This completes the basic strip. The gas parts are opened by rotating the gas cylinder lock on the right of the rear sight block.

or another have been manufactured since the late 1940s, and it is without doubt the most widely-distributed rifle in the world and the most-manufactured rifle in history.

But not all of that 50 million came from the USSR; Soviet allies soon began to produce their own.

Foreign-made AKs

Chinese AKs can be distinguished by their markings and by many having folding bayonets; East German AKs do not have the cleaning rod beneath the barrel nor do they have a trap in the butt for the cleaning kit. They also use plastic for the butt, with an odd stippled finish.

Hungarian models have a plastic stock and a front pistol grip attached to a perforated metal barrel shroud; the North Korean version has a peculiar perforated metal folding stock or, in the fixed-stock model, a fore-end without finger-rests. The Romanians use a forward pistol grip but in this case is of laminated wood and forms part of the wooden fore-end. Yugoslavian, Polish, Bulgarian and Egyptian-manufactured versions are very difficult to distinguish from the Soviet models, except by close examination of the markings.

As a service weapon the AK series have gained a reputation for robustness and reliability in the worst conditions which few weapons can equal; on the debit side, their accuracy is slightly below Western standards, but this does not seem to make much difference in practical use.

An AK-47 (nearest the camera) and AKM in action alongside an old British Lee-Enfield. The AK is designed for close-range fighting and cannot match the Enfield's long-range accuracy.

By moving this lever on the side the AK is set for safe, automatic or semi-automatic fire. It tends to make a loud click when operated, and is hard to manipulate while wearing Arctic mittens.

With the cocking handle halfway up the right-hand side of the weapon, you have to reach over with your left hand to chamber the first round.

Above: Russian paratroops armed with the latest member of the AK family: the AK-74S. This folding-stock version is chambered for the high-velocity 5.45-mm cartridge that has much the same effect as a soft-nosed bullet.

Right: A soldier of the Syrian contingent in the Gulf War sports an AKMS folding-stock 7.62-mm rifle. He wears distinctive communist-bloc chest webbing designed to carry 30-round AK magazines.

The Lebel Rifle

French soldiers with Lebel rifles on the march during World War I. This was the weapon of the French soldier from 1886 until World War II.

For many years film directors have been mesmerised by the spectacular noise and blast of modern firearms. Most 'action' movies are packed with firing sequences in which guns literally blaze away, billowing sheets of flame from the muzzle. Anyone with a little experience of guns knows this to be nonsense. While the film makers resort to all sorts of tricks to get fireballs blasting from their gun barrels, real soldiers have been doing exactly the opposite for over a hundred years. No soldier wants a rifle that pinpoints his position every time he squeezes the trigger. On the modern battlefield the trick is to see without being seen, to kill without being killed.

Modern small arms ammunition is

Like the British, the French took large elements of their colonial forces to fight on the Western Front. These Algerian soldiers are parading behind the lines in 1915.

described as 'smokeless' to distinguish it from the black powder used from the first 15th century 'handguns' to those of the 1890s. Black powder – also known as gunpowder – is simple

to produce but it does have a serious drawback. The detonation of a black powder cartridge produces a thick cloud of sulphurous smoke. By the 1860s there were rifles in production

The Lebel Mle 1886

The French army was the first to adopt a rifle capable of using a smokeless powder cartridge. But the Lebel was handicapped by its tubular magazine that could not be reloaded as quickly as a clip-fed box magazine.

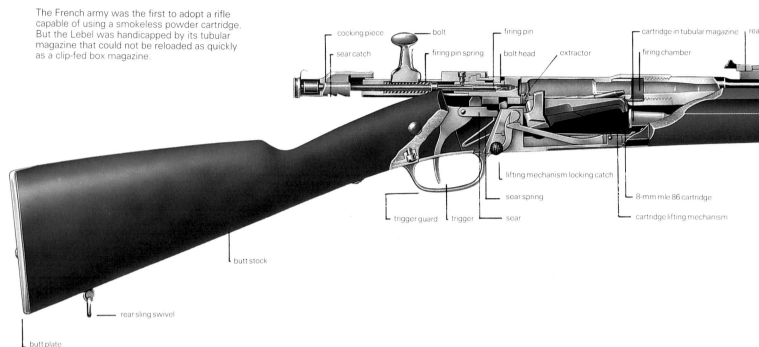

that were capable of hitting a man-sized target at 548 m (600 yd) in the hands of a good shot. But although the increasing accuracy of the weapons drove soldiers to fight in more widely dispersed groups, it was impossible to stay concealed under fire.

Smokeless powder

The French army was the first to solve the problem. In 1886 it introduced the Lebel rifle which fired a smokeless powder cartridge, the 8-mmx50R Lebel. The propellant was developed by a chemist called Vieille,

who worked in the French powder factory, and an army captain called Desalaux. The cartridge that used it was designed by Lieutenant Colonel Nicholas Lebel, commandant of a small arms training school.

The new round was not only smokeless, it produced much higher muzzle velocities than were possible with black powder. Following the ideas of Major Rubin of the Swiss army, the lead bullet was given a jacket of harder metal to stop the soft lead stripping away as it travelled along the barrel. The Lebel's 198-grain

bullet obtained the unheard of muzzle velocity of 716 m/sec (2,349 ft/sec). Its trajectory was much flatter than contemporary rifles, making it much more effective in the hands of young conscript riflemen.

At that time the French naval infantry were equipped with the Austrian Kropatschek, a black powder rifle chambered for the same 11-mm round as the Gras single-shot weapon used by the army. The Kropatschek had a seven-round tubular magazine running under the barrel. Lieutenant Colonel Lebel reworked the Kropatschek design to produce a rifle capable of firing his cartridge. It was adopted by the French army in 1866; Lebel was promoted to full Colonel and given command of the 120th Infantry Regiment in recognition of his efforts.

The French infantry were trained to leave their rifle fully loaded, chambering and firing single shots while keeping the magazine in reserve. They were instructed to use rapid bursts of fire when a good target presented itself. At close range 'fire at will' could be ordered — soldiers fired eight rounds per minute, still keeping the magazine in reserve. This could be increased to an average of 12 rounds per minute by using the magazine. French regulations expected a soldier to be

French soldiers with Lebels deployed alongside British troops armed with Lee-Enfields during the chaotic fighting that followed the German break-through in March 1918.

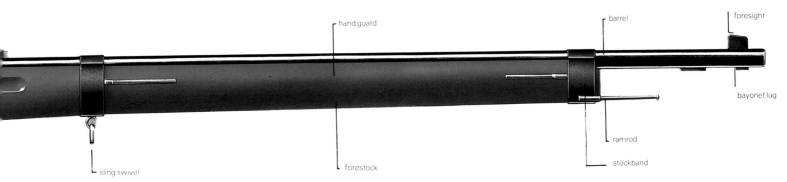

hand guard | barrel | foresight

bayonet lug

ramrod

stockband

sling swivel

forestock

Right: French troops march past the rotund figure of Marshal Joffre. A brilliant engineer officer with much colonial experience, Joffre outwitted the German high command in 1914.

able to reload the magazine in one minute.

By 1888 700,000 Lebels had been rushed out of the factory and issued to French soldiers. Many senior officers were eagerly looking forward to a war with Germany to revenge the defeats of 1870. With their new rifles the French infantrymen would have a significant advantage over their enemies. However, the crisis passed without renewed hostilities and the Lebel saw its first action not in the fields of Alsace-Lorraine but in the sweltering jungles of Madagascar and Indo-China.

Colonial experience

French soldiers found the Lebel a satisfactory combat rifle in colonial wars from South East Asia to the North African desert. The 8-mm cartridge was much lighter than the black powder round fired by the Gras and Kropatschek, so soldiers could carry much more ammunition. In Madagascar soldiers armed with Lebels were able to drive tribesmen from their stockades at ranges of nearly 2,000 m (6,562 ft).

There were some minor alterations to the design of the Lebel. In 1893 the receiver was strengthened and a gas escape hole was bored into the bolt head to release pressure in case of a breech explosion. In 1896 the round-nosed bullet was replaced by a sharply pointed one. In theory, this was dangerous, since in a tubular magazine the point of one bullet lay immediately behind the primer of the bullet in front.

In 1914 the French army finally had its chance to avenge 1870, but the Lebel was no longer in the forefront of rifle design. James P. Lee had patented his first box magazine as early as 1879 and, by the turn of the century, Britain, Germany and many other armies had adopted rifles with box magazines. Loaded through the breech with clips of bullets, box maga-

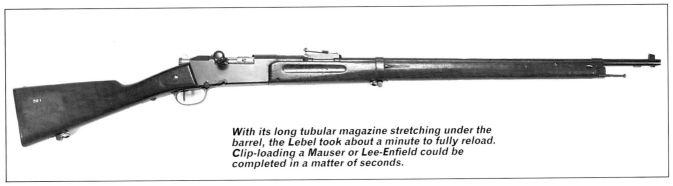

With its long tubular magazine stretching under the barrel, the Lebel took about a minute to fully reload. Clip-loading a Mauser or Lee-Enfield could be completed in a matter of seconds.

zines could be filled in seconds. The Lebel's tubular magazine was now an anachronism. German infantry were equipped with the far superior Mauser Model 1898 – a fine rifle destined to soldier on until the last battles of World War II.

The Lebel did not perform well in 1914, but this was due more to the poor marksmanship of the average French soldier than any inherent weakness in the design. An almost religious obsession with offensive tactics led tens of thousands of French

Above: In 1914 French soldiers fought wearing blue overcoats and bright red trousers. The army had tried to adopt a more modern uniform, but French politicians demanded the retention of traditional kit.

soldiers to rely more on the bayonet charge than on disciplined rifle fire. German quick-fire artillery, machine-guns and Mausers cut them down in droves.

The German invasion was defeated nevertheless and the armies found themselves locked in trench warfare for the next four years. The Lebel was used throughout the war, but a French carbine based on the Mannlicher clip-loading system was used in increasing quantities alongside it. The Berthier was adopted in 1890 by French cavalry, and this shorter, handier weapon, with its three-round internal magazine, proved very successful in trench fighting.

Between the wars

By the middle of World War I the Lebel was no longer the primary weapon of the French soldier. French infantry battalions now included 12 to 16 light machine-guns, half a dozen 75-mm or 81-mm mortars and three 37-mm 'trench guns'. Infantry sections included at least three men with their Lebels fitted to fire Vivèn-Bessières rifle grenades. The battalion heavy machine-gun companies were expanded to 12-gun sections.

The Lebel continued in service with the French army into World War II, although it was largely replaced in front-line units after 1936. It was exported to several countries between the wars, including Bulgaria, Greece, Romania, Turkey and the then newly created state of Yugoslavia.

The average height of soldiers during World War I was 1.7 m (5.6 ft): shorter than the average height of teenage girls in Western Europe or the USA today. This French Zouave is shorter than his Lebel with the bayonet fixed.

The Lee-Enfield Story

Above: British troops armed with World War I vintage SMLE rifles take up a defensive position somewhere in the south of England, as Britain prepared for a German invasion that was expected that summer of 1940.

Dating from the last years of the 19th century, the Lee-Enfield rifle has been used in combat for longer than almost all of its contemporaries. Seeing action during the Boer War, it was still being used 80 years later, in a largely unaltered form, by Afghan guerrillas and by British snipers in the Falklands. It may not be rapid firing or be made of the latest high-tech materials, but its toughness, reliability and ease of maintenance mean that Lee-Enfields will still be in use long after the current high-tech wonders have rattled to bits.

The name derives from the combination of the bolt action fed by a 10-round box magazine, designed by the American James Paris Lee, with a new rifled barrel developed at the Royal Small Arms Factory, Enfield Lock, for firing .303-calibre rounds propelled by the then new smokeless powder. The first Lee-Enfield rifles were approved for production in 1895.

Lee-Enfield Mk I

The Lee-Enfield Mk I was a long-range weapon, as was common with rifles in those days. It was effective at ranges of 1,700 m (5,577 ft) or more, although it required highly-trained troops to get the best out of the rifle at such distances. A shortened cavalry carbine was also produced.

The British Army went into the

The basic design of the Lee-Enfield rifle had already been in service for more than two decades when these riflemen prepared to go over the top on a World War I night trench raid.

Inside the Lee-Enfield Mk I

Short, Magazine, Lee-Enfield, or SMLE, was introduced in the first decade of the 20th century. It was one of the finest bolt-action military rifles ever made, and served the British Army through two world wars and beyond.

Lee action
Designed by the American James P. Lee, the SMLE's bolt action was not quite as strong as the rival Mauser action. However, the Lee was smoother and could be accurately fired much faster than its German contemporary.

Stock
As with nearly all combat rifles of its time, the SMLE had a full wooden stock. This made the rifle heavier (although it still weighed less than many modern assault rifles), but meant that in extremity the weapon could be used as a pretty good club.

Magazine
The development of the metallic centre-fire cartridge meant that rifles designed in the 1890s could carry a reasonable quantity of ammunition. The SMLE's box magazine had a 10-round capacity, double that of most of its contemporaries.

This was the rifle with which the British Expeditionary Force (BEF) went to France at the outbreak of World War I. It was an all-professional force, every man a trained shot, drilled to produce at least 15 aimed shots per minute. Many could double that rate, and such was their rapidity of fire that at Mons and on the Marne many Germans were convinced that the British had hundreds of machine-guns.

Left: Lee-Enfield armed troops on the Aisne in 1918 open fire on retreating Germans, as the Allied summer offensive pushed to bring World War I to an end.

Below: A World War II sniper aims his specially adapted No. 4 rifle from his hide. When well looked after, Lee-Enfields are capable of pinpoint shooting at ranges of several hundred metres.

Boer War armed with Lee-Enfields. The straight-shooting Boer farmers were able to inflict a number of stinging reverses on the British, and hard-won lessons were to transform the British Army after the war.

One lesson was that the cavalry, who as often as not fought as mounted infantry, did not need a special rifle, and one weapon for use by all arms made sense. In 1902, a new intermediate model of the Lee-Enfield was introduced. The Rifle, Short, Magazine, Lee-Enfield was resisted by both the infantry and the cavalry, but by 1907 the definitive version of the rifle emerged as the SMLE Mk III.

Foresight
The first models of the Lee-Enfield, such as the SMLE depicted here, had their rear sights located some distance down the barrel. On later models it was further back above the breech, allowing for a longer sight radius and better eye relief, making accurate shooting easier.

Nose cap
The most obvious difference between the SMLE and its successors is around the muzzle. The SMLE is fitted with a nose cap which extends the stock the full length of the barrel, while on later variants such as the No. 4, the last couple of inches of barrel are exposed.

reliable. It is also the fastest bolt action ever made, being much easier to use rapidly than the contemporary Mauser action. Few soldiers could manage to make use of its long-range accuracy, but they could hit obvious targets at combat ranges, which rarely exceeded 300 yds (274 ft).

The No. 5 was a shortened version of the Lee-Enfield, popularly known as the 'Jungle Carbine', and was developed for fighting in the Far East. It was not totally successful, having a kick like a mule and emitting a brilliant muzzle flash.

Below: The Rifle, No. 4 Mk I(T) was a sniper version of the Lee-Enfield, which was a selected production weapon that had been rebuilt and re-stocked before being issued to the troops.

Above: Troops from the XIVth Army use Lee-Enfield No. 4 rifles to engage Japanese positions across the Irrawaddy during the Burma campaign.

By 1915, the BEF had been superseded by larger, less well-trained armies, who fought a war in the trenches under the most appalling conditions. With basic care, such as keeping the bolt action and muzzle free of mud by wrapping them in cloth, the SMLE would keep on firing.

Rifle, No. 4 Mk I

The SMLE served on after the war and into the 1920s. However, being built to a very high standard, it was time-consuming and expensive to make. In 1931, a simplified version of the rifle appeared. This was the Rifle, No. 4 Mk I, with which the British Army was to fight through World War II. Although it featured a number of manufacturing improvements, and detail changes such as a heavier barrel, simplified sights and a shorter stock, the No. 4 was basically the same rifle as the original Lee-Enfield Mk I.

The No. 4 proved to be as good a service rifle as its predecessor, being easy to clean and maintain, and sturdy and

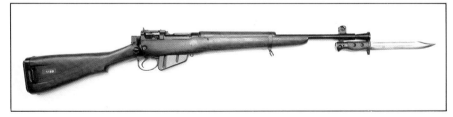

Above, centre: Designed for close combat use, such as in the jungle, the No. 5 was a shortened and lightened Lee-Enfield. It was not a success, however.

Above: The SMLE was the variant of the Lee-Enfield with which the British Army fought World War I. It is easily identifiable from its muzzle cap.

Even when the British Army began to re-equip with self-loading rifles in the 1950s, the Lee-Enfields continued to provide good service. A number of weapons were reworked to fire the new semi-rimmed 7.62-mm NATO round in place of the trusty old rimmed .303. These were used for match and target firing and for sniping. The L42A1 heavy-barrelled rifle is probably the most accurate Lee-Enfield ever made, and it was the standard British sniper rifle up until the end of the 1980s.

Over the years, Lee-Enfields have been produced in a number of countries, two million being produced in the USA and Canada during World War II alone. The last major producer of the SMLE and the No. 4 was India's Ishapore Arsenal, which continued production into the 1960s. Lee-Enfields can be found in the armouries of many Commonwealth countries, and are also still being used by guerrillas in Africa and Asia.

Below: Gurkha troops on patrol in Malaya pose with their No. 5 rifles. Unlike many other Lee-Enfield variants it had a short service career, being replaced by the FN FAL in the mid-1950s.

Below: A Royal Marine sniper takes aim with his L42 rifle. This was the last Lee-Enfield variant in British front-line service, being used into the 1980s and seeing combat in 1982 in the Falklands.

'State Security Special'
The Makarov pistol

Firing the Makarov in the stance illustrated in the Russian manual for this sturdy pistol. Note that the slide is slammed back in full recoil.

Since the Russian way of war relies on massed tank formations crewed by millions of conscript soldiers, the Red Army has never devoted much attention to pistol design. The Russians have understandably concentrated on major weapons systems that are the key to success on the battlefield. New tanks and missiles are constantly introduced as the CIS continues to spend an enormous proportion of its dwindling income on the military. As a result, the Russian army is still equipped with the same pistol that it adopted 50 years ago: the Makarov.

The Russian forces are not alone in this attitude. The US Army has only recently adopted a pistol to replace the Colt it adopted before World War I, and although the British Army is buying new SIG 9-mm pistols, these are only for the SAS and other specialists. The rest of the Army has to make do with the Browning High Power, designed before World War II.

More equal than others

In the Russian army the Makarov is issued to officers above the rank of platoon commander, to vehicle crew and other specialists whose duties preclude the use of even a folding-stock assault rifle. With the introduction of the AKSU – a cut-down version of the Kalashnikov available in 7.62-mm or 5.45-mm calibre – the Russians have effectively reintroduced the sub-machine gun. The first ones to find their way into the West came from Afghanistan, where they were being used by vehicle crew who wanted something more than a small pistol to fend off the Mujahideen guerrillas. The Makarov is a last ditch defensive weapon to be used when all else fails.

Despite its relative lack of importance to Russian forces today, the Makarov is, even so, well-made and has excellent reliability – a characteristic of Russian small arms. During World War II the Soviets used a mix-

The Makarov is seen here with its predecessor, the Tokarev TT-33. To the left of the Makarov is the (former) East German 'raindrop' camouflage holster for it. The gun rests on a tank crewman's jacket with yellow tank insignia. Note the padded tank crew helmet above. The Makarov is attached by its lanyard to the Russian holster rig on the right.

Stripping the Makarov

1 Remove the magazine and check the chamber is empty. Pivot the front of the trigger guard right down, then push it to one side to rest on the frame. Lift the rear of the slide up to disengage it from the frame.

2 The slide can be removed from the weapon forwards as shown here. Note that the trigger guard locks in this position and must be in this position for you to remove the slide.

3 The Makarov stripped for normal cleaning in the field. Re-assembly is the reverse of the stripping sequence, but one end of the recoil spring is narrower than the other. The small end fits onto the barrel.

Inside the Makarov

This is a life size cutaway of the Russian Makarov pistol. It is still in widespread use throughout Eastern Europe and the CIS.

Rear sight
For a standard low-profile miltary sight, this offers a reasonable sight picture.

Hammer
This is cocked by the firing of the first shot, so all subsequent rounds are fired single action. The rounded hammer fits snugly and does not snag when drawn from Russian breast pocket compartments.

Grips
Usually a red-brown plastic, these are cut away on the gun's right side to make room for a lanyard loop: another dated feature, but then, the 1960 manual for the Makarov does have a section on firing from horseback!

9-mm Makarov cartridge
This is the most effective round that can be safely fired from a small blowback pistol.

Barrel

Foresight

Trigger
Shooters used to a crisp and clean trigger break are usually disappointed with the Makarov. With practice, the mushy trigger can be overcome but this does require regular training with the weapon.

Magazine
The cutaway magazines make it instantly obvious to the shooter how many rounds are remaining.

Magazine latch
This old-fashioned feature is much less convenient than side-mounted release buttons. Apparently, the earlier Tokarev pistol was criticised by some soldiers for inadvertently dumping the magazine, so the Makarov adopted this slower, but more secure system.

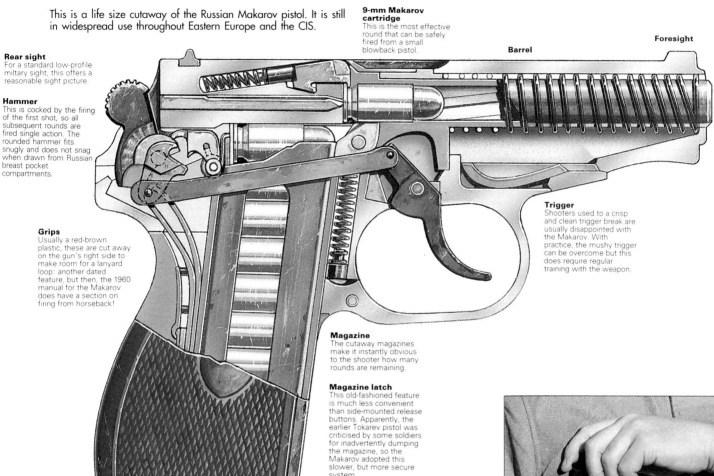

ture of ancient Nagant revolvers and the Tokarev TT-33. The latter is a bulky weapon considering its modest magazine capacity and relatively light cartridge, the 7.62-mm Tokarev. After World War II when they began to look for a replacement, the Soviets were apparently happy to settle for this cartridge again and did not follow the worldwide trend towards 9-mm Parabellum.

The Makarov introduced a new cartridge – unsurprisingly christened 9-mm Makarov – which is not as powerful as 9-mm Parabellum, but represents the most potent round that can be fired from an unlocked breech. It fires a 93-grain bullet at 320-340 m/s (1,150-1,225 km/h). The design of the Makarov is very similar to that of the German Walther PP – some authorities insist that the Russians simply copied it; but on the other hand, if you want a handy pistol that fires a 9-mm round from an unlocked breech, you are quite unlikely to arrive at anything radically different from the Walther.

The Makarov's barrel is permanently fixed to the frame, and it has a recoil spring slipped over it which bears against the front of the slide. Like the Walther (although using a different mechanism), the Makarov can fire its first shot double-action, i.e. pulling the trigger cocks and fires the gun. The hammer drops, fires the cartridge and is re-cocked as the slide returns, so subsequent shots are single-action. Like almost all pistols of this type, the first trigger pull is quite stiff. Indeed the Makarov has a very poor trigger by anyone's standards and it takes time to get used to. With practice the Makarov can shoot perfectly well at up to 25 m (82 ft), but unless in exceptionally practised hands, it is not up to the standard of, say, the Browning High Power.

Fashion accessories

Makarovs are issued in a sensible holster rig that has a pouch for a spare magazine. The Makarov's magazine holds eight rounds and is cut away so

Above: The tank crewman's right pocket includes a slim compartment for a spare Makarov magazine.

The left pocket contains the gun itself – concealing it and the ammo within the uniform is good news for tank crew who have to move in such a confined space that waist belt holsters are a problem.

Above: The Makarov at the moment of firing. Smoke blasts from the muzzle and the ejection port. As with most Russian small arms, case ejection is very positive. The Makarov is comfortable to shoot although the trigger action is usually grim.

Pistol cartridges of East and West compared: (left) 9-mm Makarov; (centre) 9-mm Parabellum; and (right) .45 ACP. The Makarov's steel case is covered with resin to prevent corrosion.

the shooter can easily see how many rounds are in it. Soldiers had criticised the Tokarev for occasionally ejecting the magazine when they accidentally banged the magazine release. So the Makarov reverted to an old-fashioned magazine release in the heel of the butt: good for magazine retention but disastrous if you need to reload in a hurry.

The Makarov was introduced into the Soviet forces during 1951, and was subsequently adopted by several Warsaw Pact armies and copied by the Chinese. East Germany manufactured a version of the Makarov that can be distinguished by its black plastic grip; Soviet and Bulgarian Makarovs have a reddish-brown grip with a lanyard loop.

The uniforms issued to tank crew and the new Russian mottled camouflage smock both include built-in holsters for the Makarov. This is a pocket on the left breast, with a pouch for a spare magazine on the right-breast pocket. For vehicle crew squeezing in and out of the cramped interior of a Russian AFV, this makes a great deal of sense.

As a military pistol the Makarov has the advantages of small size, light weight and simple operation. The safety lever flips down to fire, unlike most modern designs like the current range of Smith & Wesson automatics.

With the magazine loaded and hammer-drop safety operated, all the shooter needs to do is draw the weapon and shoot. This is particularly important since most of the personnel issued with this pistol are not going to devote much time to training with it. Tank drivers, radio operators and other specialists naturally spend most of their training time on their main job. Unfortunately, accurate pistol shooting demands regular practice and complete familiarity with the weapon. The Makarov is designed with this in mind: its lack of complexity is a positive advantage.

The West is the best

The Makarov does not compare well against contemporary Western military pistols like the Browning High Power: its low-magazine capacity and the relatively light cartridge both tell against it; it is slow to reload and the trigger is invariably grim. Yet such a direct comparison is not helpful: the Makarov does the job the Russians want it to do. Western enthusiasm for high-magazine capacity automatics firing 9-mm Parabellum has never caught on in the CIS where it is presumably believed that if a soldier requires to fire several 15-round magazines, then he might as well have an AK! The next Russian pistol to enter service continued this trend. The diminutive PSM, introduced during the 1970s, fires a very light 5.45-mm cartridge and can be slipped into a trouser pocket.

Walther Pistols: Police Specials

The Walther P38 is still going strong as the P1 of the German army. Fully silenced versions of the P1 are commercially available. The conversion unfortunately involves losing the front sight, but the weapon is not intended for target shooting and most handgun 'engagements' are well under 6 m (19.7 ft).

The Walther P38 was adopted by the German army as a replacement for the Luger, and it acquitted itself very well in action. It was back in production shortly after World War II and several different versions are now available. One of the classic 9-mm pistols, the P38 is one of a series of first-class weapons which have proved their capabilities in action.

Carl Walther went into the pistol business in 1908, producing a simple blowback 6.35-mm automatic known as the Walther Model 1. This was followed by a succession of pocket blowbacks, through to the Model 9 of 1921. The only one with military aspirations was the Model 6 of 1915, in 9-mm Parabellum and produced solely for the German army, which was not particularly happy with a blowback 9-mm and only a few thousand were ever made. The remainder did very well on the commercial market.

Revolutionary design

Walther spent the 1920s perfecting a new design, which was introduced in 1929 as the PP – Polizei Pistole. For its day it was revolutionary: a streamlined blowback pistol with a double-action lock, the first time this had been done successfully by a major manufacturer. It was followed in 1930 by the PPK – Polizei Pistole Kriminal – which was a smaller version designed for concealed carrying by plainclothes police. Needless to say, as well as being adopted by police forces, both pistols did well on the commercial market. They were produced in 7.65-mm calibre to start with, but this was then extended to 6.35-mm, 9-mm Short and, finally, .22 Long Rifle. The 6.35-mm models were never very popular and were discontinued in 1935, but the others continued in production until 1945.

In the early 1930s the renascent German army let it be known that it would like to see a replacement for the venerable Pistole '08, the Parabellum/Luger. Walther enlarged his PP to 9-mm Parabellum calibre and offered

How the Walther P5 fires: trigger and safety mechanisms

On squeezing the trigger, the first action is to release the safety sear that prevents forward movement of the hammer. Further pressure cocks the hammer and at full cock the trip lever moves up and pushes the firing pin up into line with the nose of the hammer just as it drops.

A Walther PP and associated leather wear for concealed carry. The Walther PP and PPK models are classic designs that have not declined in popularity in spite of the undoubted better choices available for most self-defence and police tasks.

it as the 'Model MP' in 1934, but there was little real hope of persuading the German army to accept a blowback pistol and the idea got nowhere. Walther therefore began exploring a locked breech design, and in 1937 took out patents (in Britain as well) which covered the essential features of what now became the 'Model AP' (for Armee Pistole). The AP used a locking wedge under the barrel, which held slide and barrel together during a short recoil; the wedge was then driven down by striking against a frame transom, releasing the slide to run back and complete the reloading cycle. The double-action firing lock of the PP was improved and incorporated into the design. The AP worked well, but the army refused it because it had an internal hammer: they preferred something with a visible indication of whether or not it was cocked.

'Heeres Pistole'

Walther reworked the design to use an external hammer, calling the new pistol the 'HP' for 'Heeres Pistole'. It was put forward for military tests, and at the same time (1938)

went into commercial production. After testing, the army requested some small changes to make it easier to mass-produce, after which it was formally taken into service as the 'Pistole 38'. Records were destroyed in 1945, and it is not possible to say how many P38s were made, but the total is probably in the region of one million.

In 1945 the Walther factory at Zella-Mehlis in Thuringia was captured by the US Army. Much of the factory's priceless collection of firearms was looted, the machinery was wrecked by rampaging refugees and ex-inmates of the nearby Buchenwald Concentration Camp, and in June the area came under Soviet control and what was left was removed to Russia as reparations. But, before that happened, the management voted with their feet and crossed over to the US Occupation Zone to start afresh.

They still held various patents covering the PP and PPK pistols, and they licensed their manufacture to Manurhin of France. With the money so obtained they were able to re-start one of their less well-known pre-war

Field stripping the Walther Model PP

1 The PPK, PP and PP super models all field-strip in this way, as do the myriad of Walther copies. First, remove the magazine and clear the pistol. Note that there is no slide stop, but there is a hold-open device.

2 Leave the weapon cocked and pivot the trigger guard down as shown. Push the guard slightly to the right or left so that the guard rests on the frame.

3 Draw the slide completely to the rear and make sure the trigger guard is still disengaged.

Inside the Walther P5

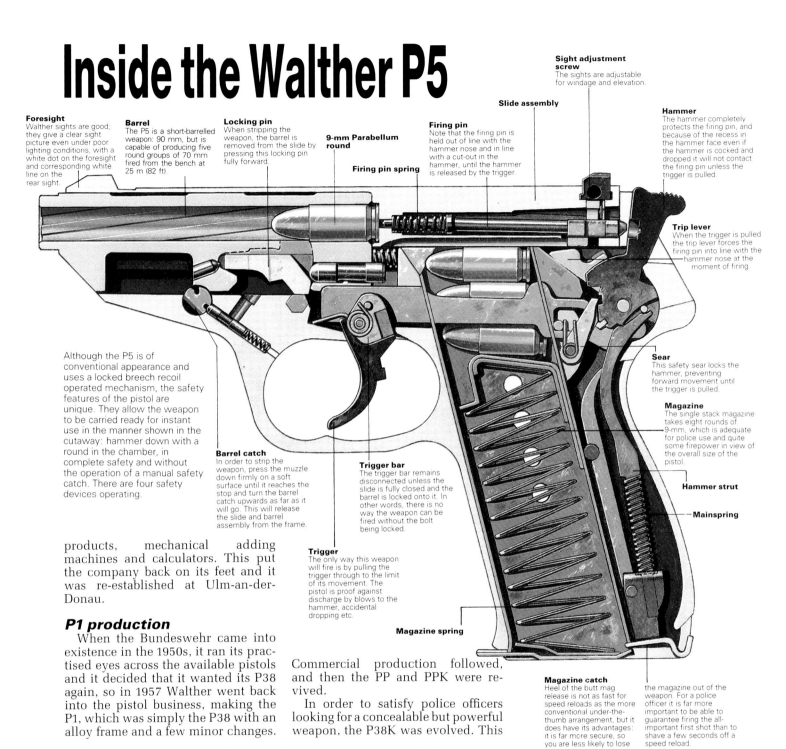

Foresight
Walther sights are good; they give a clear sight picture even under poor lighting conditions, with a white dot on the foresight and corresponding white line on the rear sight.

Barrel
The P5 is a short-barrelled weapon: 90 mm, but is capable of producing five round groups of 70 mm fired from the bench at 25 m (82 ft).

Locking pin
When stripping the weapon, the barrel is removed from the slide by pressing this locking pin fully forward.

9-mm Parabellum round

Firing pin spring

Firing pin
Note that the firing pin is held out of line with the hammer nose and in line with a cut-out in the hammer, until the hammer is released by the trigger.

Sight adjustment screw
The sights are adjustable for windage and elevation.

Slide assembly

Hammer
The hammer completely protects the firing pin, and because of the recess in the hammer face even if the hammer is cocked and dropped it will not contact the firing pin unless the trigger is pulled.

Trip lever
When the trigger is pulled the trip lever forces the firing pin into line with the hammer nose at the moment of firing.

Sear
This safety sear locks the hammer, preventing forward movement until the trigger is pulled.

Magazine
The single stack magazine takes eight rounds of 9-mm, which is adequate for police use and quite some firepower in view of the overall size of the pistol.

Hammer strut

Mainspring

Barrel catch
In order to strip the weapon, press the muzzle down firmly on a soft surface until it reaches the stop and turn the barrel catch upwards as far as it will go. This will release the slide and barrel assembly from the frame.

Trigger bar
The trigger bar remains disconnected unless the slide is fully closed and the barrel is locked onto it. In other words, there is no way the weapon can be fired without the bolt being locked.

Trigger
The only way this weapon will fire is by pulling the trigger through to the limit of its movement. The pistol is proof against discharge by blows to the hammer, accidental dropping etc.

Magazine spring

Although the P5 is of conventional appearance and uses a locked breech recoil operated mechanism, the safety features of the pistol are unique. They allow the weapon to be carried ready for instant use in the manner shown in the cutaway: hammer down with a round in the chamber, in complete safety and without the operation of a manual safety catch. There are four safety devices operating.

products, mechanical adding machines and calculators. This put the company back on its feet and it was re-established at Ulm-an-der-Donau.

P1 production

When the Bundeswehr came into existence in the 1950s, it ran its practised eyes across the available pistols and it decided that it wanted its P38 again, so in 1957 Walther went back into the pistol business, making the P1, which was simply the P38 with an alloy frame and a few minor changes.

Commercial production followed, and then the PP and PPK were revived.

In order to satisfy police officers looking for a concealable but powerful weapon, the P38K was evolved. This

Magazine catch
Heel of the butt mag release is not as fast for speed reloads as the more conventional under-the-thumb arrangement, but it does have its advantages: it is far more secure, so you are less likely to lose the magazine out of the weapon. For a police officer it is far more important to be able to guarantee firing the all-important first shot than to shave a few seconds off a speed reload.

4 Lift the rear of the slide up, and it should disengage the frame. This is fiddly; if you are having problems, you have probably not pulled the slide back far enough.

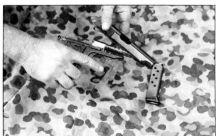

5 The slide then comes off forwards, effectively completing the field strip. The barrel is fixed, but the recoil spring can be pulled off the barrel forwards if desired.

6 These direct blowback weapons are incredibly simple, but they do tend to be very dependent on good-quality ammunition for reliable functioning. Reassembly is in reverse order, but make sure the trigger guard is fully down before attempting to replace the slide.

A wartime P38 and a modern P1. The P38 replaced the Luger as the sidearm of the German army. It is capable of reasonable combat accuracy, but do not expect too much from some of the later wartime manufacture guns.

Guarding US prisoners taken in the Ardennes in 1944. The straight-line butt configuration and positioning of the magazine release made the P38 an inferior combat pistol compared to the 9-mm Browning or Colt .45.

was simply the P38 with a short barrel and might have been more popular had the German police not soon come up with their demand for a totally new automatic pistol.

Modern looks

Walther responded with the P5. This took the basic principles of the P38 and reworked them into a more modern-looking weapon. The barrel was shorter and the slide was extended to completely conceal the barrel. Instead of the slide-mounted safety catch, a thumb-operated de-cocking lever was placed on the left side of the butt. Pressing this would lower the hammer onto the locked firing pin, after which a pull on the trigger would raise and drop the hammer in the usual double-action mode. A refinement was the incorporation of an automatic firing pin safety device. The firing pin was always locked, except during the last few degrees of trigger movement, immediately before the hammer was released. At that point an attachment to the trigger would unlock the firing pin just long enough for the hammer to drop and drive it forward. As soon as the pressure on the trigger was released, the firing pin locked once more.

The P5 was adopted by several German state police forces and was also sold abroad. However, there was still a demand for a police pistol which, while more powerful than the old 9-mm Short, was not so powerful as the 9-mm Parabellum. In response to this, the 9-mm Police cartridge had

been developed, a fraction shorter and less powerful than the Parabellum round, and was calculated to be the most powerful round which could be fired safely from an unlocked breech. Walther were quick to see the advantages of this, and they produced the 'PP Super' pistol. Basically this was the old PP, but it was slightly recontoured to look somewhat different and more modern. This, too, sold well to police and security forces.

Change of style

The most recent design to appear from Walther is the P88, and it is a considerable change of style. The locking wedge introduced with the P38 has at last been abandoned, and the new pistol uses a modified Colt-Browning system of locking in which the barrel is pulled down by a cam path and disengaged from the slide. The exterior of the barrel is shaped into a squared-off block, and this locks

into the ejection opening in the slide as the breech closes. The slide envelops the entire barrel and, in general, the pistol looks more like a Browning design than a Walther. The double-action mechanism is used, and the thumb-operated de-cocking lever of the P5 is used again, together with the automatic firing pin safety. In essence, it is the P5 but with a different barrel locking system, with the addition that the firing pin is held out of alignment with the hammer except during the final movement of the trigger.

The P38 shoots reasonably well, but do not put military 2Z ammo through or it will rattle to bits. The double-action feature, some would say, is an overcomplication on a military pistol.

Post-war French Rifles

France was the first nation to develop a small-calibre rifle firing smokeless cartridges. The 8-mm Lebel rifle entered service in 1886, later joined by the Berthier rifle, and both were used through World War I. It was seriously out of date by the 1920s, however, and the 8-mm cartridge was also less than effective, especially in machine-guns.

In 1935, the French army introduced a new 7.5-mm cartridge in an attempt to make some sense out of the multiplicity of rifle and carbine designs then in service. The 7.5-mm round had actually been in development since the early 1920s. Many of the old Berthier rifles were rebarrelled, but they still remained an archaic design and were no real comparison to the Mauser and Lee-Enfield rifles in service in Germany and the UK, let alone with the self-loading M1 Garand that the Americans were adopting at the same time. Obviously, a more modern rifle would be necessary to make use of the new cartridge.

Fusil MAS 36

The Fusil MAS 36 was the last bolt-action rifle adopted as a standard weapon by any major army. Developed by the Manufacture d'Armes St Etienne, from which the MAS designation is derived, it had a modified Mauser action but with rear lug locking like the Lee-Enfield. Unlike the

Above: For most of this century, the French army has had to struggle through wars armed with archaic or ineffective personal weapons, but since the early 1980s that has changed. The 5.56-mm **FA MAS** automatic rifle is a short and handy weapon that is as effective as any other rifle currently in service.

Left: France's standard rifle in the immediate post-war years was the **MAS 36** rifle. It was a tough, reasonably effective rifle, but it was considerably outclassed by contemporary weapons like the American M1 Garand.

Inside the MAS 49/56

The MAS 49/56 is a modified version of the MAS 49, with which the French Army re-equipped after the end of World War II. A solid, if uninspired design, its main advantage was its reliability. It can still be found in large numbers in French-speaking armies in Africa.

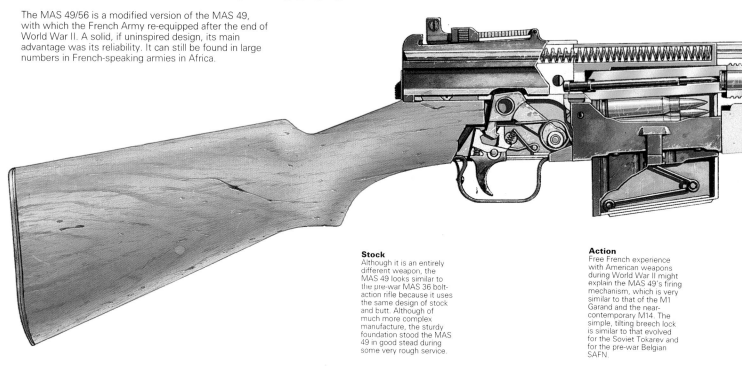

Stock
Although it is an entirely different weapon, the MAS 49 looks similar to the pre-war MAS 36 bolt-action rifle because it uses the same design of stock and butt. Although of much more complex manufacture, the sturdy foundation stood the MAS 49 in good stead during some very rough service.

Action
Free French experience with American weapons during World War II might explain the MAS 49's firing mechanism, which is very similar to that of the M1 Garand and the near-contemporary M14. The simple, tilting breech lock is similar to that evolved for the Soviet Tokarev and for the pre-war Belgian SAFN.

British rifle it was not easy to use, and the bolt handle was angled awkwardly forward in an attempt to bring it more conveniently under the firer's hand.

Production of the new rifle was slow, and few were in service by the summer of 1940 when France was defeated by Germany. Production of the MAS 36 continued during the Vichy years, and after the end of World War II it was the MAS 36 that the French army used in its attempt to re-establish the French colonial empire. The MAS 36 equipped troops in Indo-China and North Africa as France fought a series of bloody and ultimately unsuccessful colonial wars. Even when replaced in front-line service by more modern weapons, the MAS 36 was often retained for ceremonial use, and the rifle can still be encountered in police armouries in former French colonies.

French troops in Indo-China were equipped with a variety of personal weapons, from the sturdy MAT 49 SMG to war-surplus American rifles.

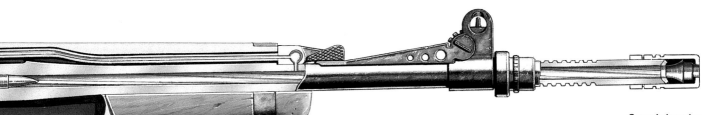

Ammunition
Although most NATO nations were standardising on 7.62-mm calibre for their rifles, the MAS 49 and the MAS 49/56 stuck with the pre-war French 7.5 mm×54 cartouche modèle 1929. It is a reasonably effective cartridge, but it was not adopted by any other army except for a few ex-French colonies.

Gas operation
The MAS 49 uses propellant gas drawn from the top of the barrel which acts directly on the bolt carrier to cycle the action. This is similar to the way the Armalite AR-15/M16 was to work some years later. Users of the MAS 49 encountered few problems caused by excessive fouling, which was in direct contrast to the American experience with the M16 in Vietnam.

Grenade-launcher
The improved model of the rifle introduced in 1956 differs from the original MAS 49 in that it has a shortened, wooden forestock, and the earlier rifle's integral grenade-launcher has been replaced by a combined flash-hider/grenade-launcher. The 22-mm (0.87-in) launching sleeve will accommodate a wide variety of standard diameter rifle grenades.

Although it was the last to introduce a new bolt-action rifle, the French army was quicker off the mark when it came to bringing a semi-automatic, self-loading weapon into service. Free French troops had been equipped with American-supplied M1 Garand rifles and M1 carbines during the final years of World War II and they could see the value of such weapons.

MAS 49

The Fusil Mitrailleur MAS 49 resembled the preceding MAS 36, primarily because it used the same two-piece wooden stock. In fact, in all essential areas it was a completely new design. Weighing in at 4.5 kg (10 lb), it was no lightweight, but its solid construction and strength proved reliable from the jungles of Vietnam to the deserts of Algeria.

The MAS 49 is gas-operated. It uses no cylinder or piston: the propellant gas acts directly on the bolt carrier. This kind of system generally causes excessive fouling and requires a considerable amount of maintenance, but the MAS 49 seemed to get by without much problem. Modifications in the mid-1950s gave rise to the MAS 49/56, which served the French army until the mid-1980s. It is recognisable by its smaller forestock and the combined muzzle break/grenade-launcher. The MAS 49/56 is 90 mm (3.5 in) shorter than the earlier model.

The MAS 49 self-loading rifle was France's standard rifle for three decades. One of its last operational uses was in central Africa, when the Foreign Legion parachuted into Zaire to rescue Europeans threatened by a local uprising in Kolwezi.

*Above: Legionnaires practise personal administration while on a training exercise. They are armed with **FA MAS** bullpup rifles, which are notable for their permanently attached bipods.*

French small arms design in the 20th century could charitably be called idiosyncratic. By the end of the 1950s, NATO armies were standardising on 7.62-mm weapons, but the French stuck obstinately with the 7.5 mm×54 cartouche modèle 1929. However, when the time came to adopt a new rifle firing the small-calibre, high-velocity rounds that were in fashion, French designers were ahead of the game. The Fusil Automatique MAS 5.56, or FA MAS, is a thoroughly modern and effective little rifle. Its small size is due to the adoption of a 'bullpup' layout, with the trigger group moved to the front of the magazine.

FA MAS rifle

In theory, this results in a highly compact rifle which is easy to use from vehicles or helicopters. In practice, it often leads to difficulties. Some bullpups, like the British SA80, cannot be fired left-handed, but the designers of the FA MAS have dealt with the problem more successfully than most, and the rifle can be converted from right-hand fire to left-hand fire in a matter of minutes. The cocking handle is mounted on top of the receiver and can be operated by either hand.

The FA MAS is easy to identify. Its unique appearance has caused the rifle to be nicknamed 'Le Clarion' in the French army, and indeed its compact length and the integral carrying handle do make it look rather like a bugle. The sights are contained within the carrying handle, and there is also an integrally fitted bipod, which folds away under the barrel when not needed.

The FA MAS can fire in single-shot, three-round burst and full-auto modes, although the 1,000 rounds per minute rate of fire in the latter is a little too fast for easy control. The choice of 5.56-mm NATO calibre for the new rifle meant, that for the first time, French soldiers would be firing the same ammunition as their allies. The FA MAS comes with a 25-round magazine, with drill holes to allow the firer to check at a glance how many bullets he has remaining. It is also capable of firing grenades without adaptation.

The first FA MAS rifles were issued in the early 1980s, and since that time, they have been used operationally in Chad, Lebanon and during the Gulf War of 1991. They have also been exported to a number of former French colonies in west Africa and to the United Arab Emirates.

*The **FR-F1** has been the French army's sniping rifle since the 1960s. Based loosely on the MAS 36 bolt action, it is a much better constructed weapon, which is capable of notable accuracy in competent hands.*

Mauser C96 'Broomhandle'

Carried by Winston Churchill at the battle of Omdurman, the Mauser automatic pistol was one of the most accurate and hard-hitting pistols in service at the beginning of this century. Today, it is one of the most widely-collected historic weapons, and versions of the Mauser C96 are still available from Communist China.

The Mauser C96 was designed by three brothers – Fidel, Fritz and Josef Feederle, who worked in the Mauser factory at Oberndorf. They started work on a pistol chambered for the 7.65-mm Borchardt cartridge in 1894. Patents followed in 1895 and Mauser put the gun into production a year later. Paul Mauser himself took a keen interest in the weapon and entered it in the German army pistol trials. However, he was to be disappointed. The German army preferred the Luger.

The Mauser C96 was aggressively marketed and was tested by several other armies, among them the British, American and Swiss. Several British officers and newspaper correspondents carried Mausers during the invasion of the Sudan in 1898, and officers and volunteers on both sides used the Mauser in the Boer War.

Service contracts

Although the Mauser had achieved some service contracts – notably from Persia, Turkey and the Italian navy – they were only for modest quantities and there were no re-orders. None of the major powers were interested, and the Mauser seemed destined for obscurity until, in 1914, Germany finally launched its long-planned war against France and Russia. The anticipated lightning campaign produced enormous casualty lists, but Paris held out. By the end of the year the German army occupied entrenched positions from the English Channel to Switzerland. Britain had entered the war too, and the Russians only narrowly prevented the Germans from overrunning the Kaiser's most easterly territories.

The 'Broomhandle' was used in both world wars by Germany. On the eve of World War II it was adopted by the SS, and some surviving weapons have had fake SS stamps added to boost their collectability.

Facing a prolonged war, the German Ordnance Department placed heavy orders for all manner of weapons. German forces were eventually equipped with 13 types of automatic pistol in five different calibres! The Mauser C96 was used in two calibres: the original 7.63 × 25-mm cartridge and in 9-mm Parabellum. Before 1915 the Mauser C96 was chambered for the 7.63-mm Mauser cartridge – basically a higher velocity 7.65-mm Borchardt – that remained the high-velocity champion of the pistol world until the advent of the .357 Magnum in 1935.

In 1915 the German army ordered 150,000 C96s chambered for 9-mm Parabellum, the cartridge it had tried to standardise on before the war. To distinguish them from the 7.63-mm

version, the 9-mm Mausers had a figure '9', usually painted red, burned into the wooden grip . They are referred to today by US collectors as 'Red Nines' for this reason. These 9-mm Mausers were used alongside the practically identical 7.65-mm Mausers that were privately purchased by many officers.

In the field there was probably not much to choose between the Luger and the Mauser C96, as neither weapon is particularly tolerant of muddy conditions. Although the Mauser looks decidedly ungainly when compared to the sinister elegance of the Luger, the C96 at least offers its owner two more shots in the magazine.

All good military weapons have at least one 'idiot-proof' feature: on the Mauser this was the large cocking ring on the hammer that obstructed your view of the sights when the hammer was forward — your final reminder that the pistol needed to be cocked. The original C96 was designed purely as a pistol and it had fixed sights, but in about 1903 the C96 was altered to have the pistol grip grooved for a shoulder stock and adjustable sights were added. The wooden shoulder stock/holster unit became a standard accessory.

Long-range sights

The sights were graduated to 500 or 1,000 m (1,640 or 3,280 ft), both of which were very optimistic. Nevertheless, a Mauser with a shoulder stock was a far more useful back up than an ordinary handgun. With nothing

A Mauser-wielding officer seen during street fighting against the Berlin Communists in 1919. After defeating its indigenous Communists, Germany decided it was safe to sell Mausers to the Russian Bolsheviks.

more than a pistol for emergency defence, the crew of a trench mortar or heavy machine-gun would have great difficulty keeping the enemy out of grenade range. Serving as a light carbine, the Mauser was much more effective, offering reasonable accuracy to 100 m (328 ft) or more.

In November 1918 Germany sued for peace and was compelled to accept the Treaty of Versailles. This imposed very strict limits on military equipment allowed to the new democratic government in Germany. One provision banned German forces from

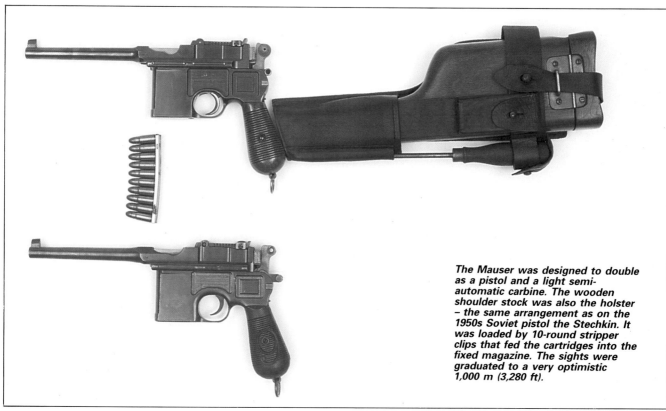

The Mauser was designed to double as a pistol and a light semi-automatic carbine. The wooden shoulder stock was also the holster – the same arrangement as on the 1950s Soviet pistol the Stechkin. It was loaded by 10-round stripper clips that fed the cartridges into the fixed magazine. The sights were graduated to a very optimistic 1,000 m (3,280 ft).

Inside the Mauser C96

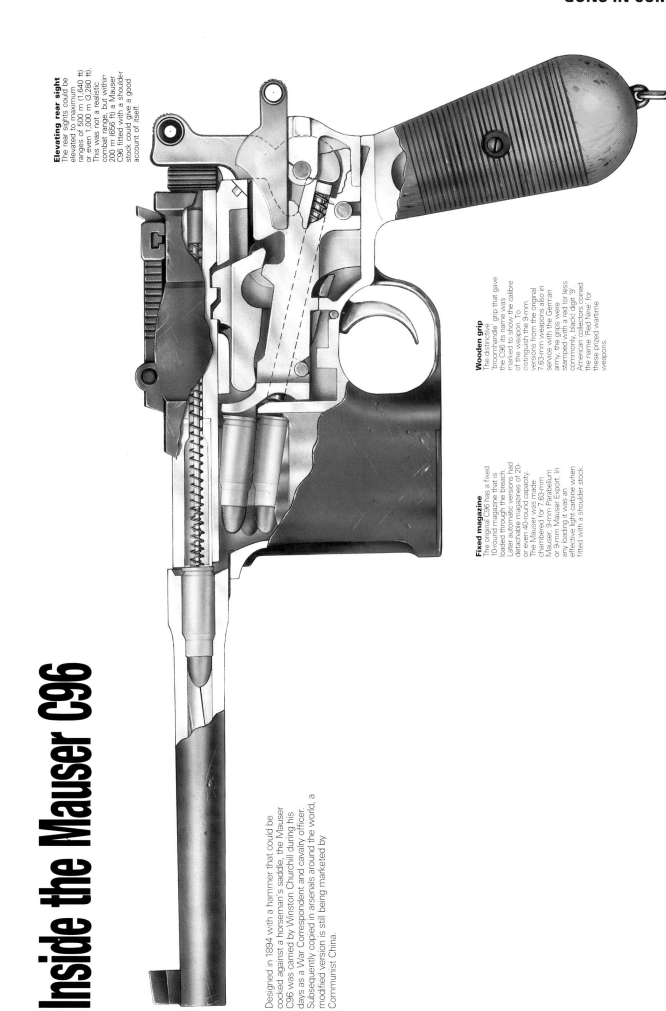

Elevating rear sight
The rear sights could be elevated to maximum ranges of 500 m (1,640 ft) or even 1,000 m (3,280 ft). This was not a realistic combat range, but within 200 m (656 ft) a Mauser C96 fitted with a shoulder stock could give a good account of itself.

Wooden grip
The distinctive 'broomhandle' grip that gave the C96 its name was marked to show the calibre of the weapon. To distinguish the 9-mm versions from the original 7.63-mm weapons also in service with the German army, the grips were stamped with a red (or less commonly, black) digit '9'. American collectors coined the name 'Red Nine' for these prized wartime weapons.

Fixed magazine
The original C96 has a fixed 10-round magazine that is loaded through the breach. Later automatic versions had detachable magazines of 20- or even 40-round capacity. The Mauser was made chambered for 7.63-mm Mauser, 9-mm Parabellum or 9-mm Mauser Export. In any loading it was an effective light carbine when fitted with a shoulder stock.

Designed in 1894 with a hammer that could be cocked against a horseman's saddle, the Mauser C96 was carried by Winston Churchill during his days as a War Correspondent and cavalry officer. Subsequently copied in arsenals around the world, a modified version is still being marketed by Communist China.

Danish resistance fighters are instructed in the care and maintenance of their weapons during World War II. A Mauser joins a motley assortment of guns that will be used against the Germans.

using pistols of a greater calibre than 8 mm and with barrels longer than 100 mm (3.9 in). Thus, many 'Red Nines' were re-barrelled to 7.63 mm and their barrels shortened from their original length of 139 mm (5.5 in). The short-barrelled Mausers are sometimes referred to as 'Bolos' – after Bolshevik – since many of them were supplied to the Red Army during the 1920s.

Spanish copies

More dramatic developments followed during the 1930s when some small Spanish gun-makers began to build Mauser copies that were capable of fully automatic fire. These met with predictable success when sold in South America and Asia. As these were some of Mauser's most profitable markets, the company felt compelled to introduce an automatic version of its own. This was known as the Model 712 and had a selector bar on the right-hand side offering semi-automatic or fully automatic fire. Fired automatically, the Model 712's cyclic rate was 850 rounds per minute.

The original C96 had a fixed magazine loaded by 10-round chargers, which was obviously not suitable for

Ethiopian Emperor Haile Selassie seen here during the war with Italy. His bodyguard on the right holds a Mauser C96 in his left hand.

an automatic weapon. Detachable 10-, 20- and even 40-shot magazines were introduced for the semi-automatic Model 711 and the fully automatic Model 712.

Mauser pistols were widely used during the 1930s. Both sides used them in the Spanish Civil War, the Chinese civil war and at least some Ethiopian troops had them to resist the Italian invasion. Although the Nationalist victory in Spain stopped unauthorised Mauser copies being produced there, new imitation Maus-

ers soon began to appear from workshops in China.

It is the Chinese copy of the Mauser that survives to this day. Chinese factories no longer produce direct copies of the C96 but now offer the 'Type 80 machine pistol'. This looks similar to the C96 but has a less sharply-angled grip, detachable 20-round magazines and a skeleton shoulder stock. Chambered for 7.62-mm Tokarev (very similar to 7.63-mm Mauser), it is reported to be still in production by North China Industries.

Mauser Gewehr '98

The rifles developed by the German company of Mauser Brothers are among the most successful military weapons of the 20th century. The Mauser Gewehr '98 was the standard service rifle of the German army from 1898 to 1945. The company manufactured numerous versions of the basic design, supplying them to many foreign armies. In 1914 Mauser rifles were issued to the soldiers of Belgium, Germany, Serbia, Spain, Sweden and Turkey. Such was the fame of the Mauser design that it was almost universally adopted in South America – the armies of Argentina, Bolivia, Chile, Columbia, Ecuador and Peru all buying them. The version known as the 98k, adopted by the Germans in 1935, was still turning up during the Vietnam War, and is currently being used by Croatian and Serbian irregular forces in the Yugoslavian civil war.

Around the world

British soldiers have been under fire from Mausers for the best part of a century. In 1898 the British Army suffered unexpected defeats in South Africa where the canny Transvaal President Paul Kruger had acquired 37,000 Mausers for the Boer commandos. In addition to facing Mauser-

Above: A German soldier dashes across enemy field fortifications, his Mauser Kar 98k clutched tightly in his hand. The Mauser was the German infantryman's weapon through two world wars.

armed Germans in both world wars, British troops have encountered the Mauser in terrorist campaigns from Ireland to Cyprus and the Middle East.

Paul and Wilhelm Mauser were sons of a gunsmith who worked at the Royal Wurttemberg arms factory at Oberndorf, and they became appren-

Left: A World War I sniper takes aim at the opposing trench line. The Gewehr '98 rifle, like most of its contemporaries, could accurately fire a full-power round out to considerable distances.

Inside the Mauser

The Mauser Infantry Rifle of 1898 was one of the most successful of all military small arms, and was manufactured by the million. It was adopted in a virtually unchanged form by dozens of armies, and was Germany's basic infantry weapon for nearly half a century.

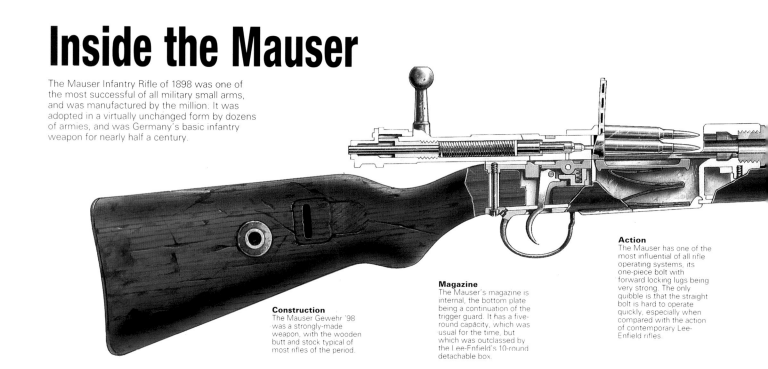

Construction
The Mauser Gewehr '98 was a strongly-made weapon, with the wooden butt and stock typical of most rifles of the period.

Magazine
The Mauser's magazine is internal, the bottom plate being a continuation of the trigger guard. It has a five-round capacity, which was usual for the time, but which was outclassed by the Lee-Enfield's 10-round detachable box.

Action
The Mauser has one of the most influential of all rifle operating systems, its one-piece bolt with forward locking lugs being very strong. The only quibble is that the straight bolt is hard to operate quickly, especially when compared with the action of contemporary Lee-Enfield rifles.

tices there before going into the gun business on their own. In the light of their contribution to the German army, it is interesting to note that their first venture was actually for France. They designed a single-shot, black powder rifle in the 1860s and tried to sell it to the French army just before the Franco-Prussian War.

The brothers' fortunes changed abruptly in the wake of that conflict. The Prussian army was already testing new rifles to replace the ageing Dreyse, and the Mauser design won. Accepted for service in 1871, this bolt-action weapon was the foundation of the Mausers' success. With the Prussian government paying royalties on the rifles they manufactured at the Spandau arsenal, the Mausers could

Left: It is 1918. This sentry wears a late pattern helmet, improvised body armour, and carries a gas mask in the can. The only item that would have been familiar to a soldier of 1914 is his Mauser rifle.

Above: More than 20 years later, in 1940, and Germany is again at war. Once more, the uniforms are different but the rifle in use is a version of the trusty Mauser Gewehr '98.

Performance
The Gewehr '98 firing spitzer ammunition with a muzzle velocity of 870 m (2,854 ft) per second was effective out to at least 1,000 m (3,280 ft), while the later Kar 98k with its shorter barrel and lower muzzle velocity still had an effective range of more than 600 m (1,970 ft).

Sights
The original Gewehr '98 had a complex tangent rearsight with ramps and slides, which was graduated up to 2,000 m (3,280 ft). It was located well down the stock, which was not an ideal position but which was never changed.

Ammunition
The 7.92-mm Gewehr Patrone round was one of the first small-calibre, high-velocity, smokeless rounds to be adopted by a major army. In 1905, a pointed, boat-tailed version was introduced. This revolutionary 'spitzer' bullet performed far better than the older round-nosed rounds.

Barrel
The original barrel on the Gewehr '98 was 740 mm (29 in) long. It contained four rifling grooves with a right-hand twist. The later 'Karabiner' and 'kurz' versions were some 140 mm (5.5 in) shorter.

afford to build their own factory. Opened in 1873, it burned down within a matter of weeks. Fortunately for the brothers, they received a contract for a further 100,000 rifles from Wurttemberg and ended up buying the Royal Wurttemberg factory at Oberndorf.

8-mm Mauser

Wilhelm died, aged 50, in 1884 just as they completed the first magazine-loading version. However, Paul Mauser continued apace, developing rifles for numerous foreign armies and producing the world's first smokeless powder, rimless cartridge case to be adopted by a major power. This round, known variously as the 7.9- or 8-mm Mauser, held a 227-grain round-nosed bullet with a true diameter of 8.07 mm. It had a muzzle velocity of 640 metres (2,100 feet) per second.

Unhappy with the Mannlicher clip-loading system that the German army insisted on fitting to its M1888 rifle, Paul Mauser continued to modify the basic design. The rifle, adopted by the Belgian army in 1889, incorporated a one-piece bolt with forward-locking lugs. The M1893 Spanish army Mauser featured an internal magazine. Five years later, Mauser's improvements came together in the shape of the Gewehr '98. Accepted by the German army, this was the ultimate Mauser design – subsequent versions differing only in relatively minor detail. The cartridge was altered in 1905 to fire an 8.2-mm, 150-grain pointed bullet at higher muzzle velocity. Some of the M1888 rifles were converted to fire the German army's new standard cartridge, but modern-day collectors are advised never to use this larger calibre round in them. Chamber pressures, espe-

cially in modern 7.9-mm ammunition, are far too high.

The Gewehr '98 proved to be a robust and reliable weapon in the horrendous conditions of World War I. So much so that the German army retained it after 1918, and Belgium and Czechoslovakia ordered new versions of it. Compared with the famous British Lee-Enfield, the weapon it would be matched against again in World War II, the Mauser had two disadvantages. Its magazine held only five rounds, as opposed to the Lee's

The problem with the Gewehr '98, even in its shortened 'Kar' and 'kurz' carbine variants, was its length. Designed for long-range performance, the Mauser was difficult to handle in confined spaces.

10, and the Mauser bolt action is slower to operate. However, it compared favourably against all others, and when the Nazis began to re-arm Germany in the 1930s, they turned again to Mauser.

In 1935 the German army adopted the Gewehr '98k as its standard service rifle. The designation is peculiar

By the time these Mauser-armed troops marched into Russia in 1941, it was clear that the Gewehr '98 was overpowered (except as a sniper weapon, seen above). This understanding was to lead to the development of the lower powered, fully automatic assault rifle.

and gives the lie to the idea of German clinical efficiency. The 'k' stands for *kurz* (short) and the rifle was actually designated as the *Karabiner* (carbine) 98k. There had been a shortened, carbine version of the Gewehr '98 used during World War I: but the Karabiner 98k was actually longer. This inconsistency was compounded in 1940 when the Germans took over production of the M1933 carbine in occupied Czechoslovakia. Manufactured at Brno, the Czech weapon was a lightened, short-barrelled Mauser that the Germans issued to their airborne and mountain troops under the designation *Gewehr* (rifle) 33/40. So they officially classed the carbine as a rifle and vice versa!

World War II use

Given the pioneering use of light automatic weapons by German troops in World War I, the decision to issue a traditional bolt-action rifle on the eve of World War II seems rather odd. The US Army was re-equipping with the M1 Garand self-loading rifle – a far superior combat weapon. The Soviet army was experimenting with several automatic rifles that the Wehrmacht would soon encounter. It would take the icy plunge of real combat ex-

perience to stimulate real interest in the firepower of the individual rifleman. Even then, Hitler's personal opposition to automatic rifles meant that the first German assault rifles were tested on the Russian Front as 'sub-machine guns'.

Paul Mauser himself had been thinking along the same lines since the introduction of the Gewehr '98. He had a working design for an automatic rifle ready as early as 1898 and spent the last years of his career working on automatic weapons. He died of a chill in 1914, caught while testing yet another design out on the range. One Mauser design – the 7.92-mm aircraft self-loading carbine – was used by aircrew and on the ground, albeit in limited numbers.

The bolt-action mechanism developed by Mauser is able to handle far more powerful loads than that of the Lee. Mauser actions are found on countless different sporting weapons as well as on military sniper rifles in use today. Almost every major army has used a Mauser rifle at some time during this century.

Mausers are in use around the world, but their heyday was probably during World War I when these German sailors were seen in action on the Belgian coast.

The MG42 in action

Produced out of the need to simplify the manufacture of the MG34, the MG42 was soon to become a weapon respected and feared by anyone who faced it. When the time came for West Germany to re-arm, the MG42 was the natural machine-gun choice, and the weapon is in use in a modernised form to this day.

The MG42 had its origins in the fact that the existing MG34 was too expensive to manufacture and too costly in materials and time for extensive wartime production. While the MG34 was an excellent weapon, the ever-expanding German forces and the increasing amounts of territory they had to cover after 1940 meant that new machine-guns were constantly in great demand at rates that German industry could not meet. From this situation the MG42 emerged.

The MG42 had its origins in 1937, when a project to produce a new and cheap form of machine-gun was initiated by the German army weapons department, the *Heereswaffenamt*, which wanted a relatively cheap machine-gun that would be reliable under all conditions and one that

Above: The MG42 was designed to match or better the performance of the excellent MG34 – the world's first true GPMG – while being far more suited to mass production in wartime.

Below: An MG42 fitted with the anti-aircraft sight and saddle-drum magazines, rather than the belted ammunition most commonly used.

Inside the MG42

Sights
The MG42 was fitted with conventional iron sights, but a special circular sight was provided for anti-aircraft use and optical sights could be fitted for long-range sustained fire.

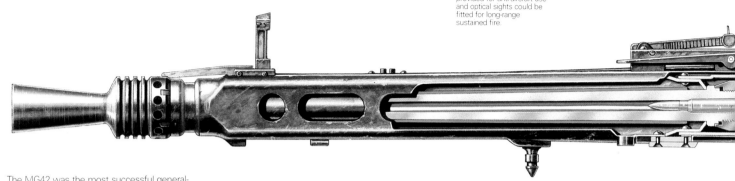

The MG42 was the most successful general-purpose machine-gun introduced during World War II, and a slightly modified version remains in service today with the German army and several other nations. Modern and World War II versions are currently being used in the Balkan wars that have followed the break-up of Yugoslavia.

Quick barrel change
The MG42's ferociously high cyclic rate of fire made it essential to change the barrel repeatedly when firing in the SF role. How the US Army ended up with the awkward system on the M60 when it began by copying the MG42 is one of the mysteries of post-war machine-gun design.

could use the accessories and ammunition feed systems of the existing MG34. In general, the expensive close tolerances of the MG34 were to be avoided to ease manufacture and assist operations in the field. From this requirement came one design with a novel breech-locking system that offered much, but none of these early submissions appeared to warrant further development. It was not until 1940 that the real impetus came, and by that time the Mauser design team had been able to examine some Czech and Polish 'paper' designs of considerable promise. By that time the principle of using mass-production techniques for weapon manufacture was fully accepted and in employment for several types of small arm, including the revolutionary MP38 and MP40 sub-machine guns.

A trials weapon, known as the MG39/41, was produced in 1941 using a new locking device that had small steel rollers set into the sides of a breech block. As the breech block was pushed into the locking position by a spring, the rollers were pushed outwards into grooves in the receiver walls, where they formed a mechanical advantage for the critical instant of firing. The system operated smoothly and reliably, and had the advantage of a high operating speed providing a high rate of fire (almost double that of existing machine-gun designs). The overall system was of the recoil type, aided by a muzzle

The MG42 proved capable of operating in the arduous conditions of the Russian Front. The fine tolerances of the superbly-made MG34 often led to problems with grit and sand.

device to trap the muzzle gas pressures.

With some slight alterations to this system the type was soon in production as the MG42. Quick introduction onto the production lines was aided by the intended fact that many existing machine tools could be easily adapted to the task and that the need for special machine tools was kept to a minimum. Great use was made of simple steel pressings, and welds were employed where pins and screws would normally have been employed. For all this ease of manufacture the MG42 worked even better than the MG34 and had a very high rate of fire. This was about 1,500 rounds per minute, and the accompanying noise was not dissimilar to that of a band saw. Thus small capacity magazines, although they could be fitted, were of limited use and reliance was generally placed on 50-round belts that could be linked together for prolonged fire. Such prolonged fire and the high fire rate made necessary some form of barrel-change mechanism, and the system used was very simple and rapid: as the lever on the side of the barrel jacket was pulled outwards a rotary device turned the barrel to release the locking lug, at the same time freeing it to be pulled out readily to the rear.

General purpose

The MG42 followed the MG34 in that it was designed as a general-purpose machine-gun. For infantry use a simple bipod was fitted, but in the heavier roles some very complex devices were introduced. The basic tripod turned out to be a special one

Trigger
The trigger of the MG42 was usually good enough for an experienced gunner to squeeze off short bursts, but it was very easy to empty a 75-round saddle drum in a moment.

for the MG42 alone and a great chance was missed to enable many of the MG34 accessories to be used with the new design despite the earlier intentions. In fact almost every accessory produced was for the MG42 alone and only a few of the existing MG34 items proved to be usable with the later weapon. Some of the MG42 mountings turned out to be very complex affairs, especially the very expensive ball mountings produced for use in fortifications and other similar ball mountings produced for mounting in the front hulls of heavy tanks such as

the Tiger and the Panther. Rather less expensive but no less complex were the various *Zwillingslafetten* (twin mountings) produced for anti-aircraft defence and often carried on small towed hand-carts.

The MG42 was in service by the end of 1942, both in North Africa and the Soviet Union. It soon proved to be a formidable weapon and was feared by all who encountered it. Some Allied troops tried to capture as many as possible for their own use, surely one of the best accolades for any weapon design, and the US Army examined the

design (and built prototypes in 7.62-mm calibre) for possible future adoption. Until 1945 the MG42 was usually reserved for front-line units only, the MG34 being gradually switched to rear support echelons; but the MG42 had not fully replaced the MG34 before 1945.

Post-war service

After 1945 large numbers of MG42s were issued to several European armies, including the French army which used the MG42 during their Indo-China campaigns. One nation

The MG42 with its weighted tripod ready for sustained fire. Its very high cyclic rate gave the MG42 a distinctive sound on the battlefield.

A German machine-gunner looks out at the English channel from an MG42 position on the Atlantic Wall. German forces today use a 7.62-mm version of the MG42.

took over large numbers of captured MG42s and completely re-equipped its front-line army units. That nation was Yugoslavia, and so impressed was it with the MG42 that it even established a national production line. The Yugoslavs even retained the 7.92-mm calibre, and to this day maintain the type in production for possible export sales. They know the MG42 as the M53 and their product is exactly the same as the original MG42, right down to accessories such as the tripod.

Germany re-arms

By 1957 the Frederal Republic of Germany was established as a full member of NATO and some thought was given to the re-arming of the West German forces. When it came to machine-guns the MG42 was the immediate choice, but as Mauser (being in East Germany) was no longer on the side of the NATO allies the production base was switched to Rheinmetall GmbH. Using an actual example as a starting point, Rheinmetall restarted production once again in 1959, but this time in the standard NATO calibre of 7.62 mm. The product was known at first as the MG42/59, but in time this was changed to MG1 to aid the export image. There are several subvariants of the MG1, including one in which the butt can be removed to aid anti-aircraft use from vehicle ring mountings. When sufficient old war stocks of MG42s were released from warehouses they too were converted to the NATO 7.62-mm calibre and

these became the MG2. Then came the MG3, with a number of minor Rheinmetall-inspired improvements, including a version with several light alloy components to reduce weight. Even this fully-modernised variant is immediately recognisable as an MG43.

Still in service

Today the German Bundeswehr continues to use the MG1 and MG3 in exactly the same manner as its predecessor used the MG42. It is still employed either mounted on its own bipod or mounted on a heavier tripod for the sustained-fire role. Leopard tanks mount MG3s where Panthers once mounted MG42s and a number of new types of vehicle mounting have been designed and produced. On the infantry side, the MG3 is still used on occasions in the anti-aircraft manner when emergency targets appear. One man of the squad acts as a temporary firing stand while another aims and fires, using his partner's back as a stand for the gun. Infantry squad tactics remain much the same, in that a section of up to eight infantrymen depends on its section MG3 for the bulk of its own supporting firepower. The squad moves only under covering fire from the MG3, and once in place the section then supplies the machine-gun team with covering fire as it moves forward. The section also carries the bulk of the machine-gun's

ammunition either hand-carried in boxes or in belts slung about their persons.

Today the MG1 (or MG3) is in licence production in several locations in countries such as Italy, Pakistan, Portugal, Spain and Turkey. Every year it appears that more nations adopt the type and the market is still far from sated. It seems that the basic MG42 design will still be in widespread service after the turn of the century. The reasons for this are not difficult to discover. The MG42 and its later derivatives are easy to manufacture, to maintain, to clean and to use in action, and have been developed to the point where no bugs remain. Add to this the ready availability of numerous accessories to suit almost any application and the ability to obtain spares from a number of easily-accessible sources, and the popularity of the type becomes clear. But these alone are not the full answer. That must lie somewhere in the overall appearance and feel of the weapon. The MG42 and its descendants all have that look of a thoroughbred design that can be relied upon. Many other weapon designs quite simply do not have this asset, but the military mind is not so simple as to rely on appearances alone. The military mind wants quality that can be relied upon under all circumstances, and the MG42 series can provide that quality.

A Russian Cossack volunteer serving with the German forces on the Eastern Front armed with an MG42.

The Bren has served the British armed forces with distinction for more than half a century. The example above is in Royal Marine hands in the Arctic, and is typical of the guns which have been modified to fire 7.62-mm **NATO** rounds. Even today it remains one of the most reliable machine-guns ever made.

The Bren Gun

Britain's soldiers have been using the Bren light machine-gun for more than half a century. The gas-operated, magazine-fed Bren is a superb weapon. Manufactured to exacting standards, it has seen service from the jungles of Malaya to the icy cold of northern Norway, and its voice has been heard on battlefields from World War II to the modern conflicts in the Falklands and the Gulf. Tough, reliable and highly accurate, the Bren was and remains one of the finest weapons of its type ever produced.

In the 1920s, the British Army was looking to replace the Lewis Gun, which had been used as a light machine-gun during World War I. Machine-guns from around the world were tested, and generally were found wanting. One weapon that showed

A Gurkha Bren gun team fires on German positions near Monte Cassino during the vicious battles in Italy during 1944. The gun's No. 2 carries spare magazines and is armed with a Thompson SMG.

Inside the Bren

The Bren light machine-gun is a quality product, manufactured to the highest standards. The Mk 3 depicted here was introduced in 1944. Lighter and with a shorter barrel, it otherwise differed little from earlier models. Modified to fire NATO 7.62-mm rounds, the Mk 3 became known as the L4A4 LMG.

Magazine
The Bren's magazine is curved to accommodate the standard British rimmed .303 rounds. A full load of 30 rounds sometimes jams, but with 28 or 29 rounds it works perfectly.

Gas tube
Propellant gas drawn from the barrel drives the under-barrel gas piston backwards, pushing the gun's working parts. Vents in the side of the piston wall allow the gas to escape once the piston has moved back far enough.

Quick release
The Bren's barrel changes easily. It is released by the large lever in front of the magazine, and the carrying handle allows it to be removed even when red-hot.

Regulator
The gas regulator under the barrel has four positions, which allow differing amounts of gas to escape from the gun barrel into the gas-piston cylinder.

promise was a Czechoslovakian design, the ZB vz.26, which was developed at the Brno factory.

During trials which began in 1930, the Czechs offered a slightly revised version of the gun, the ZB vz.27. This was clearly a superior weapon but as it fired Mauser 7.92-mm rimless rounds it was not acceptable to the British, who required a machine-gun firing the same .303-inch (7.7-mm) rimmed round that was used in the Lee-Enfield service rifle.

A series of development models culminated in the ZB vz.33. From this, the Royal Small Arms Factory at Enfield Lock developed the Bren (the name is a combination of BR from the weapon's origin at Brno and EN from its place of manufacture at Enfield). The easiest way of distinguishing the ZB series from the Bren is from the magazine – the straight box of the Czech gun evolving into the distinctive banana-shape chosen to accommodate the British .303 rimmed cartridge.

Slow production

Tooling up at Enfield began in the mid-1930s, with the first production Bren gun Mk I being delivered in 1937. Production was slow as a result of the immense amount of work needed to manufacture the weapon. The machine-gun's body required 226 separate steps to be milled from a 10-kg (22-lb) piece of high-quality steel down to a single, finished part weighing 2 kg (4.4 lb). Nevertheless, by 1940 some 30,000 Bren guns had been built. The 30-round box magazines gave some problems at first, arising from the translation of the design from the original Czech 7.92-mm rimless cartridge to the British .303-inch rimmed, but it was soon found that the

gun functioned perfectly if the magazine load was restricted to 28 or 29 rounds.

A large proportion of Britain's inventory of Brens was lost at Dunkirk, the Germans taking captured examples into service as the Leichte MG 138(e) where they were used alongside their 'half-brothers' manufactured in Czechoslovakia. The British Army had to re-equip in a hurry, and in an effort to speed up the process a new variant was developed in the shape of the Bren gun Mk 2. Generally

Although not really a general-purpose machine-gun, the Bren was used for a variety of tasks. These included air defence, on a simple anti-aircraft pintle mount.

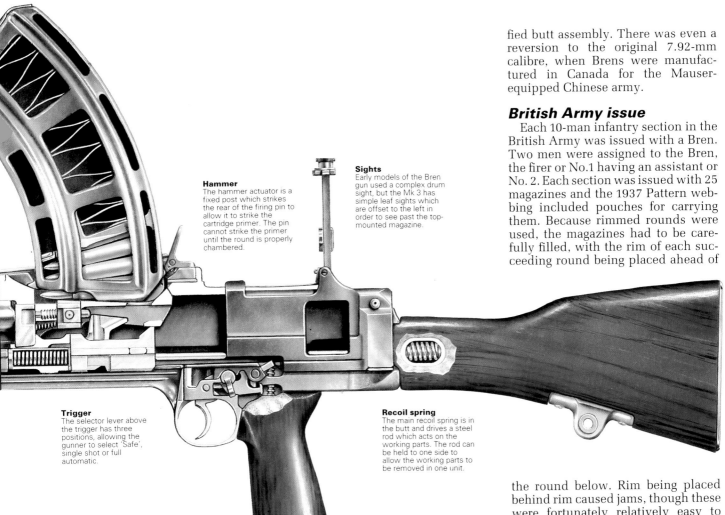

Hammer
The hammer actuator is a fixed post which strikes the rear of the firing pin to allow it to strike the cartridge primer. The pin cannot strike the primer until the round is properly chambered.

Sights
Early models of the Bren gun used a complex drum sight, but the Mk 3 has simple leaf sights which are offset to the left in order to see past the top-mounted magazine.

Trigger
The selector lever above the trigger has three positions, allowing the gunner to select 'Safe', single shot or full automatic.

Recoil spring
The main recoil spring is in the butt and drives a steel rod which acts on the working parts. The rod can be held to one side to allow the working parts to be removed in one unit.

fied butt assembly. There was even a reversion to the original 7.92-mm calibre, when Brens were manufactured in Canada for the Mauser-equipped Chinese army.

British Army issue

Each 10-man infantry section in the British Army was issued with a Bren. Two men were assigned to the Bren, the firer or No.1 having an assistant or No. 2. Each section was issued with 25 magazines and the 1937 Pattern webbing included pouches for carrying them. Because rimmed rounds were used, the magazines had to be carefully filled, with the rim of each succeeding round being placed ahead of

similar in appearance to the original gun, the Mk 2 retained the original ZB gas-operated mechanism and locking system. Out went the rather complicated drum sights that were replaced by a simpler leaf sight, and extras such as the under-butt firing handle were

omitted. The bipod was simplified, but the curved box magazine was retained.

In time, more modifications were incorporated into the basic design, the Bren gun Mk 3 having a shorter barrel and the Mk 4 being made with a modi-

the round below. Rim being placed behind rim caused jams, though these were fortunately relatively easy to clear.

The Bren was popular with armies throughout the British Commonwealth. In defence it was issued in large enough numbers to be able to provide effective interlocking fire, while in the attack it was light enough to be fired from the hip, and even from the shoulder given a reasonably large gunner. Its comparatively slow rate of fire of 500 rounds per minute made it easy to control, and with spare barrels it could sustain fire remarkably well. Even without spares it could be fired with reasonable accuracy until the barrel began to glow with the heat. Its toughness and simplicity gave the Bren a considerable degree of 'soldier-proofing', and its accuracy and reliability were proverbial. Even when foul, it could be kept firing by increasing the flow of gas through the regulator.

Accessories

Although its magazine feed means that the Bren is almost exclusively suited to light machine-gun tasks, over the years it has been fitted with a

After World War II, the Bren continued to serve British and Commonwealth infantrymen. This Iban patrol, posing with their British officer, is about to set off on a patrol during the Malayan emergency.

infantry units by the FN MAG belt-fed general-purpose machine-gun, the Bren soldiered on with second-line units. Indeed, it remained in the front line in areas where its light weight was an advantage, such as in the jungle and in the arctic.

Current service Brens

Current service Brens have been given the designation L4A4 Light Machine-Gun, or LMG. These are Bren Mk 3s that have been been converted to fire NATO 7.62-mm rounds. Their barrels are chrome-lined in order to reduce wear and increase barrel life. The 7.62-mm Brens are easily identifiable by their straight magazines, introduced to hold the rimless NATO round, and by the absence of the conical flash hider that is characteristic of .303 Brens.

The L4A4 was used by the Royal Marines in the Falklands, and 7.62-mm LMGs equipped British Army support units during the Gulf War. However, that may well be the Bren's swan song, since it is being replaced by the 5.56-mm Light Support Weapon. It is not without its supporters, however, and undoubtedly it will remain in reserve for years to come. To many people the Bren remains, more than half a century after its introduction, the world's finest light machine-gun.

Above: A Bren gunner keeps watch over a patrol in Northern Ireland's 'Bandit Country' of South Armagh. The Bren is still used in Ulster, where its accuracy is a positive factor in internal security operations.

Left: Bren guns found favour with almost every British-influenced army. This Australian Bren gunner is covering the advance of a light tank and its escorting infantry in an attack on Japanese positions in New Guinea.

Below: A South African gunner lays down supporting fire from a tripod-mounted Bren gun during operations on the Angolan border. With a plentiful supply of magazines, the Bren's quick barrel change makes it a reasonable SF weapon.

number of accessories more suited to a general-purpose machine-gun. A whole range of specialist mounts were introduced during World War II, ranging from a tripod to enable the gun to perform limited sustained fire missions to a number of complicated anti-aircraft mounts. Several methods of mounting Brens on vehicles were developed, and a 100-round drum magazine was developed but was little used.

Total production of the Bren reached about 300,000. In the years following World War II, the type remained the standard British and Commonwealth light machine-gun, and saw service in the many campaigns which marked the end of the British Empire. Even though replaced in

Firing the GPMG

A GPMG gunner during an exercise in Wales. Note the red-tipped tracer rounds in the belt of 7.62-mm ammunition.

A GPMG deployed in the SF (Sustained Fire) role. Groups of GPMGs used in this manner can sweep large areas of ground, although such 'barrage' fire demands vast quantities of ammunition that must be stockpiled near the gun-line.

*A **GPMG** gunner opens fire on an 'enemy'-held building during a **FIBUA** (Fighting in Built Up Areas) exercise. The ability of the **GPMG** to penetrate cover is one of its most important features.*

During World War I, the heavy machine-gun sat on a tripod and poured out volumes of fire, while the light machine-gun was used by infantrymen in the attack. The thought behind the GPMG was simple. What if a single weapon could do both jobs? If the conflicting requirements for machine-guns to be portable while being capable of sustained fire could be dealt with, then a new type of weapon would appear.

In the mobile and fluid conditions of modern warfare, the general-purpose machine-gun has become the pivot around which an infantry unit acts. The machine-gun became a fire support weapon, able to pour such volumes of fire onto attacking infantry or onto a position being attacked that any tactical movement on the part of

the enemy became temporarily difficult or even impossible.

By moving to a flank the machine-gun could keep the enemy engaged while the rest of the platoon or squad moved to a more favourable position or into an attack. Evolving between the two world wars, these developments became the foundation of the fire and movement tactics in use today.

The first true GPMGs were the German MG34 and MG42, which influenced post-war weapon design to a tremendous extent. Air-cooled and much lighter than preceding water-cooled heavy machine-guns, the GPMG overcame the problems of overheating generated by long periods of sustained fire by means of a quick barrel change mechanism. Spare bar-

*Above: A salutary demonstration of why hiding behind a brick wall will not save you from a dedicated **GPMG**. The machine-gun will chew through brick with concentrated bursts. Lighter material like breeze block offers even less resistance to a hail of 7.62-mm bullets.*

Firing the GPMG

The GPMG has a folding handle to allow you to carry it. If you are going to have to travel for a considerable distance it is important to apply the safety. The loaded belt can be folded over the weapon rather than left to dangle.

The famous GPMG will be retained by the British Army despite the introduction of the LSW. It will no longer be carried by dismounted infantrymen as a section weapon, but it will be fitted to virtually all armoured vehicles and to as many 'soft skinned' vehicles (lorries and Land Rovers) as possible, giving them some sort of self-protection ability.

The GPMG will also be retained in its Sustained Fire (SF) role. In this configuration, the butt is removed and it is mounted on a tripod and provided with a dial sight that allows targets to be registered and recorded. Thus, by dialling up certain co-ordinates, targets can be engaged blind in the dark or in bad visibility. Thus certain infantrymen are still trained in the use of the GPMG, some of them during their basic training.

The GPMG is 1.231 m (4 ft) long, weighs 10.9 kg (23.98 lb), is gas and spring operated and belt fed, has a cyclic rate of fire of 750 rounds per minute, and a sight range of 200-1800 m (656-5905 ft). In its SF role its weight with tripod is 13.62 kg (30 lb).

The GPMG is an automatic weapon and so is most effective when fired in bursts. You need to fire three to five rounds at longer ranges to observe the strike of shots and to correct errors in range and wind allowance. One round in four is tracer, to help with this. The length of the burst, however, is determined by the type of target, its range and your skill. A burst of eight to 10 rounds

spreads more, but gives a better chance of hitting a moving target and may be necessary at very short ranges against a mass attack.

The longer burst can be also extremely effective when firing at the front of an enemy armoured vehicle, particularly if aimed at devices that assist crew vision when the vehicle is closed down – such as periscopes, image intensification or infra-red equipment, or even headlights or spotlights.

Rapid fire is the fastest rate at which you can maintain your accuracy, and should only be used when absolutely necessary – such as when there are a large number of enemy infantry in the open at short range or when providing covering fire for an attack by your own troops.

Whenever possible normal rates of fire should be used – short bursts of 2-3 rounds – mainly because the gun is easier to control and much more accurate, but also because sustained rapid fire will overheat the barrel. This quickly wears it out and affects its accuracy.

If possible, during a lull in the fighting, you should unload the gun, cock the action and raise the top cover so that the gun can cool down after sustained rapid fire. Each gun team carries a spare barrel and this should be changed after every 400 rounds, and not used again until it is cool to the touch. Apart from anything else, ammunition is always short and resupply may be difficult.

The GPMG is no featherweight, but by carrying it like this the gunner will appear much like another rifleman to enemy observers some distance away. Actually firing it from the hip is just possible but you need the sling, plenty of practice and arms like tractors.

1 Tilt the gun to the right, open the top cover and position the belt on the feed tray. Hold the belt in place with your left hand and close the top cover.

2 Set the sights, then cock the gun with your right hand, still holding the butt up with your left.

3 Press the trigger just long enough to fire two or three rounds. Longer bursts are only needed at long range, moving targets or mass attacks.

4 As soon as you release the trigger, observe where strike lands so you can correct your aim if you misjudged the range or wind allowance.

rels kept close at hand could be fitted in a few seconds. The same weapon could be fitted with a light bipod for producing rapid aimed fire in the light machine-gun role.

Unfortunately, the general-purpose machine-gun, like all such compromises, has its limits. While the GPMG makes an adequate sustained fire weapon, it is much less successful in the light machine-gun or squad automatic weapon roles.

A bit of a handful

Most GPMGs feed via an ammunition belt. When a flapping belt is dragged through ditches and across country, it can easily snag. It creates feed problems, to say nothing of the difficulties it offers the hapless gunner, who has to take considerable care, otherwise he will spend half his time freeing the beast from undergrowth.

GPMGs also tend to be a bit on the weighty side for squad use. In many armies, the image of the machine-gunner has been of a big fellow, loaded with a heavy weapon and festooned with ammunition belts. He had to be big, because he was carrying big loads.

Things have changed dramatically in the last few years. There has been a move back to the specialist light machine-gun, which is smaller and easier to manage than the GPMG. It also fires the same small-calibre cartridges used in the squad's rifles, and is often a heavy-barrel variant of the same gun.

It is not the end of the GPMG, however. Even with heavy barrels, the new light machine-guns are not capable of engaging targets at more than about 600 metres. For real support fire, you need a more potent weapon, and the GPMG has found a new niche serving as a latter-day, heavy machine-gun.

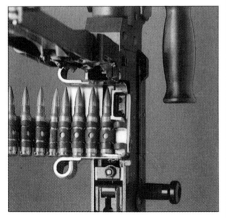

Detail of the feed tray: note that the links are uppermost and the leading round rests against the cartridge stop. Always check the links are not damaged before loading a belt.

Sustained fire role

Above and below: The GPMG mounted on a tripod for the Sustained Fire (SF) role. Its flat trajectory means that it can lay down a belt of fire up to 600 m (1968 ft) long, no bullet reaching more than 60 cm (23.62 in) from the ground.

The GPMG continues to provide valuable support for the infantryman in combat.

Each infantry company has three GPMG (SF) conversion kits consisting of tripod and dial sight. The crews of these additional GPMGs are normally drawn from the bugle or drum platoon in an infantry battalion, but this varies in different regiments. GPMGs in the light role mounted on vehicles are manned by either the vehicle commander or possibly even one of soldiers in the back of a lorry, which is why it is important that as many infantrymen as possible should still be familiar with the GPMG despite its replacement by the LSW in a rifle section.

The GPMG needs to be balanced to find the best gas regulator setting to ensure reliability combined with minimum vibration. The setting should push the working parts sufficiently far back to result in automatic fire, but not so far back as to cause accentuated wear and unnecessary vibration. This is a matter of trial and error.

When the gun is balanced you will then learn to group with the GPMG so that you can produce a 500-mm (19.7-in) group of 20 rounds at 100 m' (328 ft') range. As with the SA80 and LSW, you must then zero the weapon from the 100-m (328-ft) firing point by firing four five-round belts. When the weapon is zeroed to you, the next stage is for you to fire progressive practices at 200-400 m (656-1312 ft). When you are competent at these ranges you will learn to engage targets at 500-600 m (1640-1968 ft).

Remember that the GPMG, unless you are firing it in the SF role using a dial sight, has only a conventional iron sight, so at 500 and 600 metres it is extremely difficult to observe the strike of your rounds. This is where the gun controller comes into his own, using his binoculars and correcting the fall of shot.

SA80 The British Army's new Combat Rifle

The British Army's ultra-modern rifle, the SA80, gives the individual soldier tremendous firepower. Accurate and easy to maintain, the SA80 is a pleasure to shoot. Its light recoil keeps it on target and a special optical sight gives the soldier a clear view even in poor light conditions. The most striking feature of the SA80 is its compact layout. The 'bullpup' configuration involves the magazine being placed behind the trigger, allowing the weapon to fit a long barrel into a short overall length. The SA80's barrel is only a little shorter than that of the SLR (Self-Loading Rifle) it replaces, but it is 30 per cent shorter. As a result the weapon is easy to handle, especially in confined spaces like the back of an armoured personnel carrier.

Below: Infantrymen from the 4th Armoured Brigade on exercise just before the ground offensive in the Gulf. The leading soldier carries the standard SA80, while the man behind carries the heavy-barrelled Light Support Weapon version.

Below: A British soldier takes careful aim with his SA80 5.56-mm assault rifle. The telescopic sight magnifies by a factor of 4, giving a clear view of the target. The overall length of the gun is dramatically reduced by the bullpup layout – placing the magazine behind the pistol grip.

Inside the SA80

Firing the new NATO 5.56-mm cartridge, the SA80 produces so little recoil that you can keep the target in your sights all the time. This is a great improvement over the SLR, which tends to veer off target with each round.

Soldiers of the RAF Regiment on foot patrol: the handy size of the SA80 is readily apparent. It is well suited to fighting from cramped vehicles or in built-up areas.

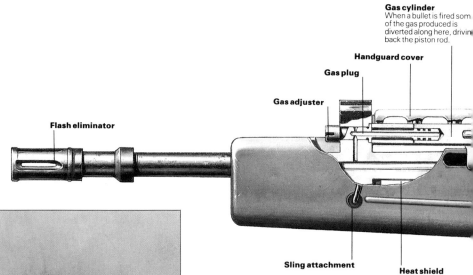

Gas cylinder
When a bullet is fired some of the gas produced is diverted along here, driving back the piston rod.

Handguard cover

Gas plug

Gas adjuster

Flash eliminator

Sling attachment

Heat shield

The compact size of the SA80 is an important advantage for the British soldier: charging through a doorway in Belfast with the long SLR was never easy. The SA80 is ideal for troops who go into action in Warrior Infantry Fighting Vehicles like those used by the British infantry regiments in Operation 'Desert Storm'.

The SA80 works well in house-to-house fighting. Its sling arrangement has delighted the men who fight with it: it can be slung across the chest, back or to one side whenever the soldier needs his hands free. The sling prevents the rifle getting in the way when hacking through jungle, snow or forest. But it still comes swiftly into

action, simply by unclipping the sling at the top.

Because of the 'bullpup' design, the SA80's empty cases are ejected from a port opposite the firer's face, so it can only be fired right-handed. But in extensive tests with the new weapon, left-handed soldiers have had little difficulty in adjusting to right-handed shooting.

SUSAT sight

The SA80 is one of the first combat rifles to be issued with a telescopic sight as a standard fitting. The sight, known as SUSAT (Sight Unit, Small Arms, Trilux) gives 4x magnification and comes with a comfortable rubber eyepiece. Through this the shooter sees a pointer – dark in daylight, illuminated by the radioactive Trilux lamp in poor light – that he places against the target. The SUSAT sight gives the British infantryman a massive advantage over conventionally-equipped enemies and lets him un-

How to fire the SA80

The SA80 fires one shot per squeeze of the trigger when set at 'R' (Repetition) as seen here. You should only switch to 'A' (Automatic) during close-quarter fighting.

Having inserted a fresh magazine, cock the weapon by pulling the cocking handle smartly to the rear. Keep your finger away from the trigger, otherwise you may shoot accidentally.

Ready to fire, you now release the safety catch by pushing the bar in from the other side.

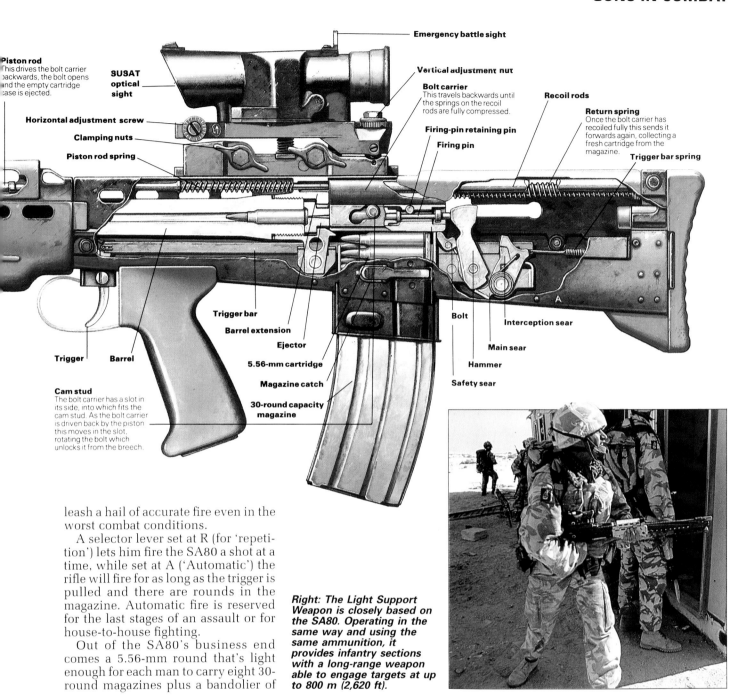

Emergency battle sight

Piston rod
This drives the bolt carrier backwards, the bolt opens and the empty cartridge case is ejected.

SUSAT optical sight

Vertical adjustment nut

Bolt carrier
This travels backwards until the springs on the recoil rods are fully compressed.

Recoil rods

Horizontal adjustment screw

Firing-pin retaining pin

Firing pin

Return spring
Once the bolt carrier has recoiled fully this sends it forwards again, collecting a fresh cartridge from the magazine.

Clamping nuts

Piston rod spring

Trigger bar spring

Trigger bar

Bolt

Interception sear

Barrel extension

Trigger

Barrel

Ejector

Main sear

5.56-mm cartridge

Hammer

Cam stud
The bolt carrier has a slot in its side, into which fits the cam stud. As the bolt carrier is driven back by the piston this moves in the slot, rotating the bolt which unlocks it from the breech.

Magazine catch

Safety sear

30-round capacity magazine

leash a hail of accurate fire even in the worst combat conditions.

A selector lever set at R (for 'repetition') lets him fire the SA80 a shot at a time, while set at A ('Automatic') the rifle will fire for as long as the trigger is pulled and there are rounds in the magazine. Automatic fire is reserved for the last stages of an assault or for house-to-house fighting.

Out of the SA80's business end comes a 5.56-mm round that's light enough for each man to carry eight 30-round magazines plus a bandolier of

Right: The Light Support Weapon is closely based on the SA80. Operating in the same way and using the same ammunition, it provides infantry sections with a long-range weapon able to engage targets at up to 800 m (2,620 ft).

Multi-purpose bayonet

The SA-80 bayonet with two scabbards showing (left) the sharpener on one side, and (right) the fold-away saw.

The bayonet and scabbard fit together to make a handy pair of wire-cutters. The bayonet is balanced to be used in the hand as well as on the rifle.

The saw is useful for cutting wood when you are building a basha or making camouflage poles.

The scabbard has a sharpening block fitted to it, so you have no excuse for having a dull blade.

ammo. Light as it is, the round is still highly effective at up to 500 m (1,640 ft), although in practice small-arms fire is rarely called for at ranges over 300 m (984 ft). The 5.56-mm round gives very little recoil, so the SA80 can be held on target for continuous firing – whereas many assault rifles tend to jump off target with each shot and thump into the firer's shoulder. However, a strong wind can affect the flight of the bullet and at long ranges the soldier needs to adjust his aim to compensate for this.

The SA80 replaces three weapons in the infantry armoury: the SLR, the 9-mm Sterling sub-machine gun and the 7.62-mm General Purpose Machine Gun. To take the GPMG's place there is another version of the

Above: Heavily camouflaged infantrymen are shown in more familiar terrain. On a European battlefield rifles are rarely used against targets more than 400 m (1,310 ft) away: the SA80 is designed to win relatively short-range firefights.

Right: A smile of victory from one of the 'Desert Rats'. Note how the SA80 can be slung to leave the hands free, but in such a way that the soldier can get it back into action with the minimum of delay.

SA80 which has a heavy barrel and a bipod. Known as the Light Support Weapon, it is virtually identical to the SA80, so the soldier only needs to be familiar with one weapon instead of three. With his new rifle in his hands, the British soldier can easily outshoot any potential opponent.

The SUSAT sight

The SUSAT sight is an invaluable aid to accurate shooting. Providing you with ×4 magnification, it is especially useful in bad light, but your immediate field of vision is limited and you must remember where your mates are when you are shooting.

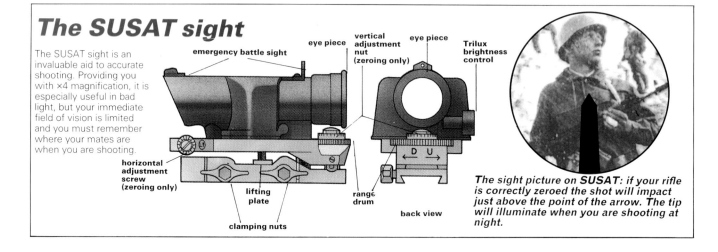

emergency battle sight · eye piece · vertical adjustment nut (zeroing only) · eye piece · Trilux brightness control · horizontal adjustment screw (zeroing only) · lifting plate · clamping nuts · range drum · back view

The sight picture on SUSAT: if your rifle is correctly zeroed the shot will impact just above the point of the arrow. The tip will illuminate when you are shooting at night.

The 9-mm Sten Gun 'PLUMBER'S DELIGHT'

After the Dunkirk evacuation of mid-1940 the British Army had few weapons left. In an attempt to re-arm quickly the military authorities put out an urgent request for simple sub-machine guns that could be produced in quantity, and using the concept of the MP38 as an example the designers went to work. Within weeks the results were adopted. It was the product of two designers, Major R. V. Shepherd and H. J. Turpin who worked at the Enfield Lock Small Arms Factory, and from these three names came the universally-accepted name Sten for the new weapon.

The first result was the Sten Mk I, which must be regarded as one of the unloveliest weapon designs of all time. It was designed for production as quickly and cheaply as possible using simple tools and a minimum of time-consuming machining. The Sten was made up from steel tubes, sheet stamping and easily produced parts, all held together with welds, pins and bolts. The main body was a steel tube

Above: A British paratrooper ready to defend his position with a Sten gun during the battle of Arnhem. A high proportion of the British airborne forces were armed with Sten guns.

Below: Sten guns were a common weapon during the fighting in Palestine that resulted in the establishment of Israel. Seen here in the hands of Jewish volunteers, Sten guns were issued to police, Jordanian and Egyptian units.

The 9-mm Sten gun

The Sten gun was designed to be mass-produced as quickly and cheaply as possible. It requires only simple tooling and little skilled labour. Used by British and Commonwealth forces, it was widely supplied to resistance forces in Europe.

Magazine well
The single column magazine of the Sten was perhaps its weakest feature and was responsible for many malfunctions. One of the Czech agents sent to assassinate Reinhard Heydrich produced his Sten from under his raincoat, aimed it at Heydrich at point-blank range, but had a stoppage on the first round.

and the butt a steel framework. The barrel was a steel drawn tube with either two or six rifling grooves roughly carved. The magazine was again sheet-steel and on the Sten Mk I the trigger mechanism was shrouded in a wooden stock. There was a small wooden foregrip and a rudimentary flash-hider. It looked horrible and caused some very caustic comments when it was first issued, but it worked and the troops soon learned to accept it for what it was: a basic killing device produced in extreme circumstances.

Simplified design

The Sten Mk I was produced to the tune of about 100,000 examples, all delivered within months. By 1941 the Sten Mk II was on the scene and this was even simpler than the Mk I. In time the Sten Mk II became regarded as the 'classic' Sten gun and it was an all-metal version. Gone was the wooden stock over the trigger mechanism, which was replaced by a simple sheet-metal box. The butt became a single tube with a flatt butt plate at its end. The barrel was redesigned to be unscrewed for changing and the magazine housing, with the box magazine protruding to the left, was designed to be a simple unit that could be rotated downwards once the magazine was removed to keep out dust and dirt. The butt could be easily removed for removing the breech block and spring for cleaning. By the time all these parts (barrel, magazine and butt) had been removed, the whole weapon occupied very little space and this turned out to be one of the Sten's great advantages. When the initial needs of the armed forces had been met, from several production lines, including those set up in Canada and New Zealand, the Sten was still produced in tens of thousands for paradrop into occupied Europe for use by resistance forces and partisans. There it found its own particular place in combat history, for the very simplicity of the Sten and the ease with which it could be broken down for hiding proved to be a major asset, and the Germans came to fear the Sten and what it could do. The Germans learned, as did many others, that the bullet from a Sten was just as lethal as a bullet from something more fancy.

Silent Sten guns

A silenced version of the Sten Mk II was produced in small numbers for Commando and raiding forces as the Sten Mk IIS, and then came the Sten Mk III. This was basically an even simpler version of the original Mk I, as its barrel could not be removed and it was encased in a simple steel-tube barrel jacket. Again, tens of thousands were produced and were widely used.

The Sten Mk IV was a development model intended for parachute troops but it was not placed into production. By the time the Sten Mk V was on the scene things were going better for the Allies and the Mk V could be produced with rather more finesse. The Mk V was easily the best of the Stens, for it was produced to much higher standards and even had such extras as a wooden butt, forestock and a fitting

Left: The Sten gun became famous as a weapon of the resistance fighters throughout Nazi-occupied Europe. Simple to operate and maintain, its only drawback was the reliability of the single-stack magazine.

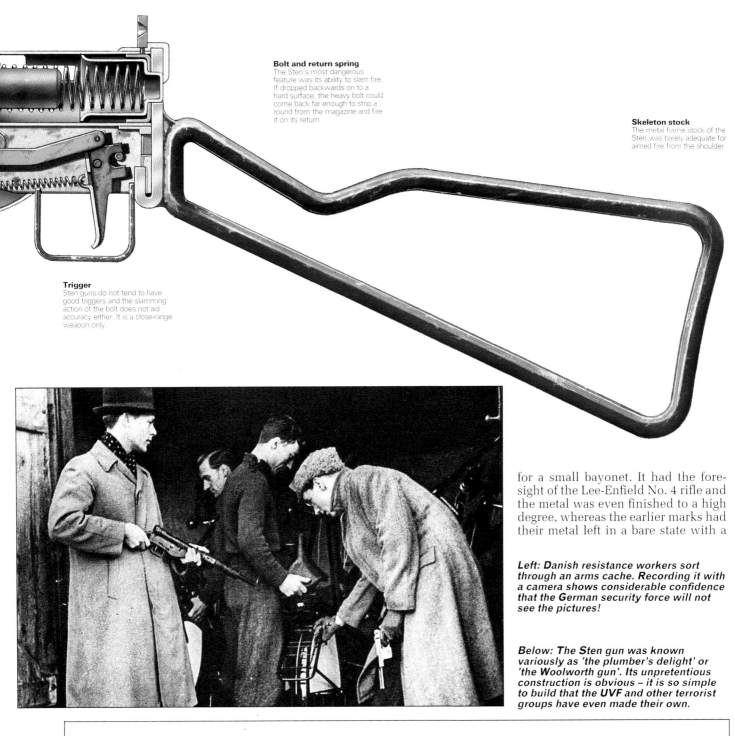

Bolt and return spring
The Sten's most dangerous feature was its ability to slam fire. If dropped backwards on to a hard surface, the heavy bolt could come back far enough to strip a round from the magazine and fire it on its return.

Skeleton stock
The metal frame stock of the Sten was barely adequate for aimed fire from the shoulder.

Trigger
Sten guns do not tend to have good triggers and the slamming action of the bolt does not aid accuracy either. It is a close-range weapon only.

for a small bayonet. It had the fore-sight of the Lee-Enfield No. 4 rifle and the metal was even finished to a high degree, whereas the earlier marks had their metal left in a bare state with a

Left: Danish resistance workers sort through an arms cache. Recording it with a camera shows considerable confidence that the German security force will not see the pictures!

Below: The Sten gun was known variously as 'the plumber's delight' or 'the Woolworth gun'. Its unpretentious construction is obvious – it is so simple to build that the UVF and other terrorist groups have even made their own.

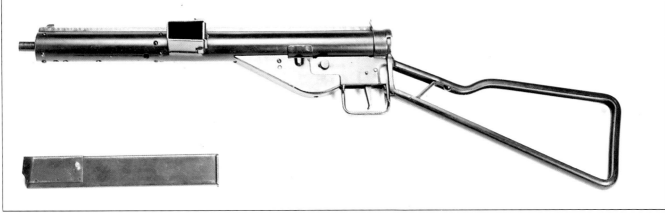

minimum of fine finish. The Mk V was issued to the airborne forces in 1944, and after World War II it became the standard British Army sub-machine gun.

The Sten was a crude weapon in nearly every way, but it worked and it could be produced in large numbers at a time when it was desperately needed. In occupied Europe it was re-vealed as an ideal resistance weapon, and all over the world underground forces have been busy copying the de-sign almost direct. The Germans even produced their own copies in 1944 and 1945. It was one of the more re-markable weapons of World War II.

Left: British soldiers in snow camouflage make contact with an American patrol on the German border in early 1945.

Below: Two British paratroopers at Arnhem in 1944. The Sten gun was an effective weapon for fighting in built-up areas.

The Ruger Mini-14 is a well thought-out, fast-handling, lightweight assault rifle with a traditional appearance, which has had some well-deserved sales in the police and security markets.

Rocking with the Ruger

Sturm, Ruger & Company of Southport, Connecticut, USA, appeared in the late 1940s with a simple .22 automatic pistol which rapidly acquired a high reputation for accuracy and reliability. Some years later, when the mania for single-action Western-style revolvers was sweeping America, they stepped in where Colt failed to tread and produced a range of excellent revolvers. After that they went on to make shotguns and hunting rifles, and rarely did they put a foot wrong.

When the 5.56-mm (.223) cartridge began to make itself felt in the military world, Ruger looked at the rifles on the commercial market and realised that they were entirely military-oriented, and that something a trifle less aggressive in appearance might well be popular. Since the recoil of the 5.56-mm cartridge is fairly low, and because the evergreen M1 carbine was always in demand, Ruger had the happy idea to weld two together, producing a light semi-automatic rifle similar to the M1 carbine and chambered for the 5.56-mm round. The result, introduced in 1973, was the Mini-14, so called because in many respects it was a miniaturised version of the contemporary US Army M14 rifle.

Military selective-fire variants of the Mini-14, like the folding-stocked AC-556K seen here, have cyclic rates of fire of about 750 rounds per minute.

Inside the Mini-14

The Ruger is a gas-operated, box magazine fed semi-automatic rifle. The rotating bolt is very similar to the M14 and MI Grand from which the Mini is developed, but the gas system of fixed piston and mobile cylinder differs from earlier service rifle designs. Ruger have combined the feel of the M1 carbine with a serious assault rifle calibre to produce an excellent weapon with a very attractive price tag.

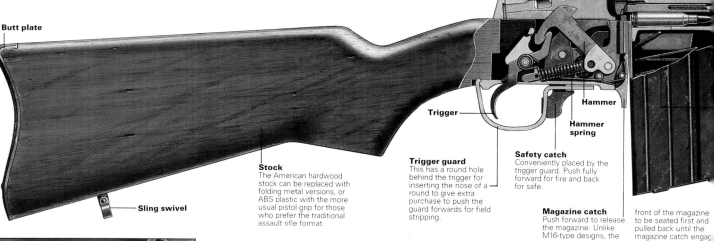

Rearsight
This is adjustable for windage and elevation using the tip of a round. The sight drums are adjustable in 1/4 turns, which adjusts the point of impact 4 cm (1.5 in) when zeroing at 100 m (328 ft). To raise the mean point of impact, turn the elevation drum anti-clockwise; to move the MPI right turn the windage dial anti-clockwise.

Bolt
The bolt rotates to lock in the same way as the M1 service rifle.

Firing p

Butt plate

Stock
The American hardwood stock can be replaced with folding metal versions, or ABS plastic with the more usual pistol grip for those who prefer the traditional assault rifle format.

Sling swivel

Trigger

Hammer

Hammer spring

Trigger guard
This has a round hole behind the trigger for inserting the nose of a round to give extra purchase to push the guard forwards for field stripping.

Safety catch
Conveniently placed by the trigger guard. Push fully forward for fire and back for safe.

Magazine catch
Push forward to release the magazine. Unlike M16-type designs, the front of the magazine to be seated first and pulled back until the magazine catch engag

It was not, though, just a matter of scaling down the Garand action. The chamber pressure of the 5.56-mm cartridge at about 3,650 kg/cm^2 (51,900 PSI) is higher than that of the 7.62-mm NATO cartridge at 3,515 kg/cm^2 (50,000 PSI), and the forces involved are still very high. The bolt is the standard rotating pattern developed by Garand for the M1, but the gas system is somewhat different.

The cocking handle is on the right of the breech, forming part of the operating rod. On pulling this back, a cam cut on the inner surface of the operating rod causes the bolt to rotate and unlock. Further movement of the cocking handle opens the bolt, and it

Field stripping the Mini 14

1 Remove the magazine by pressing forward on the release catch located to the rear of the magazine, and pull back on the cocking handle to check that the weapon is clear.

2 Push forward and pivot down the trigger guard to release and remove the trigger assembly as a single unit.

3 Remove the barrel and working parts from the stock by lifting the receiver forwards and upwards.

5 Turn the working parts over and remove the recoil spring and guide by pushing it forward to release it and then removing it to the rear. Do not separate the recoil spring from the guide rod. Watch out: the spring is under considerable pressure.

6 Pull the cocking handle connected to the operating rod to the rear, align the locking projections with the cut-outs in the receiver, and remove the whole assembly from the receiver.

7 The recoil spring cup and pin which hold the recoil spring and guide in place will drop out as soon as the tension of the recoil spring is removed. In some models these parts are a permanent fixture and cannot be removed.

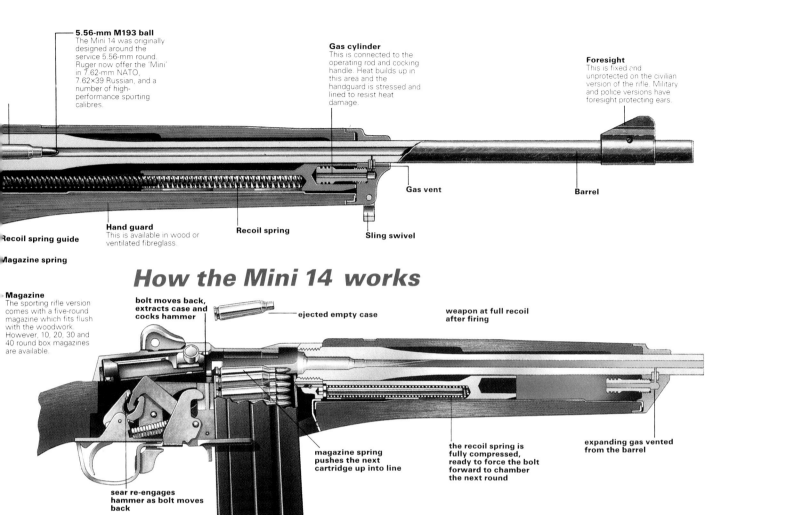

5.56-mm M193 ball
The Mini 14 was originally designed around the service 5.56-mm round. Ruger now offer the 'Mini' in 7.62-mm NATO, 7.62×39 Russian, and a number of high-performance sporting calibres.

Gas cylinder
This is connected to the operating rod and cocking handle. Heat builds up in this area and the handguard is stressed and lined to resist heat damage.

Foresight
This is fixed and unprotected on the civilian version of the rifle. Military and police versions have foresight protecting ears.

Gas vent

Barrel

Recoil spring guide

Hand guard
This is available in wood or ventilated fibreglass.

Recoil spring

Sling swivel

Magazine spring

Magazine
The sporting rifle version comes with a five-round magazine which fits flush with the woodwork. However, 10, 20, 30 and 40 round box magazines are available.

How the Mini 14 works

bolt moves back, extracts case and cocks hammer

ejected empty case

weapon at full recoil after firing

magazine spring pushes the next cartridge up into line

the recoil spring is fully compressed, ready to force the bolt forward to chamber the next round

expanding gas vented from the barrel

sear re-engages hammer as bolt moves back

4 Remove the plastic resin handguard, which snaps on and off. The handguard also covers the operating handle. The gun is available with wood handguards, which should be left in place.

8 Remove the bolt by pushing it forwards until the front of the bolt lifts out of the receiver, then align the firing pin projection at the back of the bolt within the cut-out in the receiver and remove. This is a little fiddly until you get used to it.

9 The weapon should not be stripped further. Reassembly is in reverse order. When cleaning, pay attention to the gas block under the barrel, which is usually heavily fouled with carbon.

Ruger's scoped Ranch Rifle version of the Mini-14 proves that it can be deadly accurate out to ranges of 300 m (984 ft) or more, which is ideal for most 'varmint' hunting use in the States.

can be locked open by means of a plunger if required. Releasing the bolt allows it to go forwards and load the first round. On firing, a proportion of the propelling gas is diverted through a port and into a gas cylinder beneath the barrel; this is surrounded by a hollow piston head, so that in effect the piston head is blown off the gas cylinder, driving back the operating rod to actuate the breech by means of the cam. As the bolt goes back, it cocks the hammer, and on the return stroke it collects a fresh cartridge from the box magazine underneath the breech. Magazines for 5, 10, 20 and 30 rounds are available, though the last is only supplied to military and police forces.

The safety catch is in the front of the trigger guard and is simply pushed forwards for 'fire' and pulled back for 'safe'. When the last round is fired, the bolt is held open by a catch operated by the magazine follower. The bolt can be closed by means of the bolt release on the left of the receiver or by simply removing the magazine.

In 1977 some minor changes were made to simplify the mechanism and give better protection against dust and dirt, and in 1981 a flash suppressor and radioluminous sights were fitted.

The popularity of the Mini-14 with

Britain's most notable users of the Mini-14 are the Royal Ulster Constabulary. They appreciate the assault rifle firepower coming from a less aggressive-looking weapon, which is an important point to an internal security force.

police and security forces led to the development of the Ruger Mini-14/20GB Infantry Rifle. This used the same basic mechanism but had a protected front sight and bayonet lug, grenade launcher fittings on the muzzle, a heat-resistant glassfibre handguard and a flash suppressor.

The Infantry Rifle didn't go as well as might have been expected, largely because most military forces in the late 1970s were looking for weapons with selective fire capability – in other words, they wanted something with automatic fire. So Ruger produced the AC-556 rifle, which was the Infantry Rifle with the addition of a selector switch to permit full-automatic fire at about 750 rounds per minute. This was followed by the shorter barrelled AC-556K (330 mm [13 in] instead of 470 mm [18.5 in]) and a pistol grip and folding stock. With the stock folded the length of the AC-556K is no more than 603 mm (23.7 in), whereas the standard AC-556 is 984 mm (38.7 in) long.

'Ranch Rifle'

Back in the commercial market, in 1982 Ruger produced the 'Ranch Rifle'. This was simply the Mini-14 with some small internal improvements and with the addition of integral telescope sight mounts on the receiver. It was also available in some of the smaller high-velocity commercial calibres. And in 1987 came a further addition to the family, the 'Mini-Thirty'; you might expect that, with a name like that, the rifle would be chambered for the venerable 'thirty-thirty' cartridge, but in fact the truth is more remarkable than that. It is chambered for the Soviet 7.62-mm×39 M43 cartridge, one of the very few rifles of the Western World to be capable of firing the common Soviet army round. It makes a great deal of sense, because the Mini-Thirty is capable of taking the recoil, and with its 470-mm barrel, longer than that of the Kalashnikovs, it is capable of delivering better accuracy from the M43 cartridge than any other rifle. It remains to be seen how popular this model will be in the long term.

Security Revolvers

The automatic pistol may get all the attention these days, as new designs fall over each other, but the revolver still has a faithful following. There is rarely anything exceptionally new – after all, the basic design was well and truly settled before the turn of the century, and most of the improvements since then have been in manufacturing and safety devices. Gradual and almost imperceptible refinements continue to be added, and a good revolver is a highly reliable and accurate weapon which has the added virtue of having very little that can go wrong with it.

Revolvers, like automatic pistols, can be considered in two groups – the big, heavy military-style weapons, and the light, smaller-calibre self-defence weapons. It is the second of these groups that we are about to look at, the weapons carried by police and security agents, as concealed weapons or holster weapons, as back-up weapons or off-duty weapons.

Many manufacturers

Say 'revolver' and most people think 'Colt' or 'Smith & Wesson'; but there are other manufacturers, and these others predominate in the security and small-calibre field. Ruger, Astra, Charter Arms, Rohm, Taurus, Famae, Erma, Llama, Manurhin, Rossi, Squibman . . . we cannot deal with all of them, but a few examples may be of interest.

Bill Ruger made his name with an excellent .22 automatic; then when the 'fast draw' craze swept the USA in the 1950s and Colt was slow to put the 1873 Frontier back into production, Ruger saw a market opening and proceeded to fill it with some splendid big

Above: Custom-built revolvers like this Davis .357 Special are hardly general issue to security forces, but individual officers who can make use of the phenomenal accuracy of such weapons might buy one for personal use.

Below: Police Chief Jerry Priest of the Indianapolis Police is taking no chances in arresting a suspect: his thumb is on the hammer of his Colt Python .357 Magnum, ready in an instant to notch it back for single-action operation.

Inside the Ruger Security-Six

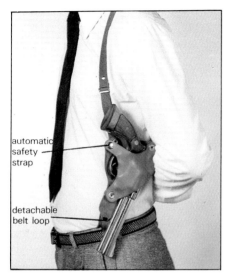

automatic safety strap

detachable belt loop

The 152.4-mm (6-in) revolver is the better option once action has commenced, but there are problems with concealed carry of the excellent but rather large Smith & Wesson Model 686. The large frame and heavy underbarrel rib make this a very accurate and easy to handle revolver.

The revolver is an obvious choice for police use: they are inherently more reliable and easier to operate safely with a minimum of training compared with automatic pistols. There are no manual safeties to operate; all the officer has to do under stress is draw the revolver and pull the trigger through on double action to fire.

Firing pin
On many revolvers this is part of the hammer assembly. They do not have the transfer bar safety feature but rely on a rebounding lock, which means that the firing pin cannot contact the cartridge without full trigger operation.

Recoil plate pin

Recoil plate

Hammer
This weapon will not fire even if the hammer is struck or dropped while being thumbed back as the hammer nose rests on the frame, not the firing pin.

Firing pin spring

Cylinder release button

Transfer bar
This safety feature means that the weapon can only be fired by pressure on the trigger; the hammer cannot contact the firing pin without the trigger pushing the transfer bar between them. The weapon cannot accidentally fire when dropped on the hammer, as the hammer nose rests on the frame.

Hammer dog pivot pin

Hammer dog spring plunger

Hammer dog

Hammer strut
This connects the hammer to the main spring.

Main spring
The main spring pressure can be adjusted so that it clobbers the percussion cap harder and produces a heavier trigger pull if required. Also, the spring can be adjusted as it wears out.

Grips
Revolvers are improved by the addition of wraparound rubber grips produced by Pachmayr or Hogue. These are designed for combat and greatly improve indexing and control when firing rapid strings of shots.

single-action revolvers. From there he moved into the security revolver market and in 1968 introduced the 'Security-Six'. This is a solid-frame revolver with side-swinging cylinder released by the usual type of thumb-catch. The ejector rod is concealed in a shroud, forged integrally with the ribbed barrel, and the lockwork includes the patented Ruger transfer bar. Actuated by trigger movement, this acts as an intermediary between the hammer and the firing pin. Unless the trigger is consciously pressed the transfer bar will not go into position, and if the hammer is thumbed back and dropped it will not reach the firing pin and fire the round.

The Security-Six has .38 Special or .357 Magnum chambering, with 2.75, 4-in (101-mm) or 6-in (152-mm) barrels, fixed or adjustable sights, and in blued or stainless steel finish. The 'Speed Six' is the same as the Security-Six but with a rounded butt and only the shorter barrel options.

The Security-Six was originally available with fixed or adjustable sights, but in 1975 the fixed-sight model became the 'Police Service-Six', now known simply as the 'Service-Six'. Like the Speed-Six it has a rounded butt to make concealment easier and only the shorter barrel options were made. As the 'Model 209', this version was also made in 9-mm Parabellum calibre, but this chambering was later extended to all the compact revolvers and the Model 209 was dropped.

New Ruger

Ruger's most recent revolver is the GP 100, in .357 Magnum calibre. The frame width has been increased in critical areas, various other constructional details have been improved, and the lockwork is contained within the trigger guard which is inserted

Smith & Wesson has dominated the US police market for years, but Colt and Ruger revolvers and some interesting automatics from Europe are now being purchased by many police forces. This police officer involved in a shoot-out in New Orleans is using a Smith & Wesson Model 57.

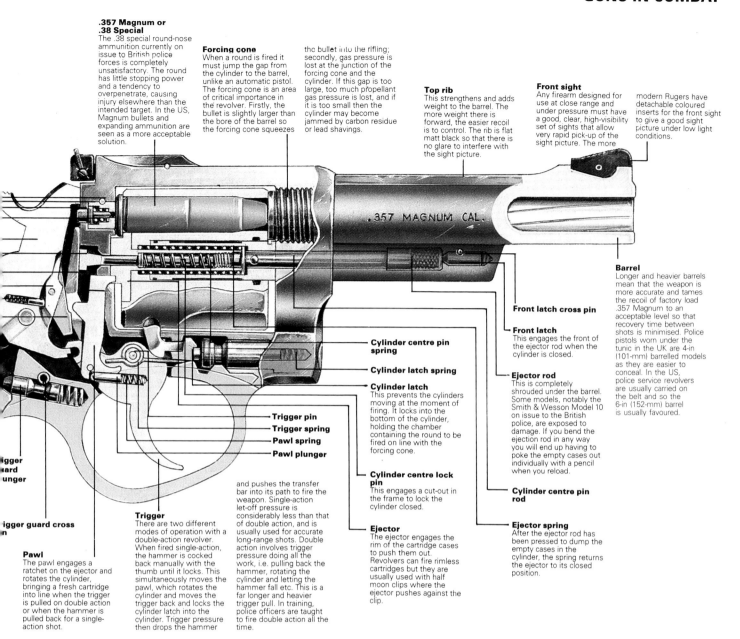

.357 Magnum or .38 Special
The .38 special round-nose ammunition currently on issue to British police forces is completely unsatisfactory. The round has little stopping power and a tendency to overpenetrate, causing injury elsewhere than the intended target. In the US, Magnum bullets and expanding ammunition are seen as a more acceptable solution.

Forcing cone
When a round is fired it must jump the gap from the cylinder to the barrel, unlike an automatic pistol. The forcing cone is an area of critical importance in the revolver. Firstly, the bullet is slightly larger than the bore of the barrel so the forcing cone squeezes the bullet into the rifling; secondly, gas pressure is lost at the junction of the forcing cone and the cylinder. If this gap is too large, too much propellant gas pressure is lost, and if it is too small then the cylinder may become jammed by carbon residue or lead shavings.

Top rib
This strengthens and adds weight to the barrel. The more weight there is forward, the easier recoil is to control. The rib is flat matt black so that there is no glare to interfere with the sight picture.

Front sight
Any firearm designed for use at close range and under pressure must have a good, clear, high-visibility set of sights that allow very rapid pick-up of the sight picture. The more modern Rugers have detachable coloured inserts for the front sight to give a good sight picture under low light conditions.

Barrel
Longer and heavier barrels mean that the weapon is more accurate and tames the recoil of factory load .357 Magnum to an acceptable level so that recovery time between shots is minimised. Police pistols worn under the tunic in the UK are 4-in (101-mm) barrelled models as they are easier to conceal. In the US, police service revolvers are usually carried on the belt and so the 6-in (152-mm) barrel is usually favoured.

Front latch cross pin

Front latch
This engages the front of the ejector rod when the cylinder is closed.

Ejector rod
This is completely shrouded under the barrel. Some models, notably the Smith & Wesson Model 10 on issue to the British police, are exposed to damage. If you bend the ejection rod in any way you will end up having to poke the empty cases out individually with a pencil when you reload.

Cylinder centre pin rod

Ejector spring
After the ejector rod has been pressed to dump the empty cases in the cylinder, the spring returns the ejector to its closed position.

Cylinder centre pin spring

Cylinder latch spring

Cylinder latch
This prevents the cylinders moving at the moment of firing. It locks into the bottom of the cylinder, holding the chamber containing the round to be fired on line with the forcing cone.

Cylinder centre lock pin
This engages a cut-out in the frame to lock the cylinder closed.

Ejector
The ejector engages the rim of the cartridge cases to push them out. Revolvers can fire rimless cartridges but they are usually used with half moon clips where the ejector pushes against the clip.

Trigger pin

Trigger spring

Pawl spring

Pawl plunger

Trigger
There are two different modes of operation with a double-action revolver. When fired single-action, the hammer is cocked back manually with the thumb until it locks. This simultaneously moves the cylinder and moves the trigger back and locks the cylinder latch into the cylinder. Trigger pressure then drops the hammer and pushes the transfer bar into its path to fire the weapon. Single-action let-off pressure is considerably less than that of double action, and is usually used for accurate long-range shots. Double action involves trigger pressure doing all the work, i.e. pulling back the hammer, rotating the cylinder and letting the hammer fall etc. This is a far longer and heavier trigger pull. In training, police officers are taught to fire double action all the time.

Trigger guard plunger

Trigger guard cross pin

Pawl
The pawl engages a ratchet on the ejector and rotates the cylinder, bringing a fresh cartridge into line when the trigger is pulled on double action or when the hammer is pulled back for a single-action shot.

into the frame as a separate sub-assembly. It has a 4-in (101-mm) barrel with full-length ejector shroud, or a 6-in (152-mm) barrel with full or short shroud.

The 'Undercover'

Charter Arms was founded in 1964. The founder had worked for Colt, High Standard and Sturm Ruger and he felt that there was a gap in the market for a short-barrelled pocket revolver. Failing to convince any of his employers, he set up in business and proved his point. The 'Undercover' was the model which first appeared, a .38 Special five-shot solid frame weapon of conventional form but high quality, later produced in other calibres and with various barrel lengths. It was soon followed by the 'Undercoverette', designed for female police officers. Chambered for .32 Long, with a 2-in (51-mm) barrel and a slender butt contour, it proved popular but was discontinued.

Good as these were, customers were

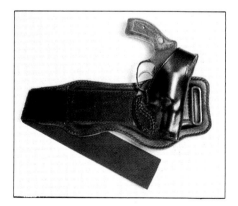

The Smith & Wesson Model 36 is excellent as a back-up gun for concealed carry in an ankle holster, but not something you would like to carry as a service weapon. Unfortunately this is exactly what was issued to British police forces in the recent past.

The successor to the Ruger Security-Six is the innovative GP-100. This is a very solidly-built weapon that is ideal for police use. The heavy barrel and .357 Magnum calibre make it a better choice than the British police issue heavy-barrelled Smith & Wesson Model 10s.

asking for more power, and Charter came up with the 'Bulldog', a .44 Special five-shot with a 3-in (76-mm) barrel of 19oz (540g). It was later made in .357 Magnum calibre. Then came the 'Police Bulldog' in .38 Special chambering and with a 2-in (51-mm) or 4-in (101-mm) barrel, a heavy or standard barrel, and with a spurless hammer as an option for people who liked to carry them in their pockets. All the Charter Arms revolvers are currently available (except the Undercoverette) and they have a high reputation for reliability.

A less well-known company is Astra-Unceta of Guernica, Spain; it has been in the pistol business since the turn of the century, supplying the Spanish army for many years. It is now the principal Spanish gunmaker and it produces a wide range of revolvers in every size and calibre. Its Model 680 is available in .22, .32 and .38 Special calibres with a 2-in (51-mm) barrel. The grip is slender but the trigger guard is well proportioned, and the 680 is a good undercover weapon. Like all Astra revolvers, in the butt it has an ingenious and simple adjusting device which permits the strength of the mainspring to be adjusted.

The 'Police 357' is similar to the 680 but rather more substantial and with a heavier butt, giving a better grip. The front sight is small, to avoid snagging when drawing the weapon, and the rear sight is simply a groove in the frame. It is widely used by Spanish police and has a good reputation for reliability.

Mauser is not, perhaps, thought of as a revolver maker since it gave up making them in the 1890s in favour of automatic pistols. But in the late 1970s it introduced an excellent 2-in (51-mm) barrel, six-shot .38 Special solid-frame revolver which was a beautifully-made weapon, ideal for concealed carry. Mauser found it to be a slow mover in the market, so it licensed production to Renato Gamba of Gardone Val Trompia, Italy, who sold it as its 'Trident'. It did rather better, but then ran into difficulties in other directions and it went off the market for a while, but recent information indicates that it is once more in production.

South American models

Finally, a nod in the direction of South America; the Amadeo Rossi company of Sao Leopoldo, Brazil, makes a wide range of revolvers, from .22 target models to heavy service holster patterns. Among its range, which is largely one of near Smith & Wesson patterns, is the 'Pioneer 87' in .38 Special, with a 1.8-in (47.7-mm) barrel and five-shot cylinder. It has a

Police forces on the continent and in South America are equipped with a range of very good Smith & Wesson copies. The Taurus from Brazil (top) and the Llama (bottom) from Spain are good guns, but do not match Colt's high standards.

The Llama 'Comanche' features good high-visibility adjustable sights. With a bit of practice you should be able to load the cylinder with two rounds at a time.

Police revolvers tend to have 4-in (101-mm) barrels. However, the 6-in (152-mm) barrel performs considerably better in terms of accuracy at longer range and damage to the target. The shorter barrel does mean a faster draw, which may be important in some circumstances.

US Police Special Weapons and Tactics teams usually carry what they personally feel happy with, in this case a 6-in (152-mm) barrelled Smith & Wesson .357 Magnum. This officer is moving a hostage to safety after an assault using tear gas.

solid stainless steel frame and a separate firing pin in the standing breech.

The selection of a security revolver is thus a matter of personal choice; there are plenty of them about. In general, none of them is going to be particularly accurate at anything but short range, and none of them has very sophisticated sights. In the heavier loadings they can be noisy, with lots of muzzle blast and a hefty recoil. But when the need arises, a lot of small faults can be overlooked.

M60: the Pig

One image that evokes the Vietnam War more than any other is that of the GI peering through the jungle, draped with ammunition belts and cradling a machine-gun; and the machine-gun is always the M60. The Americans finished World War II with a collection of machine-guns from the drawing board of John Browning. They were all of World War I origin, and American exposure to the weapons of their enemies and Allies had shown that there were other ways to make machine-guns; and some of them were more practical than the Browning for various applications.

One wartime innovation that attracted the Americans (and others) was the German concept of a general-purpose machine-gun, a weapon that could be a squad automatic on a bipod, light enough to be carried by one man but robust enough to operate in sustained-fire weapon when fitted on a tripod. The German MG42, it was felt, was the way to go.

In 1944 a captured MG42 was dissected and American designers set

about adapting it to their concept of a machine-gun. When the result appeared it proved to be a failure due to a draughtsman's misreading of a vital dimension; by that time the war was over so the project was scrapped.

A second attempt produced a design with heavy German overtones. The belt feed mechanism was lifted straight from the German MG42, while the gas operating mechanism was taken from the German FG42. paratroopers' rifle.

An M60 gunner blasts rounds downrange during preparation for the invasion of Iraq. From an unpromising start, the M60 has matured into an effective, if heavy, general-purpose machine-gun.

Inside the M60

Back sight
The M60 has a fixed front sight, so you have to zero on the back sight; this means you have to remember what the correct zero setting is for whatever barrel is in the gun. This is all but impossible, so the same zero setting is used for all barrels, with consequent loss of accuracy.

Firing pin spring

Actuating cam roller

Bolt plug

Buffer locking plate

Feed cover

Operating rod
This has a post which rides in the hollow interior of the bolt.

Barrel locking leve

Buffer plunger

Operating rod drive

Buffer

Spring guide

Operating rod drive spring

Operating rod yoke

Hinged shoulder rest

Firing pin
When the bolt is locked into place the piston post can run forward and drive the firing pin on to the cap and fire the cartridge.

Bolt
After firing the piston post rotates the bolt, unlocking it, and pulls it open. As the bolt travels back it moves the feed arm, bringing a fresh cartridge into line.

Trigger pin

Trigger
The M60 only fires on fully automatic, but it is easy to squeeze off single shots.

Sear notch

Sear

Trigger spring

Sear spring in sear plunger

The resulting machine-gun went into service in 1957 as the M60, chambered for the 7.62-mm NATO cartridge and acting as partner to the new 7.62-mm M14 rifle.

The operating system of the M60 is even older than the German FG42, since it is almost the same as the World War I Lewis Gun. The gas piston has a vertical post at its rear end, which engages in a helical groove in the hollow bolt. Inside the bolt, on top of the piston post, is the firing pin.

Firing mechanism

The gun is cocked by pulling back the cocking handle until the bolt is held to the rear. The top cover is then opened and the end of the cartridge belt laid in. The cover is closed, and the trigger pressed. The piston is released, to run forward driven by a spring, and the piston post pushes the bolt, which is restrained from rotating by longitudinal grooves in the gun body.

The topmost lug on the bolt pushes the cartridge from the belt in the feedway and into the chamber. As it enters, the bolt comes to the end of the

A Marine stands on the hood of a 'Humvee' light vehicle outside Khafji on the Saudi/Kuwaiti border. The machine-gun is an M60E3, a specially lightened version in widespread service with the Marines.

The US Army adopted the M60 as its general-purpose machine-gun 40 years ago when rifle squads were equipped with M14 7.62-mm rifles. The M60 was never an out-standing weapon and is now supplemented by the 5.56-mm Minimi produced by FN. But the new lightweight M60 offers major improvements, and the gun will remain in US service as a GPMG for many years to come.

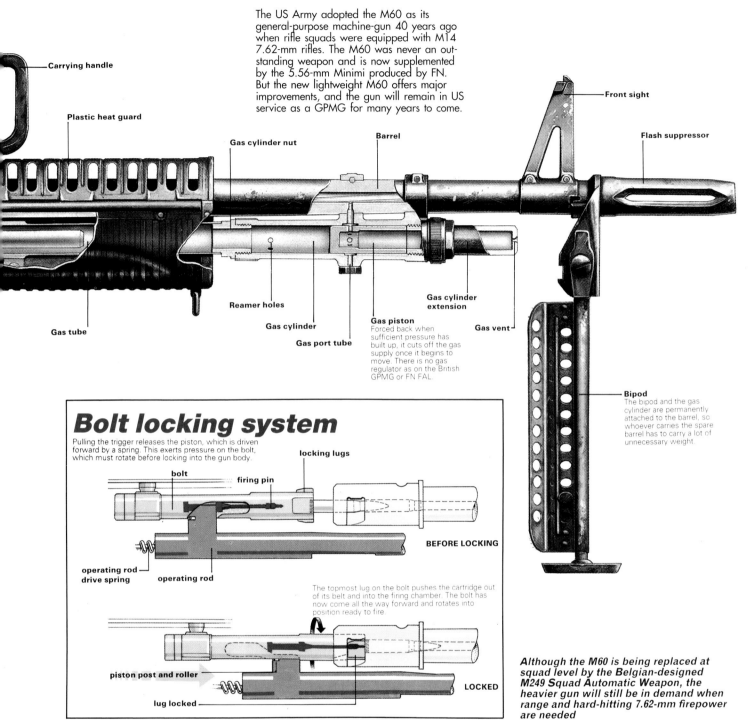

Carrying handle

Plastic heat guard

Gas cylinder nut

Barrel

Front sight

Flash suppressor

Gas tube

Reamer holes

Gas cylinder

Gas port tube

Gas piston
Forced back when sufficient pressure has built up, it cuts off the gas supply once it begins to move. There is no gas regulator as on the British GPMG or FN FAL.

Gas cylinder extension

Gas vent

Bipod
The bipod and the gas cylinder are permanently attached to the barrel, so whoever carries the spare barrel has to carry a lot of unnecessary weight.

Bolt locking system

Pulling the trigger releases the piston, which is driven forward by a spring. This exerts pressure on the bolt, which must rotate before locking into the gun body.

bolt

firing pin

locking lugs

BEFORE LOCKING

operating rod drive spring

operating rod

The topmost lug on the bolt pushes the cartridge out of its belt and into the firing chamber. The bolt has now come all the way forward and rotates into position ready to fire.

piston post and roller

lug locked

LOCKED

Although the M60 is being replaced at squad level by the Belgian-designed M249 Squad Automatic Weapon, the heavier gun will still be in demand when range and hard-hitting 7.62-mm firepower are needed

longitudinal grooves, and the piston post, pushing in the helical groove, now rotates the bolt so that its lugs lock into the rear of the barrel.

Once the bolt has rotated to the locked position, the piston post lines up with a straight section of the groove in the bolt and can run forward, driving the firing pin onto the cap and firing the cartridge.

The forward movement of the bolt has also driven a feed arm in the gun's cover to one side, latching onto the next cartridge in the belt. As the bullet passes up the barrel, a portion of the propelling gas passes through a port and into the gas cylinder. Here it

US Marines on a Search and Destroy mission near Da Nang. The M60 earned the nickname 'The Pig' because it was heavy for a squad machine-gun, and its design faults were not calculated to win it popularity.

A crewman returns fire at ambushing Viet Cong from the back of a US Navy patrol boat on the Bassac River in Vietnam. The M60 has a relatively low rate of fire of 550 rounds per minute, which means that it is fairly easy to control.

builds up pressure and pushes a piston-head backwards for a short distance, giving an impulsive blow to the front end of the piston rod.

The piston rod moves back, and the piston post rotates the bolt to unlock, then pulls the bolt open, ejecting the spent case. As the bolt goes back it moves the feed arm again, bringing the fresh cartridge into line, so that when the bolt comes forward it will reload the gun.

The M60 fires at about 550 rounds per minute, slow enough for a trained gunner to be able to loose off single shots or short bursts without the need for a special selector lever. It was also the first US machine-gun to have a quick-change barrel, but experience in combat showed that the designer hadn't quite got it right.

Difficult reload

The barrel carried the front end of the gas cylinder and the bipod, so that when the gunner shouted "Change!" and released the locking lever, his assistant had to grasp the bipod and heave the barrel out of the gun while the gunner held it up in the air – or dropped it in the mud. The gunner had to keep holding it up while the assistant put the hot barrel to one side

and inserted the new one, complete with its bipod; not the easiest of tasks on a dark night with a hot barrel, which is why a heavy asbestos glove was part of the assistant's kit.

After some combat experience with this, the M60E1 appeared. This redesigned the barrel and gas cylinder assembly so that the gas cylinder was now part of the gun and carried the bipod, while the barrel was a single assembly and fitted with a handle.

Some other changes also came along. The M60C was a modification that removed the stock and fitted a remote firing control, so that the gun could be slung on helicopters and fired by the pilot. The M60D had a

spade grip fitted at the rear, for firing from helicopter doors. And the M60E2 was designed for use as a fixed tank coaxial gun, with a long exhaust tube and barrel extension to carry the propellant fumes out of the tank.

As a sustained-fire gun on a tripod the M60 was fine; as a squad automatic, on a bipod, it was still somewhat heavy for its job, and eventually the Maremont Company developed what it called the 'Lightweight M60', which is now going into service as the M60A1.

Weighing some 2 kg (4.4 lb) less than the original M60, the M60A1 has at last given the US Army a useful and practical 7.62-mm light machine-gun.

SIG

Solid performer

The vast majority of military handguns are a compromise between capability and cost. The SIG series of automatic pistols is among the finest sidearms available, but their price tends to count against them unless an army's budget is unusually generous. Only a few rivals can match their accuracy, and the P226 passed the US Army's rigorous trials with flying colours, only to be ruled out because of the price tag.

The Schweizerische Industrie Gesellschaft, or SIG to most people, opened its doors in 1853 as a manufacturer of railway trucks, but it very soon turned to the manufacture of percussion muzzle-loading rifles for the Swiss army and then went on to make Vetterli bolt-action rifles and the Schmidt-Rubin straight-pull bolt action rifle, which was the mainstay of the Swiss army for most of this century. Although the Swiss government has its own arsenals, SIG has always been part of the manufacturing base for the army, and today they are busy producing the 5.56-mm StG 90 assault rifle with which the Swiss are currently being re-equipped.

Their venture into pistols began

shortly before World War II when they acquired a number of patents taken out by Charles Petter. Petter is something of a mystery man; we know that he served some time in the French Foreign Legion in the 1920s and was invalided out after being wounded in North Africa. He then went into engineering in France and developed a pistol which eventually became the French MAS-35. In 1937 SIG bought rights to the patents and began examining them, since they appreciated that before long the Swiss army would probably be looking for a replacement for the 7.65-mm Luger pistols they had been using since 1900.

The price is wrong

Their perfected design appeared in 1947 as the 9-mm SIG SP 47/8, the latter figure representing the number of rounds in the magazine. Adopted by the Swiss army, it then went on the commercial market as the SIG P210. Although an expensive pistol, it soon acquired a very high reputation for reliability and accuracy and is still made in small numbers today for those who demand the very best. The only other army ever to adopt it in any quantity

The SIG P210 ranks as one of the finest military pistols ever made. Built to the very highest standards, it shoots superbly and was adopted by the Swiss army in 1947. For a variety of political and economic reasons, it failed to achieve any major export sales.

was Denmark's; most other armies looked at it but decided they could not afford it in the numbers they needed.

Apart from exquisite workmanship and fit, it is difficult to see why the SIG is so good, though perhaps workmanship and fit say it all. The action is very similar to that of the Browning High Power, using a lug beneath the barrel into which a shaped cam path is cut; this, acting on a frame pin, pulls the breech down and unlocks the barrel from the slide. The most obvious novelty is that unlike almost every other automatic pistol of slide and frame construction, the SIG slide runs *inside* the frame, a system which gives it exceptional support throughout the recoil stroke. The usual barrel bushing is not used, the SIG engineers having developed some ingenious internal contours which ensure that the barrel remains parallel with the slide until after the bullet has left the muzzle, which helps to account for the outstanding accuracy.

However, being a gunmaker in Switzerland is not without its problems; Swiss laws make it very difficult to sell weapons to other countries. As a SIG engineer once observed, "We are only allowed to sell weapons to people who don't need them." So in order to gain access to a larger market, SIG entered into an agreement with J.P. Sauer & Son of Eckernforde, West Germany; SIG would design the pistols and licence manufacture to Sauer, who could then sell them around the world under the rather less restrictive Federal German regulations. SIG, of course, do still make their own pistols, selling to those markets to which they are allowed access.

The first of these collaborative efforts was the SIG P220, which appeared in 1974. The idea was to develop a pistol as reliable as the P210 but simpler to manufacture, and the principal change lay in the locking of the breech. The same sort of shaped cam was used to control breech movement, but instead of the carefully-machined ribs on the barrel and mating grooves in the interior of the slide, the breech end of the barrel was shaped into a squared-off lump and the ejection slot was expanded to cover the whole top of the slide. Locking was done by lifting the squared breech section until it locked into the ejection slot; very simple and very effective, one of those ideas which makes you say, "Why didn't anybody think of that before?"

The P220 also introduced a double-action trigger, with a de-cocking lever lying just behind the trigger on the left side, where it falls under the thumb of a right-handed firer. With the pistol loaded and cocked, pressing down on this lever releases the hammer, which drops and is held by a safety notch on

P220 in action

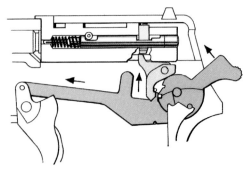

Firing
When firing double action, squeezing the trigger cocks the hammer via the trigger rod. The safety lever presses against the lock pin. The sear moves away from the hammer and the firing pin is released by the lock pin. Lastly, the hammer drops and the shot is fired.

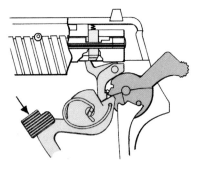

The de-cocking lever
Pressing the de-cocking lever releases the hammer into the safety notch so that you can carry the gun in complete safety. The firing pin is blocked during and after de-cocking.

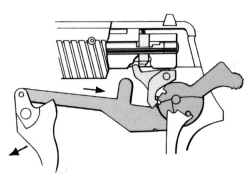

Firing pin safety
In this condition the gun can only be fired by pulling the trigger. You can drop it loaded, with the hammer cocked, and it will not go off. This allows you to get off the first round without releasing an external safety catch.

The P225 was developed to meet the West German Federal and State Police requirement for a new sidearm to replace their .32 calibre Walther PPs and PPKs. It won the competition and is now the most popular police handgun in Germany.

Stripping the P210

1 Check that the chamber is empty and remove the magazine. Pull the slide back. Look through the ejection port until you find the cut-out in the slide and match the slide stop with it.

2 Holding it in this position, press the slide stop shaft through from right to left until it is clear of the slide.

3 The slide stop comes away from the slide.

4 Take the slide off the frame forwards.

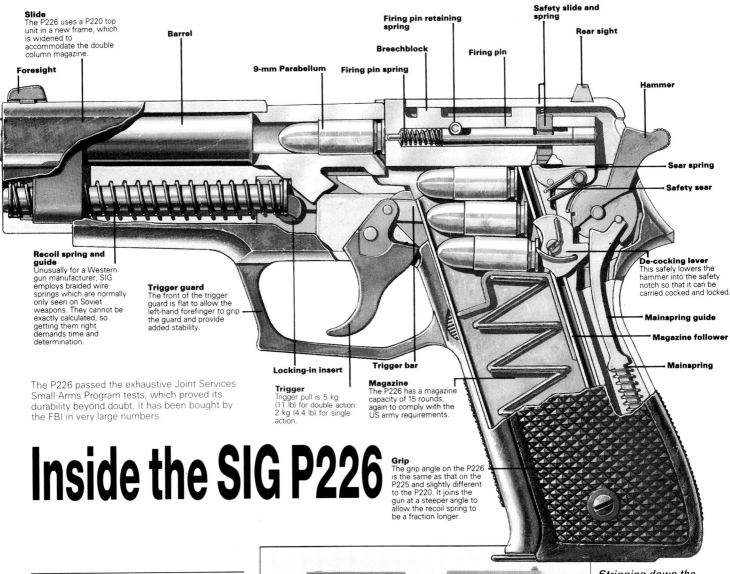

Slide
The P226 uses a P220 top unit in a new frame, which is widened to accommodate the double column magazine.

Foresight

Barrel

9-mm Parabellum

Firing pin spring

Firing pin retaining spring

Breechblock

Firing pin

Safety slide and spring

Rear sight

Hammer

Sear spring

Safety sear

De-cocking lever
This safely lowers the hammer into the safety notch so that it can be carried cocked and locked.

Mainspring guide

Magazine follower

Mainspring

Recoil spring and guide
Unusually for a Western gun manufacturer, SIG employs braided wire springs which are normally only seen on Soviet weapons. They cannot be exactly calculated, so getting them right demands time and determination.

Trigger guard
The front of the trigger guard is flat to allow the left-hand forefinger to grip the guard and provide added stability.

Locking-in insert

Trigger
Trigger pull is 5 kg (11 lb) for double action: 2 kg (4.4 lb) for single action.

Trigger bar

Magazine
The P226 has a magazine capacity of 15 rounds, again to comply with the US army requirements.

The P226 passed the exhaustive Joint Services Small Arms Program tests, which proved its durability beyond doubt. It has been bought by the FBI in very large numbers.

Inside the SIG P226

Grip
The grip angle on the P226 is the same as that on the P225 and slightly different to the P220. It joins the gun at a steeper angle to allow the recoil spring to be a fraction longer.

5 Lift the back of the return spring guide out of engagement with the barrel. Hold the cam lug and pull the barrel back and up.

6 The hammer mechanism lifts out as a single unit and the field strip is completed.

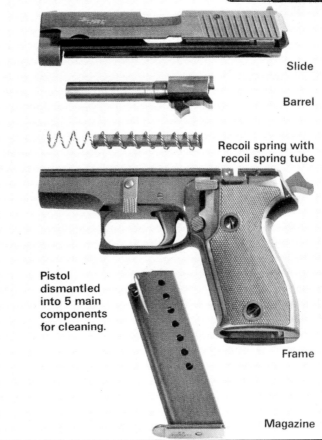

Slide

Barrel

Recoil spring with recoil spring tube

Pistol dismantled into 5 main components for cleaning.

Frame

Magazine

Stripping down the P226 reveals the braided wire return spring, which took SIG some time to develop but seems to have worked very well. The SIG introduced some new technology that proved a source of a few teething problems – trigger return springs and breechblock retaining springs tended to break. However, more than 10 years of constant military and police testing have ironed out all the bugs and left the P220 range as one of the finest series of autos available.

the sear. Pressing the lever again will raise the hammer and engage the trigger mechanism ready for firing.

Automatic safety

There is also an automatic firing pin lock, one of the first of its kind, which ensures that the firing pin is positively locked except during the last few degrees of trigger movement and as the hammer is released to fire. Because of this automatic firing pin safety there is no manual safety catch.

The P220 was introduced in 9-mm Parabellum calibre as standard, with a nine-shot magazine; in addition it was made in 7.65-mm Parabellum, .38 Super Auto and .45 ACP calibres for those who wanted them, but the 7.65-mm variation has been dropped for lack of customers.

The next design from SIG was in answer to the German Federal Police specification issued in the middle 1970s. The resulting SIG P225 is little more than a slightly smaller P220 with one round less in the magazine and has only ever been made in 9-mm Parabellum calibre. There are some minor changes in the trigger mechanism but the basic system of operation remains the same, with the addition of an internal safety device which prevents the pistol firing even if it is dropped in a cocked condition. The P225 was adopted by the Swiss police and by several German local police forces and has had wide foreign sales; rumour has it that the US Secret Service use it, but SIG refuses to comment.

In 1980, with the US Army demanding a new pistol, SIG made some modifications to the P225 to produce the P226. Made in the USA under licence by the Maremont Corporation, it came within a hair's-breadth of acceptance, being pipped at the post by the Beretta 92F solely upon price.

The squat profile of the SIG P226 identifiable by the three catches along the top of the receiver. The one above the trigger is the slide catch, next is the de-cocking lever and the slide release is at the back. Developed for the US Army pistol trials, the P226 is now used by the British SAS.

Above: Unlike practically every automatic pistol of slide and frame construction, the SIG P210's slide runs inside rather than outside the frame. The barrel also remains parallel with the slide until after the bullet leaves the muzzle, which contributes to its excellent accuracy.

Ambidextrous operation

Eighty per cent of the P226 parts are from the P220 or P225 production lines, and really it is a P220 with a larger magazine capacity and with the magazine release catch fitted to function from either side of the weapon, so accommodating left- or right-handed firers. Two magazines are available, holding either 15 or 20 rounds of 9-mm Parabellum.

Parallel with these heavy-calibre pistols, SIG was also producing the P230, introduced at about the same time as the P220. This was a simple blowback pocket pistol for police use, chambered either for the 9-mm Short or the 7.65-mm ACP cartridges. Apart from the lack of a breech lock, the mechanical specification was close to that of the P220, since it had a double-action trigger, de-cocking lever and automatic firing pin lock. It was, though, a good deal more streamlined and smoother in outline than any of the bigger pistols, and it has achieved wide sales among Continental and American police forces.

The latest SIG pistol is the P228, which is essentially an improved P225 with a 13-shot magazine as standard, and the options of using the 15- and 20-shot magazines from the P226 if preferred. In appearance it resembles the P226 except for some very small changes in contours here and

there, and the mechanical specification is the same. There are some small internal differences in manufacture, such as a new impact-resistant floorplate in the magazine which can withstand being dropped more readily than the earlier designs, but a large number of the parts of the P228 will interchange with the P225 and P226 pistols. Nearly 450,000 examples of the SIG P220 family have been built to date, and SIG pistols are in service around the world.

The magazine catch is located in the heel of the pistol grip, which is the only real weakness of the SIG P210 as a combat weapon. Thumb-operated releases on the side of a pistol allow you to drop the magazine with one hand while the other reaches for a fresh one.

SKS
Cold War
Carbine

When the Kalashnikov assault rifles were adopted by the Soviet army, they replaced a conventional self-loading rifle chambered for the same cartridge. The SKS had already been copied by North Korea, Yugoslavia and China, and it continues to turn up in the hands of armies and guerrilla movements all over Africa and Asia.

Sergei Simonov had a long apprenticeship in the weapons business. Born in 1894, by 1917 he was working with Federov on his automatic rifle. After the Revolution, Simonov studied engineering and in 1926 was Inspector at Tula Arsenal. In the following year he was in the design department, once again working under Federov. In the early 1930s he designed the AVS automatic rifle, which was taken into Soviet service in 1936; chambered for the 7.62×54R full-power cartridge, it had selective fire capability and was a bit of a hand-

Top: A rifleman in the old one-piece camouflage opens fire with an SKS. On test it produced groups of 10-12 cm (3.9-4.7 in) at 100 m (328 ft).

Above: Although the Soviets adopted the Kalashnikov instead of the SKS in 1947, they retained the latter for parades, and it can still be seen in the ceremonial role.

137

Inside the SKS

The SKS is a conventional gas-piston operated, tilting block locked, semi-automatic rifle. It is no longer in Soviet service except for ceremonial purposes. However, it is still in use in several Asian countries and equipped communist backed guerrilla organisations such as SWAPO in Namibia. Large quantities of Chinese SKS Type 56 carbines were used against the Soviets by the Mujahideen in Afghanistan.

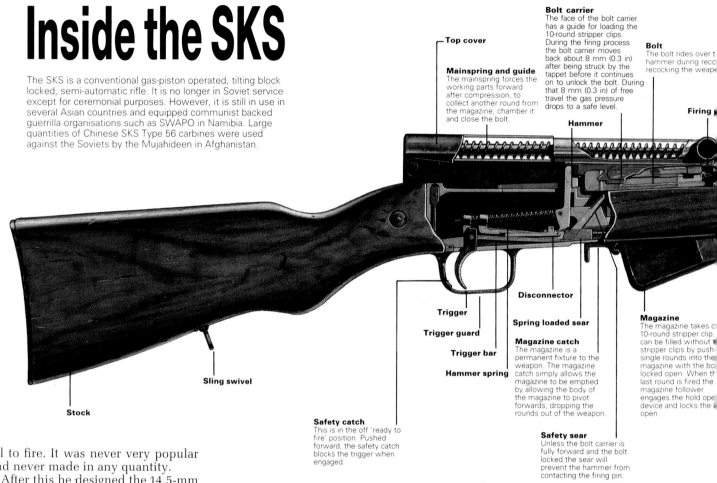

Top cover

Bolt carrier
The face of the bolt carrier has a guide for loading the 10-round stripper clips. During the firing process the bolt carrier moves back about 8 mm (0.3 in) after being struck by the tappet before it continues on to unlock the bolt. During that 8 mm (0.3 in) of free travel the gas pressure drops to a safe level.

Bolt
The bolt rides over t hammer during reco recocking the weap

Firing

Mainspring and guide
The mainspring forces the working parts forward after compression, to collect another round from the magazine, chamber it and close the bolt.

Hammer

Disconnector

Trigger

Spring loaded sear

Trigger guard

Magazine catch
The magazine is a permanent fixture to the weapon. The magazine catch simply allows the magazine to be emptied by allowing the body of the magazine to pivot forwards, dropping the rounds out of the weapon.

Trigger bar

Hammer spring

Magazine
The magazine takes c 10-round stripper clip. can be filled without t stripper clips by push single rounds into the magazine with the bo locked open. When th last round is fired the magazine follower engages the hold ope device and locks the open.

Sling swivel

Stock

Safety catch
This is in the off 'ready to fire' position. Pushed forward, the safety catch blocks the trigger when engaged.

Safety sear
Unless the bolt carrier is fully forward and the bolt locked the sear will prevent the hammer from contacting the firing pin.

ful to fire. It was never very popular and never made in any quantity.

After this he designed the 14.5-mm PTRS self-loading anti-tank rifle, which was effective against smaller armoured vehicles, and finally, in about 1945-46, he amalgamated the best features of the PTRS and the AVS and produced the SKS − the Samozaryadnyi Karabin Simonova.

The SKS was the first Soviet weapon to be chambered for the 7.62×39-mm M43 cartridge. The fullpower 7.62 round gave excessive blast and recoil − so much so that a hefty muzzle brake had to be added to the AVS of 1936 to make it tolerable.

Gas operation

The SKS carbine uses a gas operating system, with the gas cylinder above the barrel: a similar arrangement to that used in the Kalashnikov rifle. The bolt system had been first used by Simonov with his PTRS rifle and was carried over to the SKS. The bolt is held in a bolt carrier, and interconnecting cams on bolt and carrier are arranged so that as the carrier goes forwards to load, the bolt pushes a cartridge into the chamber and its rear end is then forced down by the carrier to lock in front of a lug in the receiver. On firing, gas tapped from the barrel enters the gas cylinder and drives a piston backwards; this strikes the

1 All the different types of SKS field-strip in the same way. Pull the magazine catch back to empty the mag of cartridges. Clear the weapon and leave it cocked. Release the bayonet and pivot it down through 90 degrees.

2 Remove the cleaning rod, pulling it out forwards. Next, locate the takedown lever on the right-hand side of the weapon at the base of the top cover. Rotate the lever anti-clockwise 180 degrees and you will then be able to pull the lever out.

6 Slide the bolt out of the recesses which hold it in the carrier. The bolt will usually drop out, so have a careful look at the way it goes together for reassembling.

7 The gas parts are removed by rotating the take-down lever on the rear-sight mounting upwards.

Cocking handle
The cocking handle is permanently attached to the bolt carrier. After loading with a 10 round clip and removing the stripper clip, the first round is chambered by pulling back on the cocking handle and releasing.

Rear sight
This is a conventional ramp type sight as on the AK-47 which is adjustable in 100 m (328 ft) settings. The 'v' notch and post give a clear sight picture.

Tappet
The tappet acts as a connecting rod between the gas piston and the face of the bolt carrier.

Gas piston
The gas piston is forced back against spring pressure by the gas tapped off from the barrel and forces the bolt carrier back via a tappet unlocking the action. After the initial blow from the piston the working parts move back, extracting and ejecting the empty case and recocking the hammer.

Gas port
When the weapon fires, expanding gases behind the bullet are vented through this hole to act against the piston rod in the gas tube.

Barrel
The barrel is longer than that of the AK-47 and the weapon is generally more accurate than the Kalashnikov designs.

Foresight
This is a conventional protected post which is adjustable for windage and elevation.

Muzzle
The bayonet ring fits over the muzzle by pulling the bayonet grip sleeve out against spring pressure and slotting it over the muzzle to lock it in place.

Chamber

Finger groove

Piston spring
This returns the tappet and piston to its original position after the gas pressure has compressed it during the firing sequence. It is a short stroke action.

Bayonet
Russian SKS rifles have this type of folding knife bayonet that is permanently fixed to the rifle. Later models of the Chinese Type 56 carbine have folding spike type bayonets.

Cleaning rod
Cleaning rods are a lot more effective for cleaning the barrel than the pull through. The rod has to be removed prior to field stripping and is locked in place by the bayonet that has to be pivoted downwards to release it.

7.62mm×39 Russian
This round is the intermediate round used in the AK-47, AKM, and RPK etc. It is not as powerful or accurate as the 7.62mm NATO but is effective over normal battlefield engagement ranges.

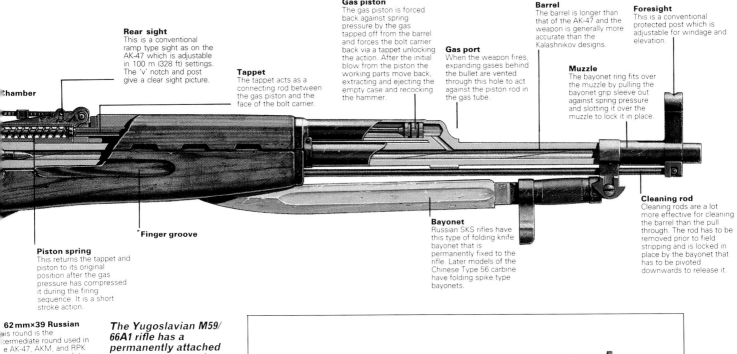

The Yugoslavian M59/66A1 rifle has a permanently attached spigot-type grenade launcher. Launching the grenade involves folding up the grenade sight and cutting off the gas to the gas piston by pressing in the cut-off valve.

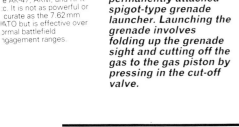

3 The lever releases the top cover, which can then be lifted off to reveal the recoil spring and guide and the bolt and bolt carrier.

4 Push in on the back of the recoil spring and lift it out of the retaining catch to remove backwards from the weapon.

5 Slide both the bolt and bolt carrier back until you can lift them out of the receiver when the carrier corresponds to the cut-outs in the receiver. When you put the working parts back in, remember to press the magazine floor plate in to release the hold-open device.

8 The gas tube and piston will then lift up and to the rear. The piston and the tube and the area of the vent from the barrel tend to be fouled with carbon after firing and will need careful cleaning.

9 The gas piston will simply drop out of the gas tube forwards.

10 The SKS field-stripped with a few 10-round chargers of 7.62×39. Reassemble the weapon in reverse order. Although very dated, it is a solid weapon that, like the AK, handles well and will put up with a lot of abuse and misuse.

front of the carrier and forces it back, so that the cam surfaces lift the rear end of the bolt free of the lug and then carry the bolt back to extract the spent case, eject it, and then cock the hammer.

The SKS retains the old style of fixed magazine, loaded from a 10-round charger or by adding loose rounds. To empty the magazine quickly, the rear end can be released, allowing the casing to swing down from a front hinge so that the rounds drop out into your waiting hands (or the waiting mud, as the case may be). The stock is also traditional: a long, good-quality wood stock with a separate handguard covering the gas cylinder; but later models often use a form of resin-bonded plywood. The most distinctive feature is the permanently-attached blade bayonet which is hinged beneath the barrel and lies in a slot in the fore-end of the stock. To 'fix' it, pull the handle to the rear to release a spring catch, and swing the bayonet through 180 degrees until it latches onto a lug beneath the foresight. This lug also acts as the front guide for the cleaning rod.

The rear sight is a U-notch on a hinged arm; there is a slider which, when moved, hinges the arm up to give the necessary elevation. A 'battle' setting covers everything out to 300 m (984 ft), after which you have to set the

range required, in 100-m (328-ft) steps to a maximum of 1,000 m (3,280 ft). The foresight is a hooded post which can be screwed up or down with the issued combination tool to alter the point of impact when zeroing the rifle.

The SKS weighs over 4 kg (9 lb), which, strangely enough, is considerably less than the original AK-47 but about the same as the AKM. But it feels more like a rifle than the AKs do, and is comfortable to shoot, being well-matched to the cartridge. Although it was superseded in Soviet

The North Vietnamese army was supplied with large quantities of the SKS. It was a popular souvenir with US soldiers who were not allowed to take home fully automatic AK-47s.

service by the Kalashnikovs (because they were cheaper and easier to make), the SKS is still carried for ceremonial purposes. It has, of course, been exported in great quantities to wherever Soviet influence has been making itself felt over the past 30-odd years, so you are likely to run into the SKS anywhere in the world.

The SKS with its appropriate accessories: Soviet helmet and belt with pouch for 10-round stripper clips. The ammunition in the clips is recently-manufactured Chinese 7.62-mm. The rifle was captured by British troops from the Egyptians in 1956.

Shooting with the Garand

The M1 Garand is one of the most successful military rifles of all time. Adopted by the US Army in 1932, it is still in production today as a sporting rifle and it remains a stalwart performer in the annual summer rifle championships at Camp Perry, Ohio. The Garand was last used in combat by US soldiers during the early days of the Vietnam War, although the National Guard and the US Navy retained M1s for many years after this.

The Garand was the first self-loading rifle to be introduced as the standard service weapon by any army. Entering service in 1936 and equipping most American infantry units by 1942, it gave US soldiers a major advantage over their German and Japanese opponents. Some 4,040,000 Garands were manufactured before the war and another 600,000 were produced during the Korean conflict. The overwhelming majority of Garands were made at the Springfield Armory.

Several armies had long recognised the advantages of a self-loading rifle, and British, German and Russian arms manufacturers had produced self-loading weapons before and during World War I. Without the need to work a bolt to manually chamber the next shot, a self-loading rifle allowed soldiers a very rapid second shot without disturbing their aim.

The Garand is a robust weapon and combat experience soon proved that it was a reliable and accurate service rifle. US Marines, still equipped with bolt-action Springfield rifles in the Guadalcanal campaign, recognised the Garand's superiority when they fought alongside Army units. In the tangled undergrowth of the Pacific islands there were few opportunities to exploit the Garand's long-range accuracy; most battles with the Japanese were decided by desperate close-quarter fighting. Here, the Garand's high rate of fire was most valuable. It could not be matched by the average soldier armed with a bolt-action rifle. The veteran soldiers of the

Above: South Vietnamese soldiers armed with M1 Garands and an M16 examine equipment abandoned by the Viet Cong after a successful assault on an enemy camp.

Top: American soldiers enjoyed a unique advantage during World War II – their M1 Garands were the first self-loading rifles to be issued as standard service weapons.

1914 British Expeditionary Force could fire 15 well-aimed rounds per minute from their bolt-action Lee-Enfields, but ordinary conscripts were never as competent.

American know-how

While most World War II armies issued sub-machine guns to boost their infantry's close-range firepower, most infantrymen went into action with the same rifles that their fathers had used in 1914. Only the Americans managed to field a self-loading rifle in time. While the Red Army and the German forces did receive self-loading weapons during World War II,

they were only available in limited quantities and never supplanted the older guns. The British Army had to wait until the 1950s before new rifles were on offer.

The Garand's operating system has proved highly reliable, from Pacific atolls to the mud of north-west Europe. It is gas-operated, with some of the propellant gases diverted through a gas port into the cylinder. The piston and operating rod are driven back, compressing the return spring which is beneath the barrel. The piston travels back freely for 8 mm while the gas pressure in the chamber falls, then the operating rod

Inside the M1 Garand

The Garand rifle was the first self-loading rifle to be adopted for regular military service. Robust and accurate, it automatically ejects the empty clip with the eighth round.

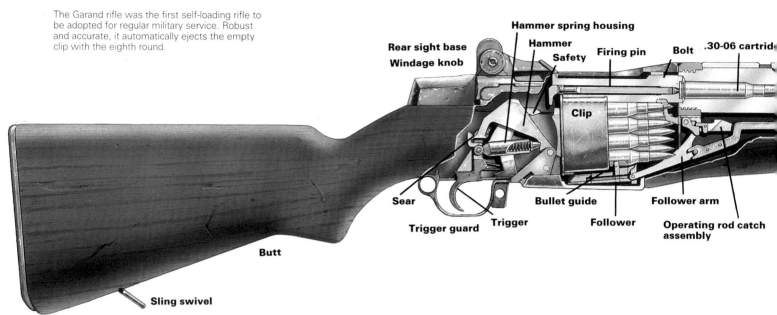

Rear sight base
Windage knob
Hammer spring housing
Hammer
Safety
Firing pin
Bolt
.30-06 cartridge
Clip
Sear
Trigger guard
Trigger
Bullet guide
Follower
Follower arm
Operating rod catch assembly
Butt
Sling swivel

Below: Two GIs cautiously approach a Japanese position with M1 Garands levelled. From the arctic chill of the Aleutians to the tropical jungle of Guadalcanal, the M1 Garand stood up to the worst conditions.

Barrel | Rear hand guard | Front sight | Gas cylinder lock | Lock screw | Bayonet boss | Gas cylinder | Stock ferrule swivel | Operating rod | Follower rod

*Below: **Street fighting takes place in Italy during 1944. The rapid fire of the Garand was appreciated by US troops facing German units equipped with a high proportion of automatic weapons.***

the noise could be heard by every Chinese soldier for miles.

The Garand fires the .30-06 cartridge – the US equivalent of the British Army's .303-in round fired by the Lee-Enfield. This no-nonsense 220-grain bullet travels at 853 m (2,800 ft) per second: perhaps overly powerful for the short-range infantry battles of World War II, the .30-06 is an accurate round with undoubted stopping power. Some of the last Garands in service with the US Navy were modified to fire 7.62-mm NATO.

In 1957 the M1 was replaced by the M14 7.62-mm rifle. This new weapon

*Below: **US troops scan the jungle for a Japanese sniper lurking somewhere ahead. The Garand is not just quick shooting – it is an accurate weapon too.***

contacts the bolt lug and lifts it. The bolt rotates to the left, unlocking the lugs in the receiver, and is carried back by the operating rod. The hammer is forced back from the firing pin, which withdraws into the bolt. The empty case is pulled from the chamber by the spring-loaded extractor which flings it out of the rifle.

The return spring is compressed fully and works against the magazine follower arm, which lifts the follower, pushing up the remaining bullets in the eight-round clip. The return spring then forces the operating rod and the bolt forward. The bolt collects the next round from the clip and feeds it into the chamber. When the round is chambered, the bolt stops but the operating rod keeps going. The cam action then rotates the bolt, locking it in place.

The Garand's clip holds its bullets double-stacked and is ejected along with the last cartridge case. Anyone who has encountered the Garand soon learns to recognise the distinctive sound of the clip zinging out of the now empty rifle. On a cold night in Korea, Americans understandably felt

was essentially a modified Garand, fitted with a 20-round box magazine and capable of fully-automatic fire. The Garands were passed to the National Guard and many foreign allies of the United States, from central America to North Africa and Asia. The South Vietnamese army also received M1 Garands, which led to the curious situation of small-statured Asian soldiers labouring with this 4.3-kg (9.5-lb) rifle while big Americans wielded the 2.8-kg (6.2-lb) M16. Although the Garand is often described as heavy, it should be remembered that the excellent FN FAL weighs the same and the British Army's new SA80 is even heavier!

Garand variants

Ten different versions of the M1 were developed during World War II, but most were experimental projects that did not enter full-scale production. The most significant variants were the T26 and the M1C. The former was similar in concept to the British SMLE No. 5 jungle carbine: simply the standard rifle with the barrel cut down from 610 to 450 mm (24 to 17.7 in). The US forces in the Pacific requested 15,000 T26s in July 1945, but cancelled the order a month later as the war ended. These are still available commercially, but their excessive blast and muzzle flash make them an acquired taste. At up to 300 m (984 ft) their accuracy compares favourably with a standard M1.

Above: South Vietnamese paratroopers parade with M1s in Saigon during the early 1960s, wearing French-style camouflage and very natty jump boots.

Below: South Vietnamese sailors develop upper body strength with help from their 4.3-kg (9.5-lb) Garand rifles.

The M1C was the sniper version of the Garand, fitted with a Griffin and Howe scope mount and an M73 Lyman Alaskan or M73B1 Weaver 330 scope. The M1C was also fitted with a leather cheek-piece and removable flash-hiders were provided from January 1945.

In 1974 Springfield Armory (Inc.) acquired the rights to the Springfield Armory name as well as to parts and tooling machinery from the government's arsenal. This company specialises in the production of US service weapons for sports shooters – their versions of the M1 rifle and M1911 .45 pistol have won many competitions over the years. They offer the standard M1 Garand in .30-06 or 7.62-mm and also produce a Match Grade M1 for the dedicated competitor. Springfield's range includes the sniper rifle and the T26, the company describes it as "a powerful brush gun for hunting in dense forests and thick undergrowth, it can't be beat." For owners of old M1s, Springfield offer a reconditioning deal, restoring elderly rifles to tip-top condition. The M1 has left the Army after a long and distinguished career, but its voice will continue to be heard on shooting ranges across the USA.

Pepper them with the PPSh

Right: The PPSh-41 looks crude, but it has quality where it matters. All a combat soldier wants is that his weapon is reliable, which is what the PPSh is.

Below: Cheerful sailors of the Black Sea Fleet pose for the camera. Within months, their PPSh SMGs were in constant use in the face of the German invaders.

Towards the end of the Sam Peckinpah Eastern Front movie Cross of Iron, James Coburn empties the magazine of a PPSh sub-machine gun into one of the villains. Even at the brisk rate of 900 rounds per minute, it takes nearly five seconds to work your way through a drum magazine that can take up to 72 or 73 rounds – and longer still if you film it in Peckinpah-style slow motion! This enormous magazine capacity is just one of the reasons that made the PPSh one of the most successful sub-machine guns of all time. Used by both sides on the Russian Front, throughout the Korean and Vietnam Wars, the PPSh can still be encountered in Third World trouble spots from Beirut to Ethiopia.

Like many armies, the Soviet forces had acquired SMGs during the 1930s, but without any great enthusiasm. Indeed, some of the place-serving senior officers who rose to prominence during Stalin's purges wanted to stick to bolt-action rifles. In 1939, the Soviets signed a non-aggression pact with Nazi-Germany and promptly invaded most of the small countries with which they shared a border. All were overrun quickly except for Finland. In the bitter Winter War of 1939-40, Finnish soldiers inflicted horrendous casualties on the Red Army. One of their key weapons was the Suomi sub-machine gun. Issued with a stick magazine or 71-round drum, it endowed small Finnish ski patrols with devastating short-range firepower. Lumbering columns of Russian troops were repeatedly ambushed in the trackless forests north of Lake Ladoga.

Wartime production

The Soviet army had little time to absorb the lessons of the Winter War before the Germans broke the treaty and invaded the USSR. With most factories either overrun or being hurriedly re-located far to the east of Moscow, the Soviets needed new weapons quickly. In particular they needed rifles and SMGs that could be mass produced with the minimum use of skilled labour and expensive tooling. Gun designer Georgi Shpagin had one answer: a simple sub-machine gun that fitted the bill perfectly. Entering production before the end of 1941, it was manufactured throughout the war, and by the end of the conflict some five million examples had been delivered to the Soviet forces.

The PPSh-41 exhibits the classic strengths of Soviet small arms design. All the crucial parts are well made. The barrel is chromed to help it withstand the twin threats of Soviet corrosive primers and heavy use between cleanings. Soviet ammunition has tra-

Barrel
The PPSh was one of the first mass-produced weapons with a chrome-lined barrel. This is expensive but it has a number of benefits, not least of which is greatly extending barrel life and making it more resistant to bad maintenance.

Inside the PPSh

The PPSh-41 is one of the most effective small arms ever developed. At first glance it looks crudely made, and, indeed, it is a brutally simple weapon. Like all sub-machine guns it is not much use at anything beyond short range, but since most firefights are at short range anyway, and the Soviet tactical system always valued firepower above accuracy, that is no handicap. As with so many Soviet-designed guns, the greatest strength of the PPSh is its rugged reliability, and it will keep firing under the worst of conditions.

Magazine
Nominally of 71-round capacity, the drum magazine of the PPSh is almost a straight copy of that developed in the 1930s for the Finnish Suomi sub-machine gun. Having so many rounds available gave the PPSh twice the firepower of the MP40 machine pistols used by the Germans.

ditionally employed mercury-based primers, which are the most reliable method of ignition in sub-zero temperatures. Unfortunately, they are highly corrosive and can cause serious damage to barrels.

Blowback operation

The PPSh operates by direct blowback. Pulling the trigger sends the heavy bolt slamming forward under spring pressure. It strips a round from the magazine, rams it into the chamber and fires it. The gas pressure created sends the bullet up the barrel and the bolt slamming backwards, compressing the recoil spring completely. If the trigger is still held down, the bolt is propelled forward again to repeat the process. The recoil spring has a buffer on the end to reduce the vibration caused by the bolt bouncing back. This was supposed to be made of rubber, a commodity in very short supply in wartime Russia. The Soviets ended up using a lump of waxed papier maché instead, and this worked equally well – possibly better, since 50-year old PPShs can still be found functioning with them.

The receiver hinges open to let you get at the bolt and return spring. Even the dullest conscript, unused to anything more mechanically advanced than a shovel, can be taught to operate the PPSh. Earlier models have a selector in front of the trigger that can set the weapon for semi- or fully automatic operation, but later versions were full auto only. Firing the 7.62 × 25 mm Russian cartridge, the PPSh has next to no recoil and is accurate enough within 150–200 m (492–656 ft). It is exceptionally robust and is hefty enough to double as a club when all else fails.

Choice of magazine

Early PPSh-41s had tangent rear sights that were soon replaced by flip-up battle sights. The 71-round drum magazines could usually accommodate a couple of extra bullets without any difficulty, the only problem being the time it took to cram in so much ammunition. As an alternative, curved 35-round box magazines were also issued. These were built to traditional Russian standards also, with the feed lips protected by a stout metal shroud.

While most armies during World War II issued SMGs to one or two men

The PPSh was a favourite with German soldiers, who valued its reliability and its high magazine capacity. They often discarded their MP40s in favour of the Soviet weapon. The second soldier seen here has done just that.

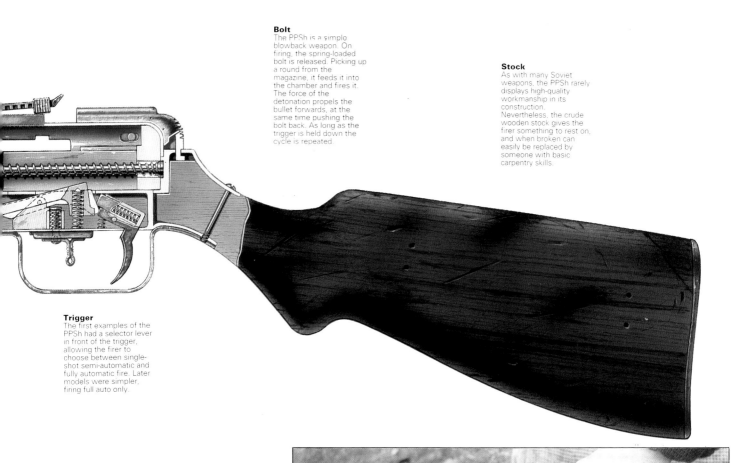

Bolt
The PPSh is a simple blowback weapon. On firing, the spring-loaded bolt is released. Picking up a round from the magazine, it feeds it into the chamber and fires it. The force of the detonation propels the bullet forwards, at the same time pushing the bolt back. As long as the trigger is held down the cycle is repeated.

Stock
As with many Soviet weapons, the PPSh rarely displays high-quality workmanship in its construction. Nevertheless, the crude wooden stock gives the firer something to rest on, and when broken can easily be replaced by someone with basic carpentry skills.

Trigger
The first examples of the PPSh had a selector lever in front of the trigger, allowing the firer to choose between single-shot semi-automatic and fully automatic fire. Later models were simpler, firing full auto only.

The PPSh is easy to use. The bolt handle is on the right-hand side, and is pulled back to cock the weapon (right). The 71-round drum magazine (below) gives the PPSh notable firepower. Unfortunately, it is the least reliable part of the weapon and charging it by hand is a somewhat laborious task.

in each section, the Soviets often equipped whole battalions with them. Whether this was the result of a conscious tactical decision or just the way the weapons were delivered has never emerged. Either way, the PPSh-41 was admirably suited to the Red Army's needs. Its close-range firepower was ideal for the savage house-to-house fighting at Stalingrad that marked the turning point of the war. As the Soviets began the long campaign to drive back the invaders, the PPSh proved equally suitable for offensive operations. For the assault troops that rode into battle on top of T-34 tanks, the PPSh was far better than a rifle. If all went according to plan, the tanks could carry the infantrymen right up

The compact length of the SMG made it an ideal weapon for cavalrymen. These are Vlassov Cossacks, nationalists who needed little persuasion by the Germans to change sides and fight against the Soviets.

to the enemy positions and bring on a close-quarter battle in which the SMG's short range was no disadvantage. What counted was volume of fire – always the PPSh's strong point.

After World War II the PPSh was supplied to most subject nations of the Soviet Empire. It was superseded in the Red Army by the revolutionary AK-47 assault rifle, which combined greater range and a more powerful cartridge with the same high standard of reliability. The PPSh was also passed to Communist China and played a leading role in Chinese expansion – equipping the millions of Chinese troops that flooded into Korea to fight the United Nations' forces. The weapon's brute strength and reliability suited it well to the harsh climate and poor training standards of the Chinese soldiers.

The PPSh-41 is one of the classic weapons of the 20th century, being used in wars from Korea to Angola. More than four million were manufactured between 1941 and 1945, and many have continued in use to this day.

Stechkin

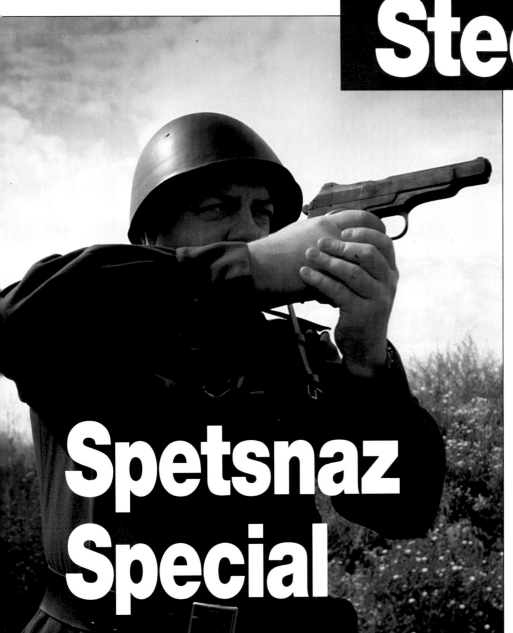

Spetsnaz Special

holster that doubles as a shoulder stock, the Stechkin can be fired like a sub-machine gun and the sights go up to 200 m (656 ft). Thus, it is similar to the Beretta 93R, but the Italian pistol's metal skeleton stock looks far more up to date than the huge lump of wood tacked onto the back of the Stechkin. The Soviet weapon seems to have more in common with the 'broom handle' Mauser pistols that were in vogue at the turn of the century.

Most Western reference books deride the Stechkin as bulky, over-complicated and unnecessary. Since it was only in production for the first half of the 1950s, this is understandable. Unusually among Soviet infantry weapons, the Stechkin was never exported to Warsaw Pact armies. Nor was it supplied to the armies of client states in the Third World – although a few in presentation boxes were given to particularly favoured dictators.

When Stechkins left the USSR they

Left: The Stechkin is one of the rarest guns around. It was made in limited numbers and was never exported from the USSR. Although often derided by Western writers who have never handled one, it is in fact one of the few reasonably successful attempts to make a true automatic pistol.

Below: Although the Stechkin is fairly large for a hand-held weapon, especially when compared to the Makarov service pistol or the tiny PSM police pistol, it is not excessively so, and can be easily handled by any competent operator.

The Stechkin is a fully automatic pistol that was issued to Soviet forces during the 1950s. It is one of the few successful 'machine pistols': not too big to be used as a pistol, yet still effective as a fully automatic weapon. Its association with Soviet special forces units and the fact that only a handful have ever been seen outside the USSR give the Stechkin an element of mystery. Why was it developed? What purpose did it serve?

Quite why the Red Army ordered the weapon has never been made public, although now that Soviet weapons designers are able to travel, the origins of the Stechkin will no doubt be revealed soon. It is a curious combination of the old and the new: some features of the weapon are distinctly old-fashioned, yet the final product is a very useful weapon for special forces. Issued with a wooden

The Stechkin fires the 9-mm×18 Makarov round. This is a little less powerful than the NATO standard 9-mm Parabellum, and makes controlling the weapon on full auto a little easier.

did so only in the hands of Soviet soldiers. For the Stechkin is a fine weapon, superbly engineered with a blued finish equal to anything seen on commercially-made guns in the USA. It is not heavy and fits comfortably in the hand. The light recoil of the 9-mm Makarov cartridge is soaked up well and on full-auto short bursts it can be kept on a man-sized target at up to 25 m (82 ft). The Stechkin was issued to specialist units including KGB and MVD detachments, and it is certainly still in use: a Bulgarian arrested for spying on NATO facilities in Holland during 1989 had a loaded Stechkin in the cab of his lorry.

The Stechkin operates by direct blowback using an unlocked breech. Its cartridge, the 9-mm Makarov, is relatively low-powered so a locked breech is not necessary. When the Stechkin is fired, the breech remains closed, held by its weight and the recoil spring. Gas pressure eventually overcomes the resistance, propelling the slide to the rear, cocking the hammer and ejecting the empty cartridge case. The recoil spring then drives the slide forward again, chambering another round and shutting the breech. When the selector is positioned for fully automatic fire, the hammer is tripped as the breech

The Stechkin is often called a failure. But if this was true it would not have been issued to front-line units and to special operations forces, who were and remain the main users of the weapon.

closes. On semi-automatic, the trigger stays disengaged until pressed again.

Like the Czech Skorpion machine pistol, the Stechkin is available in a silenced version, although the more powerful 9-mm Makarov cartridge makes the Russian weapon a far more effective weapon. The KGB unit that stormed the Afghan Presidential Palace in 1979 made plentiful use of silenced Stechkins during the initial phase of the assault. The Stechkin silencer fits on without obstructing the sights. Instead of the wooden holster/shoulder stock unit, the silenced Stechkins have a collapsible wire stock. It may look about as elegant as a bent coathanger, but it does work, providing a special forces assault team with a very compact automatic weapon.

Accuracy

The Stechkin has a rear drum sight which can be set for 25, 50, 100 or 200 m (82, 164, 328 or 656 ft), although even with a shoulder stock attached, 200 m (656 ft) is wildly optimistic. But it is easy to shoot the Stechkin accurately at 100 m (328 ft) – the effective range of most dedicated sub-machine guns. The hammer drop safety/fire selector can be set for single shots or fully automatic fire. A weight forced against the hammer spring serves to reduce the rate of fire to a controllable level by delaying the hammer release. It also works as a buffer, slowing the movement of the slide. However, although the Stechkin is one of the most controllable full-auto weapons ever made, it has a severe disadvantage as an automatic weapon. Rapid reloading – an essential feature

Above: The holster supplied with the Stechkin is hardly a quick-draw device, being a bulky wooden item. It doubles as a detachable stock, however.

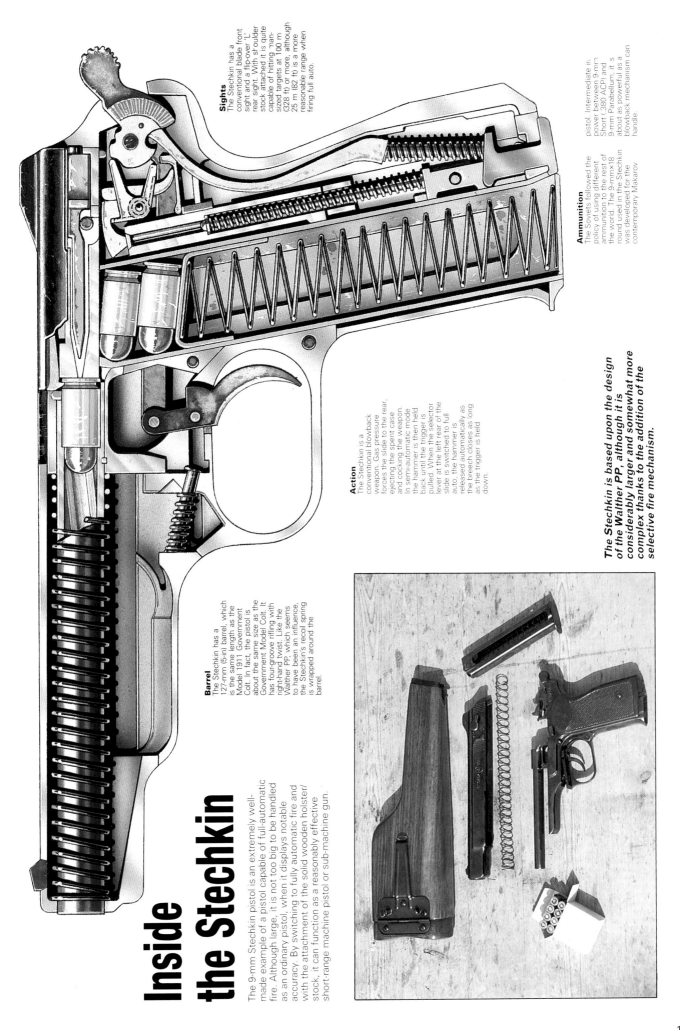

Sights

The Stechkin has a conventional blade front sight and a flip-over 'L' rear sight. With shoulder stock attached it is quite capable of hitting 'man-sized targets at 100 m (328 ft) or more, although 25 m (82 ft) is a more reasonable range when firing full auto.

Ammunition

The Soviets followed the policy of using different ammunition to the rest of the world. The 9-mm18 round used in the Stechkin was developed for the contemporary Makarov pistol. Intermediate in power between 9-mm Short (.380 ACP) and 9-mm Parabellum, it s about as powerful as a blowback mechanism can handle.

Action

The Stechkin is a conventional blowback weapon. Gas pressure forces the slide to the rear, ejecting the spent case and cocking the weapon. In semi-automatic mode the hammer is then held back until the trigger is pulled. When the selector lever at the left rear of the slide is switched to full auto, the hammer is released automatically as the breech closes as long as the trigger is held down.

The Stechkin is based upon the design of the Walther PP, although it is considerably larger and somewhat more complex thanks to the addition of the selective fire mechanism.

Barrel

The Stechkin has a 127-mm (5-in) barrel, which is the same length as the Model 1911 Government Colt. In fact, the pistol is about the same size as the Government Model Colt. It has four-groove rifling with right-hand twist. Like the Walther PP, which seems to have been an influence, the Stechkin's recoil spring is wrapped around the barrel.

Inside the Stechkin

The 9-mm Stechkin pistol is an extremely well-made example of a pistol capable of full-automatic fire. Although large, it is not too big to be handled as an ordinary pistol, when it displays notable accuracy. By switching to fully automatic fire and with the attachment of the solid wooden holster/stock, it can function as a reasonably effective short-range machine pistol or sub-machine gun.

Above: The Stechkin comes with a 20-round magazine. The release is located at the heel of the butt, which is secure but a little too awkward to permit rapid magazine changes.

weapon. The very high standard of production had to be paid for even in a planned economy with no inflation! Having made enough for their own purposes, the Soviets simply closed the assembly line. If, as has been suggested by some Western gun writers, the Stechkin had proved unsuccessful, then it would have been delivered by the shipload to African dictators or Asian guerrilla armies, like the obsolete SMGs and SKS rifles dished out throughout the 1950s and 1960s.

The Stechkin has been replaced as a machine pistol by the AKSU cutdown Kalashnikov rifle. For airborne forces, tank crew or other specialists, the AKSU provides considerably more firepower and longer range accuracy and it is no larger than a conventional SMG. The Stechkin – especially in its silenced form – remains a useful weapon for special operations and will continue to be encountered.

– is rendered impossible by the location of the magazine release latch in the heel of the grip.

At its cyclic rate of about 750 rounds per minute, a Stechkin empties its 20-round magazine in less than two seconds. The Soviet reluctance to put a push-button magazine release on the side of the grip can be traced back to their experience with the Tokarev TT-33 pistol during World War II. Some officers found their pistols jettisoning their magazines involuntarily. On the Makarov pistol that replaced the Tokarev, the magazine release was moved to the heel of the butt where it was less likely to be knocked. The decision to favour security over speedy reloading stuck Stechkin-wielding special forces with a clumsy reload procedure, which could explain the Spetsnaz's enthusiasm for using sharpened shovels like throwing axes!

Built like a watch

The reason that the Soviets retained the Stechkin solely for their own use may simply reflect the cost of the

Stechkin pistols are very well made, and although somewhat large they are not excessively so. In trained hands, the Stechkin is capable of hitting targets at ranges of 100 m (328 ft).

Stalwart Sterling

Wherever you go in the world today, you are very likely to find the Sterling sub-machine gun in use by military or police forces. Over 55 countries have adopted it since the British Army gave the lead by taking the Sterling into service to replace the Sten in 1953. Strangely, you will very rarely see terrorists carrying Sterlings; for one thing, the Sterling Armaments Company has always been very careful to supply these weapons only to authorised users, and secondly the Sterling is a gimmick-free weapon that doesn't seem to appeal to the lurid imagination of the average terrorist. It's a working weapon, not a fashionable toy.

The story of the Sterling goes back farther than most people imagine; in fact the weapon first went to war with the British Army at Arnhem in 1944. Although the Sten was in mass production throughout World War II, the Army was well aware that it was hardly the most elegant and reliable of weapons, and it was constantly looking for something to replace it.

Sterling had been manufacturing the Lanchester sub-machine gun from 1941; this was simply a British-made

For over 40 years the Sterling has been the British Army's sub-machine gun, used for close-quarter fighting and as the personal weapon of heavy weapon and tank crew. Sturdy and reliable, the Sterling is an effective conventional SMG but looks increasingly dated when compared to the new generation of sub-machine guns.

Above: A British patrol heads into the jungle during an exercise in the central American state of Belize. Until 5.56-mm rifles were issued to British soldiers operating in the jungle, patrols often included several Sterlings. At short range this simple SMG is a very useful weapon.

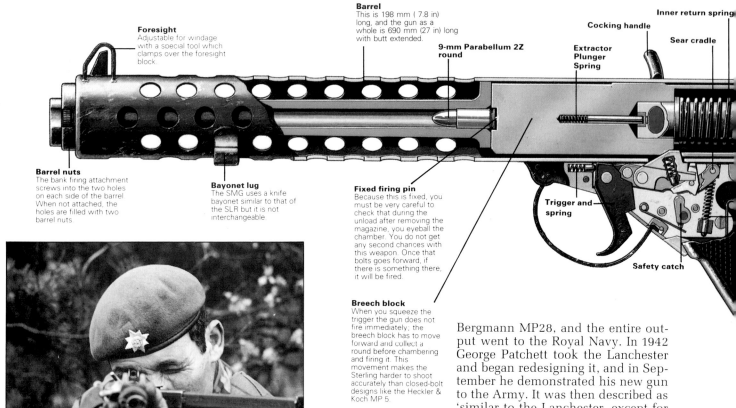

Foresight
Adjustable for windage with a special tool which clamps over the foresight block.

Barrel
This is 198 mm (7.8 in) long, and the gun as a whole is 690 mm (27 in) long with butt extended.

9-mm Parabellum 2Z round

Extractor Plunger Spring

Cocking handle

Inner return spring

Sear cradle

Barrel nuts
The bank firing attachment screws into the two holes on each side of the barrel. When not attached, the holes are filled with two barrel nuts.

Bayonet lug
The SMG uses a knife bayonet similar to that of the SLR but it is not interchangeable.

Fixed firing pin
Because this is fixed, you must be very careful to check that during the unload after removing the magazine, you eyeball the chamber. You do not get any second chances with this weapon. Once that bolts goes forward, if there is something there, it will be fired.

Trigger and spring

Safety catch

Breech block
When you squeeze the trigger the gun does not fire immediately; the breech block has to move forward and collect a round before chambering and firing it. This movement makes the Sterling harder to shoot accurately than closed-bolt designs like the Heckler & Koch MP 5.

Eyeball to eyeball with the business end of the Sterling. Within the usual limitations of a sub-machine gun, the Sterling is a reasonably accurate weapon firing single shots, but its true role is a long burst from the hip at an opponent the other side of the same room.

Bergmann MP28, and the entire output went to the Royal Navy. In 1942 George Patchett took the Lanchester and began redesigning it, and in September he demonstrated his new gun to the Army. It was then described as 'similar to the Lanchester, except for the trigger mechanism, and without butt or sights' but even at that early stage some recognisable features were there.

The pistol grip was centrally located near the point of balance and there was a change and safety lever which gave 'safe', 'repetition' and 'automatic' fire by a simple flick of the thumb. When set at 'safe', the bolt was securely locked in the forward position.

Passing the test

On trial it functioned well, and Patchett was encouraged to carry on with his development. Other tests

Stripping the Sterling

1 Remove the magazine, cock the gun and check that the chamber is clear. Squeeze the trigger and let the bolt go forward under control. Now press the butt catch as shown here to let the stock down.

2 Press in the locking lever. At the same time press the return spring cap with your thumb to release the stock.

3 The stock folds forward and clips underneath the barrel. Pull the butt slightly out to engage the catch. Move the safety catch to 'A'.

Inside the Sterling

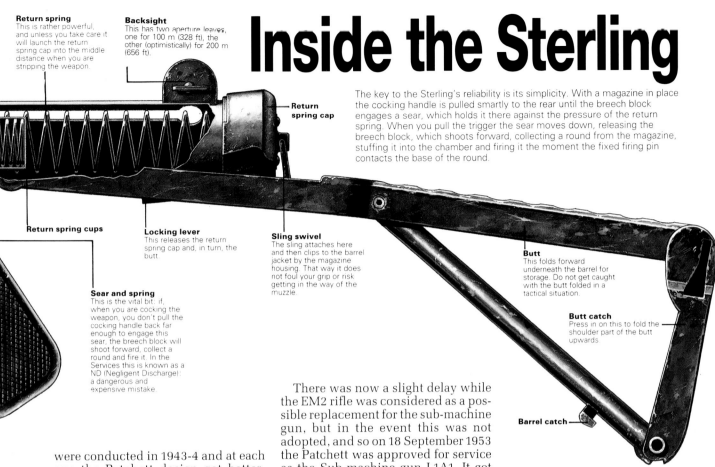

Return spring
This is rather powerful, and unless you take care it will launch the return spring cap into the middle distance when you are stripping the weapon.

Backsight
This has two aperture leaves, one for 100 m (328 ft), the other (optimistically) for 200 m (656 ft).

Return spring cap

The key to the Sterling's reliability is its simplicity. With a magazine in place the cocking handle is pulled smartly to the rear until the breech block engages a sear, which holds it there against the pressure of the return spring. When you pull the trigger the sear moves down, releasing the breech block, which shoots forward, collecting a round from the magazine, stuffing it into the chamber and firing it the moment the fixed firing pin contacts the base of the round.

Return spring cups

Locking lever
This releases the return spring cap and, in turn, the butt.

Sling swivel
The sling attaches here and then clips to the barrel jacket by the magazine housing. That way it does not foul your grip or risk getting in the way of the muzzle.

Butt
This folds forward underneath the barrel for storage. Do not get caught with the butt folded in a tactical situation.

Butt catch
Press in on this to fold the shoulder part of the butt upwards.

Barrel catch

Sear and spring
This is the vital bit: if, when you are cocking the weapon, you don't pull the cocking handle back far enough to engage this sear, the breech block will shoot forward, collect a round and fire it. In the Services this is known as a ND (Negligent Discharge): a dangerous and expensive mistake.

were conducted in 1943-4 and at each one the Patchett design got better, until by April 1944 it was considered good enough to warrant a batch of 100 being made by the Sterling company for troop trials. These were issued to the 6th Airborne Division and were used in Normandy and at Arnhem. They were well spoken of by the paratroopers, and by the end of 1944 the Ordnance Board had announced that 'with regard to accuracy, functioning, endurance and penetration, it is considered that the Patchett is suitable for service.'

There was now a slight delay while the EM2 rifle was considered as a possible replacement for the sub-machine gun, but in the event this was not adopted, and so on 18 September 1953 the Patchett was approved for service as the Sub-machine gun L1A1. It got the name 'Sterling' from the name of its manufacturers but there was a fair amount of confusion as people called it different things for its first few years of service.

The Sterling is perhaps the last sub-machine gun that uses a side-mounted magazine, something that originated with the Bergmann of 1918 and was continued in the Sten. In spite of objections, the fact remains that it gives a very reliable feed (provided the magazine is properly de-signed, as the Sterling magazine is), and by resting the magazine on the forearm you get a very steady hold.

Firing the Sterling

Insert the magazine, pull back the cocking lever, and the gun is ready to fire. Pull the trigger and the bolt is released, to run forward, collect a 9-mm Parabellum cartridge from the magazine, and thrust it into the chamber. Due to the position of the magazine,

4 Take hold of the return spring cap with your left hand, and press the locking lever in with the thumb of the right hand. Twist the cap anti-clockwise while pressing down to remove it.

5 Press the trigger and move working parts to the rear using the cocking handle. Pull the cocking handle out and remove the large and small return springs and their cups all in one piece. NB Do not separate them! The breech block will follow them up.

6 The component parts: re-assembly is a tricky business. Make sure you align the hole in the return spring cup to the hole in the breech block which corresponds to the hole in the body. Then insert the cocking handle and make sure it is the right way round.

Be careful to keep your finger away from the trigger when cocking the Sterling. Cock the gun with the forefinger and thumb of your left hand and always remember that it is depressingly easy to discharge a short weapon like an SMG in the wrong direction.

Forget the Hollywood image of the SMG always on full auto; except at point-blank range, you are better off firing quick aimed shots from the shoulder with the safety set at 'R'. For close-quarter battle, aim or point the Sterling like a shotgun and keep both eyes open.

The Sterling Mk 5 is a fully automatic silent sub-machine gun used by British forces under the designation L34. There is nothing to wear out in the built-in silencer and the weapon uses standard 9-mm ammunition.

the round is angled inwards as it is being rammed, so that the cap is not in line with the firing pin on the face of the bolt.

As the cartridge enters the chamber it is aligned with the axis of the barrel and, as the extractor snaps into the groove on the case, the firing pin touches the cap. The friction between the cartridge and the chamber will slow the cartridge sufficiently for the fixed firing pin to give the cap a blow strong enough to fire it while the bolt is still moving forward.

The rapid development of pressure in the chamber brings the bolt to a rapid stop and reverses the movement, blowing the case out of the chamber and thrusting the bolt backwards. But because the bolt was moving forwards at the instant of firing, the explosion first had to stop the bolt and then reverse it, and this 'differential locking' or 'advanced primer ignition' system means that the return spring can be less strong and the bolt less heavy than would be necessary if the bolt came to a complete stop before the cartridge fired.

For British military use the Sterling is fitted with a folding steel butt; it is also possible to have it fitted with a fixed plastic butt, and for police use it is available as a semi-automatic-only weapon, firing single shots. It is also available as the 'Mark 6 Carbine', semi-automatic with a 16-in (406-mm) barrel, which makes it a legal weapon for civil ownership in the USA.

Silenced version

In 1956 Patchett began development of a silenced version of the L2A3, as did the Royal Armaments Research & Development Establishment. Both designs were tried and it was decided to adopt the RARDE system, which was much the same as that already used on the silenced Sten

Mark 2S. This uses a long barrel with 72 radial holes drilled in it, surrounded by a sleeve containing sound baffles. Since the holes reduce the velocity, and hence the recoil, the bolt is lightened and the return spring made less stiff. The gun was adopted as the L34A1, and it has one notable advantage over the earlier Sten in that it can safely be fired at 'automatic', whereas the Sten 2S was safe only at single shots. Sterling also markets the silenced version in semi-automatic form as the 'Police Carbine Mark 5'.

Most recently, Sterling has adapted the basic design to produce a family of weapons suitable for use in confined spaces. Known as the 'Mark 7 Para Pistol', it is available in four versions. The Mark 7A4 and Mark 7A8 fire from an open bolt, as do the L2A3 and L34A1, and have 4-in (101-mm) and 8-in (203-in) barrels. The Mark 7C4 and Mark 7C8 fire from a closed bolt, using a newly designed firing mechanism which gives greater accuracy, and

with the same four-inch and eight-inch barrels.

The closed-bolt option has now been fitted to a full-sized weapon, known as the 'Single Shot Mark 8'. This is a semi-automatic of the same size and appearance as the standard L2A3, but uses the closed bolt to give very high accuracy to ranges of up to 200 m (656 ft).

Trucial Oman scouts are seen being instructed with the Sterling in Sharjah during the early 1970s. You can fire by 'sense of direction' by keeping your head high so that the target is not obscured by the foresight.

Zap it with the Steyr

The Steyr AUG is an excellent combat rifle despite its unorthodox appearance. The optical sight provides x1.5 magnification and has a black ring as its reticle. Place this over a man-sized target at up to 300m (984 ft) and you should nail him every time.

The Steyr AUG looks quite unlike any other modern rifle, and seems more like a prop from a Star Wars movie than a serious military weapon. However, despite its unconventional appearance, the Steyr is an excellent gun and is proving increasingly successful in the cut-throat world of international firearms.

The AUG was developed by the Steyr-Daimler-Puch company for the Austrian army, which wanted to replace its ageing FN FALs. The Steyr factory still manufactures the splendid Mannlicher sporting rifles, but to meet the military requirements they produced a revolutionary weapon.

Bullpup design

First, Steyr decided to make a bullpup rifle. A bullpup is a rifle which has the action set back in the stock so that the breech is alongside the firer's face and the magazine, therefore, is behind the trigger. Bullpups were not exactly new, but they had only ever been proposed for a military rifle once before – the British EM1 of 1950, which failed to reach service.

Second, they decided to utilise modern plastic material instead of wood. Third, the rifle was to be modular, so that the component parts could be shuffled around to produce a number of different weapons – hence the name 'AUG', for Army Universal Gun. And it had to be in 5.56-mm calibre, since that appeared to be the coming thing.

The plastic stock has the trigger,

The AUG system

The carbine version of the AUG is 69 cm (27 in) long. Barrel length is reduced to 407 mm (16 in), 101 mm (4 in) less than the rifle.

The HBAR (Heavy Barrel Automatic Rifle) is the LMG version of the AUG and is fitted with a 42-round magazine.

The AUG rifle (above) and the paratrooper's carbine version, at 62.6 cm (24.6 in) long and with a fixed barrel grip instead of the flexible one on the rifle.

Inside the Steyr AUG

The revolutionary Steyr is rapidly becoming the most popular bullpup assault rifle in the world. Now sold to Australia and New Zealand and Oman, it is under consideration by several other armies. The simplicity of the sights makes it easier to teach recruits to shoot with and the interchangeable parts allow an army to buy a whole weapons system built around common elements.

Telescopic graticule adjusting screws

Cocking handle
With forward-assist locking button on its rear end, which when pressed locks the handle to the bolt mechanism and allows you to slam the bolt closed on a sticky cartridge.

Barrel

22-mm bearings
These allow the AUG to fire any NATO standard rifle grenade.

Bayonet lug
This is not fitted to all models of the AUG.

Flash eliminator

Gas regulator
This can be adjusted to admit more gas to the piston to overcome dirt in the weapon or a dry mechanism. It can also be entirely shut off for grenade firing.

Barrel release
Press this down and back to unlock the barrel for removal.

Front grip
This is either in this position or folded forward to lie underneath the barrel. It also acts as a handle when you are changing the barrel.

Trigger operating rod
This carries the trigger movement back to the firing mechanism.

Left: The Steyr AUG is designed to be a light and handy assault rifle. Unlike the SA80 it can be modified for left-handed operation, and by swapping the component parts you can make an LMG or SMG instead.

rod, safety and locking catches incorporated; everything else is then added in removable form. The receiver is fitted with lugs to accept the barrel in the front end and the bolt in the rear, and it has the gas cylinder formed on the right side and a spring cylinder on the left.

The bolt carrier is attached to two rods, which slide into these cylinders and have the return springs permanently attached. The bolt locks into the carrier by a pin which, riding in a curved slot in the carrier, gives the bolt a rotary motion to lock and unlock. The receiver and bolt unit then slip into the plastic stock and are retained by a simple catch.

The barrel then slides in and locks into the receiver lugs. An all-plastic hammer unit slips into the rear of the stock and is retained in place by the butt plate. The receiver is shaped into a carrying handle, which also holds a 1.4x optical sight. The magazine is a transparent plastic unit holding 30 rounds in a double column.

Front grip

There is a folding handle fitted to the barrel, which helps when removing it and also acts as a front grip; you can grip it upright or fold it forward for a more 'rifle-like' grip. The aiming mark on the telescope is simply a circle. Place the circle around the target, press the trigger, and you invariably hit what you aimed at. Give the trigger a harder squeeze and the rifle then fires full-automatic at 650 rounds a minute; there is no change lever to adjust.

Optical sight

The circle in the sight is designed to cover a 1.8 m (6 ft) diameter at 300 m (984 ft) range, which means that it can be a useful aid to rangefinding; if the circle almost fits around the average

The Steyr field-stripped:

1 Barrel assembly
2 Housing assembly
3 Bolt assembly
4 Stock
5 Hammer group
6 Magazine
7 Butt plate

NOTE: The Steyr's take-down catch is on the right-hand side by the ejection port.

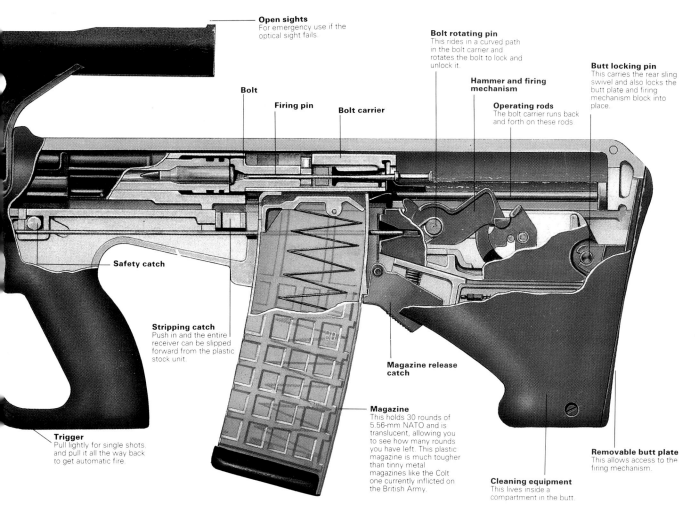

Open sights
For emergency use if the optical sight fails.

Bolt rotating pin
This rides in a curved path in the bolt carrier and rotates the bolt to lock and unlock it.

Butt locking pin
This carries the rear sling swivel and also locks the butt plate and firing mechanism block into place.

Hammer and firing mechanism

Bolt

Firing pin

Bolt carrier

Operating rods
The bolt carrier runs back and forth on these rods.

Safety catch

Stripping catch
Push in and the entire receiver can be slipped forward from the plastic stock unit.

Magazine release catch

Magazine
This holds 30 rounds of 5.56-mm NATO and is translucent, allowing you to see how many rounds you have left. This plastic magazine is much tougher than tinny metal magazines like the Colt one currently inflicted on the British Army.

Cleaning equipment
This lives inside a compartment in the butt.

Removable butt plate
This allows access to the firing mechanism.

Trigger
Pull lightly for single shots, and pull it all the way back to get automatic fire.

man, he must be about 300 m (984 ft) away. But, in fact, rangefinding is scarcely vital with this weapon; the trajectory is so flat that you can take the same point of aim at any range to 350 m (1,148 ft) and hit the target. And because there is only one aiming device, the recruit no longer has to worry about getting two sights and the target in perfect alignment, so that teaching men to shoot with this rifle is very easy.

Enormous strength

All very well, you say, but who wants a rifle with plastic furniture and a cast aluminium receiver in combat? At a demonstration at Steyr some years ago, an AUG was thrown on to stony ground and run over repeatedly by a variety of vehicles; after surviving 10 passes by a Land Rover, 10 by a 1-ton (1.02-tonne) and 10 by a 3-ton (3.05-tonne), it survived three from a 6-ton (6.09-tonne) before the receiver sight bracket cracked. The rifle was still perfectly serviceable, and the plastic was not only unbroken, but unscarred.

In another test a loose bullet was driven into the bore by a hammer and punch, after which the rifle was assembled, loaded, and fired – from a man's shoulder. Nothing untoward happened, except that it kicked

The Steyr can take a scope mount in place of the integral optical sight. This allows it to carry almost any scope you like. Quick-change mounts allow you to swap sights rapidly without having to re-sight the weapon.

Above: Austrian troops wade through a marsh, keeping their AUGs clear of the mud. Note how the man on the right has folded down the foregrip.

Left: The sights on the AUG are easy to learn how to use and provide a high degree of accuracy. Like the SUSAT sight on the SA80, the Steyr's sight is a great improvement over iron sights when shooting in bad light conditions.

The Steyr AUG has proved itself to be a very sturdy piece of kit despite fears that a largely plastic gun would not be strong enough for service use.

The AUG can be fitted with an optical night sight, shown here fitted to the alternative receiver group. This is capable of mounting any NATO standard scope. A full 1 kg (2.2 lb) lighter than the British SA80, the AUG is easier to manage with heavy optics attached.

slightly more than usual and the cap of the cartridge blew out into the plastic stock. But the barrel was perfectly undamaged. Also, a barrel has been filled with water over a loaded round and fired without damage. Try that on your . . . , well, perhaps better not. Very few rifles will survive that sort of treatment.

Choice of barrels

As to the 'Universal' part: you can swap four barrel lengths: 621 mm (24.4 in) for the light machine-gun, 508 mm (20 in) for the rifle, 407 mm (16 in) for the carbine and 350 mm (13.7 in) for the sub-machine gun.

You can fit a bipod and 42-round magazine if you are using it as a light machine-gun. You can remove the receiver with optical sight and replace it with one having a NATO-standard mounting bracket, which will accept any kind of optical sight or night vision sight.

You can take out the hammer unit and replace it with one which gives semi-automatic fire only; or with one which gives single shots or three-round bursts; or with one which allows you to select full automatic or three-round bursts by moving a switch on the unit before you fit it into the rifle.

Sub-machine gun

The last adaptation appeared in 1985; the '9-mm AUG Para'. This is something of a major refit, but it still uses the basic components. The 5.56-mm short barrel is changed for a 9-mm barrel, the locking bolt and carrier unit are exchanged for a blowback bolt, and an adapter in the magazine well accepts a new magazine carrying 32 9-mm cartridges. The result is a very effective and accurate sub-machine gun.

International service

The Austrian army adopted the AUG as the 'Sturmgewehr 77'. After that it was taken up in some numbers by the Moroccan, Omani and Saudi armies, and is now the standard service weapon of the Australian and New Zealand armies.

Snap Shooting with the Steyr

Above: The cocking piece on the MPi 69 is the forward sling mount. The safety catch is a push-through type with three positions: 'safe' locks both the trigger and the bolt; half-way through permits single shots only; and pushing the safety bar all the way through means single shots on the first trigger pressure and full-auto when you pull the trigger all the way back.

The Austrian firm of Steyr-Mannlicher is best known for the futuristic AUG assault rifle, but it also produces a very successful 9-mm sub-machine gun, the MPi 69. An extremely robust weapon, the MPi 69 employs a wrap-around bolt like the Uzi to reduce overall length while keeping a respectably long barrel. It is comfortable to grip, simple to operate and groups well firing single shots.

Steyr-Mannlicher GmbH is the latest title for a company which has been around since 1864, when it was founded by Josef Werndl to make rifles for the Austro-Hungarian army. It became the Waffenfabrik Steyr, and when Austria was annexed by Germany in 1938 it was swallowed by the Hermann Goering Werke, was dis-

Left: The Steyr handles and shoots exceptionally well. The wrap-around bolt, as with the Uzi, means a decent length of pipe with short overall length. The only real problem is the cocking handle.

Inside the Steyr

Front sight
The conventional post foresight is adjustable for windage and elevation, although a wide range of optical sights can be fitted by drilling the top of the body and adding sight mount bases.

Cap nut
This secures the barrel in position.

gorged in 1945 to become Steyr-Daimler-Puch, and in the late 1980s changed its title while remaining part of the S-D-P empire.

In all that time rifles and pistols have been the company's principal products, but it has made two ventures into the sub-machine gun business in the past. Its first venture is shrouded in mystery; there has been a brief mention of a design developed in 1918 by Steyr, few of which were made and all of which were destroyed by the Allied Disarmament Commission. Nothing exists at Steyr to confirm the former existence of this mysterious weapon, not even in its museum, and the company says, "It's all in Leningrad, or somewhere . . . we were liberated by the Red Army."

Steyr produced a much more successful weapon in 1930, the Steyr-Solothurn, so called because it was made by Steyr and marketed through a firm in Solothurn, Switzerland. In fact the design came from Rheinmetall of Germany, for whom the Solothurn firm was a 'front' organisation in the days when Germany was forbidden to make such weapons. It was a solid and

The weapon shoots very well on single-shot, producing 20-round zeroing groups well under 150 mm (5.9 in) fired from kneeling at 25 m (82 ft). There were no malfunctions in our tests, with loads ranging from dodgy 1960s Yugoslavian sub-machine gun ammo to semi-jacketed soft point pistol ammunition.

reliable weapon, and was still in use in the mid-1970s with the Portuguese National Guard.

A sound job

But in the 1960s Steyr decided to build a design of its own, since the time seemed ripe for a fresh look at sub-machine guns. The weapon it produced was adopted by the Austrian army as the Maschinen Pistole 69 – MPi 69 – and has since been adopted in several other places. It is, like all Steyr products, a sound and workmanlike job, though it avoids the startling elements of design which make the Steyr AUG such a recognisable item.

The essentials of the MPi 69 are simple enough. A pressed-steel receiver, welded into a hollow box, carries a 260-mm barrel retained by a finger-tight nut at the front. The bolt is

The Steyr MPi 69, when introduced, was the first military weapon to be developed in Austria since the 1930s. The Steyr is a compact weapon which, like the UZI, has a long barrel but a short overall length. The bolt telescopes round the barrel for about two-thirds of the barrel length.

severely cut away and encloses the rear end of the barrel when forward, and has apertures to admit the cartridge and allow the empty case to be ejected. A single return spring is wrapped around a guide rod along which the bolt moves in recoil.

Mags in the dark

There is a simple collapsible wire butt, and the magazine (25 or 32 shots) is inserted into the pistol grip. This latter is a good feature, since it makes changing magazines in the dark a great deal easier, as anyone who has ever tried changing a Sten or Thompson magazine in darkness will testify.

Like the AUG, the MPi 69 uses a two-stage trigger as a selector: a first

Field stripping the Steyr MPi 69

1 After clearing the weapon, let the bolt forward under control and release the cap nut locking button which is on the right of the front sight. This will allow you to unscrew the cap nut which holds the barrel in position.

2 Remove the cap nut and then pull the barrel assembly out from the frame forwards. This is exactly the same procedure as on the Uzi and the Beretta PM12.

3 To remove the working parts, locate the takedown button, which protrudes through and locks a hinged plate covering the back of the body. Press in on the button and rotate the plate upwards.

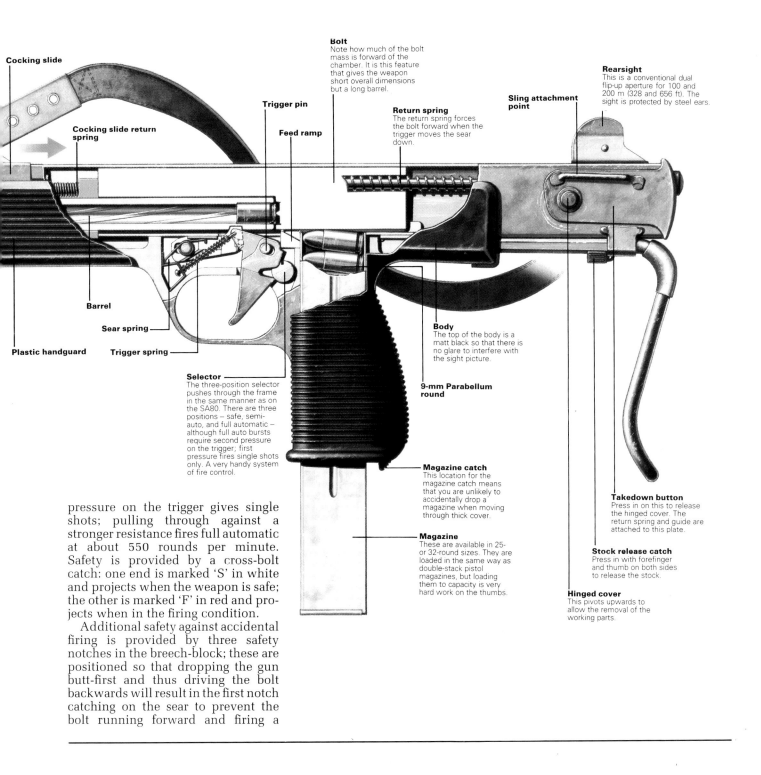

Cocking slide

Cocking slide return spring

Barrel

Sear spring

Plastic handguard

Trigger spring

Trigger pin

Feed ramp

Bolt
Note how much of the bolt mass is forward of the chamber. It is this feature that gives the weapon short overall dimensions but a long barrel.

Return spring
The return spring forces the bolt forward when the trigger moves the sear down.

Sling attachment point

Rearsight
This is a conventional dual flip-up aperture for 100 and 200 m (328 and 656 ft). The sight is protected by steel ears.

Body
The top of the body is a matt black so that there is no glare to interfere with the sight picture.

9-mm Parabellum round

Selector
The three-position selector pushes through the frame in the same manner as on the SA80. There are three positions – safe, semi-auto, and full automatic – although full auto bursts require second pressure on the trigger; first pressure fires single shots only. A very handy system of fire control.

Magazine catch
This location for the magazine catch means that you are unlikely to accidentally drop a magazine when moving through thick cover.

Magazine
These are available in 25- or 32-round sizes. They are loaded in the same way as double-stack pistol magazines, but loading them to capacity is very hard work on the thumbs.

Takedown button
Press in on this to release the hinged cover. The return spring and guide are attached to this plate.

Stock release catch
Press in with forefinger and thumb on both sides to release the stock.

Hinged cover
This pivots upwards to allow the removal of the working parts.

pressure on the trigger gives single shots; pulling through against a stronger resistance fires full automatic at about 550 rounds per minute. Safety is provided by a cross-bolt catch: one end is marked 'S' in white and projects when the weapon is safe; the other is marked 'F' in red and projects when in the firing condition.

Additional safety against accidental firing is provided by three safety notches in the breech-block; these are positioned so that dropping the gun butt-first and thus driving the bolt backwards will result in the first notch catching on the sear to prevent the bolt running forward and firing a

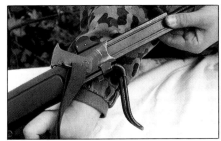

4 Take hold of the return spring and guide, which is connected to the bolt, and pull the whole assembly out of the back of the body. You should not strip the weapon further in the field.

5 You can remove the body from the plastic fore-end and pistol grip by pulling the body to the rear. However, you must support the cocking piece while you do this as it is a very fiddly job to reassemble the cocking piece and spring.

6 The weapon field-stripped shows a remarkable resemblance to the Uzi. Reassembly is in reverse order: be careful when placing the metal body back into the plastic fore-end, as it is the plastic fore-end that holds the cocking piece of the sling in place.

Combat use of the sling

The test model looks dangerous at first, in that when the weapon is loaded it could make itself ready and fire a round if the firer was carrying the weapon on the sling and, for example, jumped off the back of a truck.

The sling cocking device could be quite useful in some situations, where you need to go from load to ready at speed. When carrying the weapon across your body with a sling, all you have to do is knock the safety catch off and push the weapon away from you firmly.

The point of balance of the weapon is slightly forward of the pistol grip. Bursts over five rounds disappear off the target over the right shoulder. Bursts of two to three rounds can be kept on a Figure 11 at 25 m (82 ft) from the hip or underarm assault position with a little practice.

Left: The 'show clear' is a bit of a problem, as when the bolt is fully back it is difficult to see if the chamber is clear. Pulling the bolt back onto the second sear with a firm grip of the sling gives the best view of the chamber. Like all Steyr products, the weapon is very well made.

round. The second notch is designed to catch the bolt in the case of a weak cartridge not providing enough impulse to drive the bolt back far enough to engage the normal firing notch in the sear. One way and another, accidental discharge of the Steyr is impossible.

The most novel feature, and one which arouses different opinions, is the method of cocking. The cocking handle is at the front left end of the receiver, and forms the forward attachment point for the sling, so that cocking the weapon is simply a matter of holding the pistol grip with one hand and jerking back the sling with the other. This is fine, as long as you don't try to loop the sling around your arm for steadiness when firing, which places tension on the cocking lever and prevents the bolt from closing, so

the gun will fail to fire. Leave the sling free and you'll have no trouble.

Firing port model

To cater for those who dislike this system, the MPi 81 was developed; this is exactly the same weapon except that the sling is attached to a conventional sling swivel riveted to the receiver, and a normal type of cocking handle is fitted. In addition, in this model the rate of fire has been increased to about 700 rpm by slight internal changes.

Another version of the MPi 81 is the 'firing port model'. This has a longer-than-normal barrel with a prominent collar about half way along, and is intended for use by troops firing out of armoured personnel carriers. The long barrel protrudes well through the firing port, keeping the smoke and

gases out of the vehicle, and the collar lodges on to the sill of the port and prevents the weapon accidentally being drawn inside if the vehicle lurches during firing. It is also fitted with the 1.4× optical sight of the AUG rifle, carried in special brackets at the rear of the receiver, a position which allows the sight to be used behind a vision block above the firing port.

Sound suppressor

It is possible to fit a sound suppressor to the MPi 69 or to the standard MPi 81, by simply unscrewing the retaining nut and removing the barrel, then inserting a special barrel and suppressor unit, the latter screwing on to the receiver and acting as the retaining nut. This is a very efficient assembly, reducing the noise by something like 30 dB and still allowing full automatic fire.

Firing the MPi 69 is much the same as firing any other sub-machine gun; it has no vices, is as accurate as you have any right to expect, and never seems to give any trouble. The firing port model is remarkably accurate due to its longer barrel and optical sight, though it is hardly the weapon for street-fighting. The MPi 69 may lack the glamour of some other designs, but Steyr has been producing it now for over 30 years without complaints, and it looks like continuing.

Police Sniper Rifles

Left: Israeli police forces are equipped with the excellent sniper version of the 7.62-mm Galil. The weapon is a little heavy for police use and features folding stock with cheek piece, a superb Nimrod scope, bipod and 35-round magazines!

Below: A scoped-up and reworked SLR is capable of acceptable sniper accuracy out to around 600 m (1,970 ft) in the hands of a competent shot. The Home Office went through a phase of imposing military weapons on police forces, but common sense has now largely prevailed and individual police forces can pick the weapon best suited to their needs.

The 1960s saw the arrival of the psychotic sniper in the USA, men who took to a high point with a rifle and shot at anyone in sight — and, as a result, police forces had to think of using snipers in retaliation.

But, as far as crime goes, what America thinks today the rest of the world thinks tomorrow. Over the past 20 years virtually every country has suffered from snipers, terrorists and similar disastrous affairs that can usually be dealt with only by accurate and lethal gunfire.

The Parker Hale T4 is a very solid long-range 7.62-mm bolt action which is again a bit cumbersome for vaulting over walls and running across roofs with. The heavy barrel makes it good to shoot from prone, but a little tiring from other positions.

The long shot

The requirement of a police sniper is somewhat different to that of a military sniper. The military sniper needs a weapon with which he can hit hard and accurately at long range. His targets are never less than 600 m (1,970 ft) away, and in most cases the range is over 1,000 m (3,280 ft). For this you need a heavy bullet and high muzzle velocity so that the trajectory is as flat as possible, the time of flight short, and the terminal energy sufficient to kill at the longest ranges.

The service 5.56-mm rifle is outclassed in this contest; the light bullet and high velocity are fine out to 300 or 400 m (984 or 1,310 ft), but after that the limitations begin to show and the accuracy is nowhere near what is required for sniping. Moreover, at long range the 5.56-mm bullet simply does not have the residual energy to ensure maximum effect.

As a result, military sniping rifles are usually designed around an old-style, full-power cartridge, such as the 7.62-mm NATO, the 7.92-mm Mauser or the 7.62×51 Soviet. Indeed, some firms have designed them to fire non-military rounds such as the .300 Winchester Magnum, claiming that these give better consistency and accuracy than out-of-the-box service ammunition.

Close-in sniping

But the police sniper is rarely interested in 1,000-m (3,280-ft) shots; his problem is the terrorist holding a hostage in an airport or building, or the crazy sniper on a rooftop, or the cornered gunman in a building site.

None of these is likely to be over 300 m (984 ft) away, and the police sniper's principal problem is not so

Inside the SSG 69

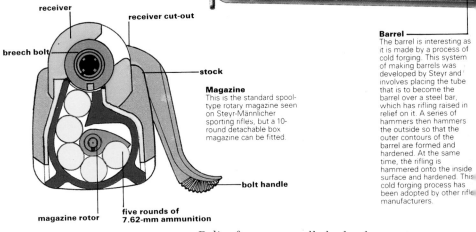

Foresight
This is a conventional protected post. The iron sights are only intended for emergency use if the scope is damaged.

Bore
The Steyr process also produces a slightly tapered bore towards the muzzle, which enhances accuracy.

Kahles ZF 69 telescope
Not surprisingly, the lens quality in these scopes is excellent and they can be internally adjusted to 800 m (2,624 ft) in 100 increments to eliminate the need to hold over targets. The sights are attached to the rib cut-in the receiver by clamped rings. In theory, you can remove and refit the scope quickly without altering the zero of the weapon.

Rear sight
This is a flip-up 'V' notch that can be drifted for windage.

The Model 69 is now the standard sniping rifle of the Austrian army. The rifle's full title is 'Steyr-Mannlicher-Scharfschützengewehr'. The Steyr police rifle is basically the same as the SSG with an extra-heavy barrel, an oversize match bolt handle and an adjustable shooting sling fitted in a fore-end rail. A 6×42 scope is fitted as standard.

Sling swivel

receiver

receiver cut-out

breech bolt

stock

Magazine
This is the standard spool-type rotary magazine seen on Steyr-Männlicher sporting rifles, but a 10-round detachable box magazine can be fitted.

Barrel
The barrel is interesting as it is made by a process of cold forging. This system of making barrels was developed by Steyr and involves placing the tube that is to become the barrel over a steel bar, which has rifling raised in relief on it. A series of hammers then hammers the outside so that the outer contours of the barrel are formed and hardened. At the same time, the rifling is hammered onto the inside surface and hardened. This cold forging process has been adopted by other rifle manufacturers.

bolt handle

magazine rotor

five rounds of 7.62-mm ammunition

The rotary magazine ensures reliable functioning and the see-through plastic plate allows a quick inspection of ammunition state.

much range as simply getting into a position where he can see his target without exposing himself. Thus the logical conclusion is that the full-power sniping rifle is over-powered for police use and something lighter and smaller could be sufficiently effective.

But, like every argument about weapons, it all comes back to the ammunition. You cannot be certain that shots over 300 m (984 ft) will never be needed, so you take out insurance by adopting the full-calibre sniping rifle anyway. There were police forces in the past who used things like .220 Swift and .275 Rigby sporting rifles for their precision requirements, and very successfully too. But today anything outside the standard calibres is virtually unusable unless you choose to hand-load or pay exorbitant prices.

An Austrian police sniper team uses the SSG. The rifle is accurate enough to place 10 shots in a 400-mm (15.75-in) group at 800 m (2,620 ft) with RWS target ammo. At more realistic police ranges the rifle will group 10 rounds in 90 mm (3.5 in) at 300 m (984 ft) and put five rounds into 15 mm (0.6 in) at 100 m (328 ft).

Police forces generally look askance at such solutions.

So it comes back to the military-pattern sniper, though perhaps with some refinements. A good example is the Steyr Police Rifle. Steyr-Mannlicher produced an excellent military sniping rifle in the 1960s, calling it the SSG69. This uses the Mannlicher-Schoenauer rotary magazine, a turn-bolt action, and has a plastic stock, usually coloured olive drab.

The Police Rifle starts from the same basic action but uses the heavy barrel from the Steyr UIT Match rifle, the bolt with extended handle from the same source, adds a bipod, does away with iron sights and uses a 6×42 telescope as standard.

Above: A close-up of the SSG demonstrates the advantages of the clear back to the 10-round magazine. Note that the safety catch is pushed forward off safe, revealing the red dot behind it, and the pin protruding from the rear of the bolt shows the weapon is cocked.

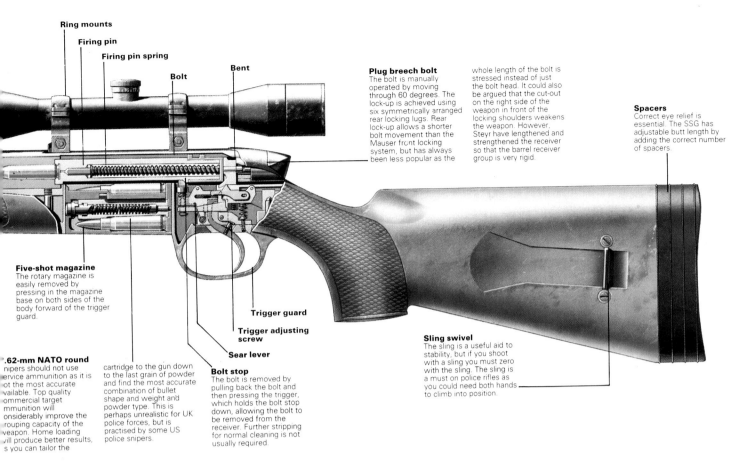

Ring mounts

Firing pin

Firing pin spring

Bolt

Bent

Plug breech bolt
The bolt is manually operated by moving through 60 degrees. The lock-up is achieved using six symmetrically arranged rear locking lugs. Rear lock-up allows a shorter bolt movement than the Mauser front locking system, but has always been less popular as the whole length of the bolt is stressed instead of just the bolt head. It could also be argued that the cut-out on the right side of the weapon in front of the locking shoulders weakens the weapon. However, Steyr have lengthened and strengthened the receiver so that the barrel receiver group is very rigid.

Spacers
Correct eye relief is essential. The SSG has adjustable butt length by adding the correct number of spacers.

Five-shot magazine
The rotary magazine is easily removed by pressing in the magazine base on both sides of the body forward of the trigger guard.

Trigger guard

Trigger adjusting screw

Sear lever

.62-mm NATO round
nipers should not use ervice ammunition as it is ot the most accurate vailable. Top quality ommercial target mmunition will onsiderably improve the rouping capacity of the veapon. Home loading ill produce better results, s you can tailor the cartridge to the gun down to the last grain of powder and find the most accurate combination of bullet shape and weight and powder type. This is perhaps unrealistic for UK police forces, but is practised by some US police snipers.

Bolt stop
The bolt is removed by pulling back the bolt and then pressing the trigger, which holds the bolt stop down, allowing the bolt to be removed from the receiver. Further stripping for normal cleaning is not usually required.

Sling swivel
The sling is a useful aid to stability, but if you shoot with a sling you must zero with the sling. The sling is a must on police rifles as you could need both hands to climb into position.

Old hat?

But why, you may ask, does this excellent rifle rely upon a mechanism relatively unchanged since the turn of the century? For the Steyr-Mannlicher of 1969 used the same bolt and magazine as the Mannlicher-Schoenauer of 1903 – with which the Greek army was equipped until World War II.

Why not something more modern, a semi-automatic of some sort? After all, Steyr make the AUG, a classic automatic weapon, which is in wide use.

The answer is difficult, but it comes back to the primeval belief that semi-automatics are not as accurate as bolt actions. And there is some warrant for this belief. The standard military rifle is not a precision weapon, by any measure; it is built to reach a specified standard of accuracy but, more important, it is built to withstand a battering that would make most rifles fall to pieces. Reliability takes first place, so accuracy comes second, and when people tried to make the first semi-automatics shoot accurately they found them lacking.

Today, 40 years on, the production

The Steyr Police rifle fitted with the UIT heavy barrel is even more accurate than the military version. Note also the over-large bolt handle to avoid fumbling; chances are if you do need a second shot, it will be taken under considerable stress.

problems have been overcome, and it is now quite possible to make mass-produced semi-automatic actions that will shoot accurately enough to be sniping rifles. Heckler & Koch use the same delayed blowback action in their hunting rifles as they do in their military rifles, and they are excellent weapons.

But there is still a reluctance to place faith in a semi-auto for sniping.

Bearing in mind that, among others, the standard Soviet Dragunov sniper, the Galil, the German H&K PSG-1 and Walther WA2000 are all semi-autos, it has to be said that there is a certain amount of reactionary prejudice.

How it looks

So far as police forces are concerned, though, they have another reason for avoiding military semi-

automatics: appearance. Some foreign forces don't care; but the British and some others have no wish to be seen as some sort of oppressive para-military force carrying what look like military weapons.

For this reason, a wood-stocked bolt action, basically a sporting rifle, is favoured for police work in many places. Even some of the specialised weapons – the Steyr, the Beretta Sniper, the FN Sniper – have the appearance of 'civilian' weapons until

you look closer.

There is, of course, a highly practical reason for the military to use semi-auto rifles; after firing a semi-auto it reloads, and the sniper doesn't have to move his arm to work a bolt and thus, possibly, reveal his position. He is not there for just one shot; he hopes to make three or four.

The police sniper, on the other hand, rarely needs more than one good shot to do what is required, and reloading is no problem. So, once

US police forces and SWAT teams favour the Remington 700 bolt action sporting rifle, which is relatively light and fast-handling. The 700 was modified for use by US Marine Corps snipers in Vietnam and designated the M40A1. It has a fibreglass stock and heavy barrel.

again, the bolt action is perfectly adequate for his needs. And, the final clinching argument for most police forces: accurate bolt actions are cheaper than accurate semi-automatics.

Left: A German border police sergeant demonstrates the Mauser sniper rifle Model 66, as used by GSG-9. The weapon uses the Mauser front-locking short action and has an adjustable trigger, cheek piece and recoil pad.

Above: The mighty Mini 14 is a cheap and effective urban counter-sniper rifle for short- and medium-range work. The synthetic stock is as supplied to certain UK police forces. It cannot compete with 7.62 at long range, but is useful for most police encounters.

The Tommy Gun

The sub-machine gun was born in the close-quarter battles of World War I. In the confined combat which took place in trenches, troops began to feel the need for some kind of small weapon which would be easy to handle, yet could provide real firepower when needed. This need was first met by the German MP18 machine pistol, which was probably the first true sub-machine gun. It was that same requirement, however, that was to inspire the development of one of the most famous weapons of the 20th century, the Thompson.

There can be few people who are not familiar with the Thompson, thanks to Hollywood. Star of countless gangster films in the 1930s and featuring in many of the war movies of the 1940s and 1950s, the Thompson so caught the public's imagination that for many years any sub-machine gun was known as a 'Tommy Gun'. Yet the Thompson has always been much more than a movie prop.

'Trench Broom'

The origin of the Thompson gun dates back to the last year of World War I. The American Army was receiving its first full taste of trench warfare, and it didn't like the experience.

Winston Churchill poses with one of the thousands of M1928 Thompsons bought by Britain during the early years of World War II. The Germans tried to use copies of this photo as crude propaganda, likening the Prime Minister to a Hollywood gangster.

Troops called for a kind of 'Trench Broom', that would sweep the trenches clear of an enemy. Since this sweeping was to take place at short range, it was obvious that a weapon firing full-power rifle cartridges, accurate to a thousand yards or more, would be a waste of time.

The Germans had come to the same conclusion and their MP18 was chambered for the 9-mm Parabellum round, a calibre that was to become pretty much the worldwide standard over the next 50 years. On the American side, General John T.

By the end of the war, Thompsons could be found in every theatre. These US Marines are attacking a Japanese bunker on Okinawa in April 1945. The gunner is using an M1A1 Thompson.

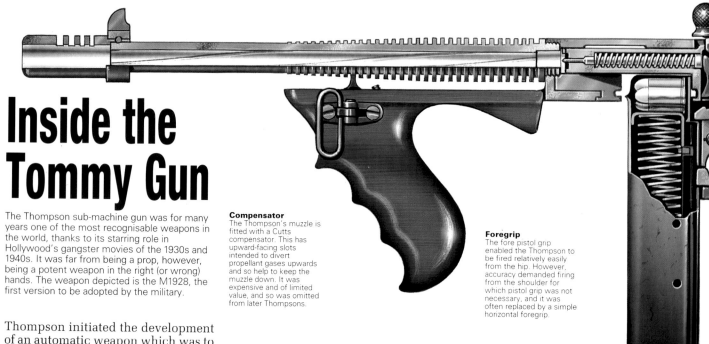

Inside the Tommy Gun

The Thompson sub-machine gun was for many years one of the most recognisable weapons in the world, thanks to its starring role in Hollywood's gangster movies of the 1930s and 1940s. It was far from being a prop, however, being a potent weapon in the right (or wrong) hands. The weapon depicted is the M1928, the first version to be adopted by the military.

Compensator
The Thompson's muzzle is fitted with a Cutts compensator. This has upward-facing slots intended to divert propellant gases upwards and so help to keep the muzzle down. It was expensive and of limited value, and so was omitted from later Thompsons.

Foregrip
The fore pistol grip enabled the Thompson to be fired relatively easily from the hip. However, accuracy demanded firing from the shoulder for which pistol grip was not necessary, and it was often replaced by a simple horizontal foregrip.

Thompson initiated the development of an automatic weapon which was to use the US Army's standard .45 Colt automatic pistol cartridge.

By the time the new weapon was ready for production, World War I was long over. The Thompson gun made its debut on the commercial market in 1921. The weapon was an immediate hit, though not with the law enforcement and military bodies for which it had been designed. This was the era of prohibition in America,

and the bootleggers and gangsters soon developed a taste for the Tommy Gun. Police, federal and prison agencies followed suit, and shoot-outs between the criminals and law men became staple fodder for the press of the time and a little later for Hollywood. It was not until 1928 that the military began to acquire the Thompson, when the Sub-machine gun, Caliber .45-in, M1928A1 entered service.

Complex and expensive

The Thompson was a complex and expensive piece of gunsmithing, which required some skill to keep in working order. It was cocked by a knob projecting through the top of the receiver. Pulling the trigger released the bolt, which activated a hammer to strike the firing pin. The early models of the Thompson were delayed blow-back weapons, using the friction between two sliding blocks of metal to hold down the rate of fire. In practice, the gun fired perfectly well without the inertia wedge block which provided the friction, although with a slightly increased rate of fire.

The gun was fitted with a selector switch allowing the choice of single shot or automatic fire, and the rate of fire was between 600 and 800 rounds per minute. The barrel was fitted with a Cutts compensator. The slots of the muzzle-mounted compensator diverted some of the propellant gases upwards, counteracting muzzle climb, which is an inevitable result of

A New Zealander fires his Thompson during the fierce battle for Cassino which took place in the spring of 1944. Firepower and ease of handling made the sub-machine gun ideal for urban combat.

automatic fire. The Thompson was available with 20- or 30-round box magazines and 50- or 100-round drum magazines. The 100-round drum was not a success, however, being very heavy and prone to feed problems. Although adopted by the military, the gun's complexity and a price tag of more than $200 meant that few were taken into service.

It was not until 1940 that large-scale production got under way. German

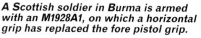

A Scottish soldier in Burma is armed with an M1928A1, on which a horizontal grip has replaced the fore pistol grip.

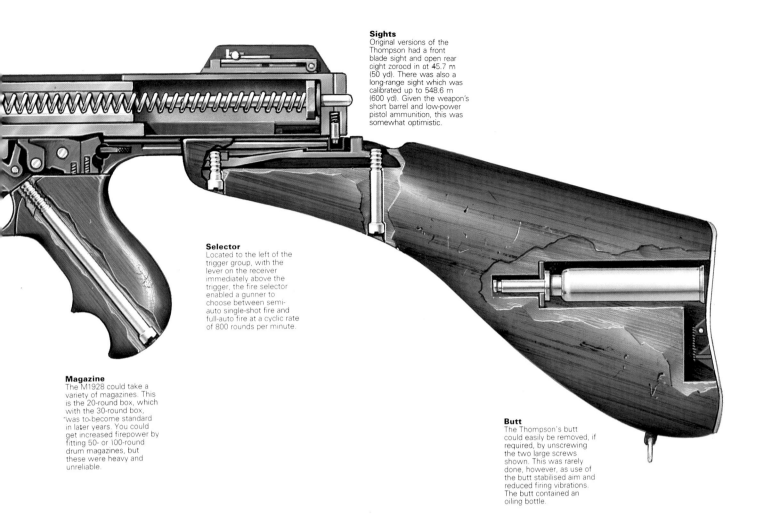

Sights
Original versions of the Thompson had a front blade sight and open rear sight zeroed in at 45.7 m (50 yd). There was also a long-range sight which was calibrated up to 548.6 m (600 yd). Given the weapon's short barrel and low-power pistol ammunition, this was somewhat optimistic.

Selector
Located to the left of the trigger group, with the lever on the receiver immediately above the trigger, the fire selector enabled a gunner to choose between semi-auto single-shot fire and full-auto fire at a cyclic rate of 800 rounds per minute.

Magazine
The M1928 could take a variety of magazines. This is the 20-round box, which with the 30-round box, was to become standard in later years. You could get increased firepower by fitting 50- or 100-round drum magazines, but these were heavy and unreliable.

Butt
The Thompson's butt could easily be removed, if required, by unscrewing the two large screws shown. This was rarely done, however, as use of the butt stabilised aim and reduced firing vibrations. The butt contained an oiling bottle.

troops were plentifully equipped with sub-machine guns, and after Dunkirk the British Army demanded similar weapons. The Thompson was the only example available and in production, so the British placed large orders for M1928s which served until deliveries of the crude Sten gun began. Mass production of the Thompson was difficult because of the large number of processes involved in machining it.

The M1 and M1A1

Once the war widened to include the United States, the US Army also had a need for large numbers of sub-machine guns. The Thompson was again chosen, but in considerably modified forms as the M1 and M1A1. Operation was now by simple blow-back, and the separate bolt, hammer and firing pin were replaced by a fixed firing pin mounted directly onto the bolt. The cocking handle was moved to the right-hand side of the receiver and the Cutts compensator was deleted. The large, awkward and noisy drum magazines were also no longer fitted.

The M1 still used the wooden butt and pistol grip of the earlier Thompsons, but the fore pistol grip was replaced by a straight wooden stock. In service the M1 was popular, espe-

Above: The M1928 Thompson was a well-made weapon. Identification features include a muzzle-mounted compensator, ribbed barrel, fore pistol grip and the cocking knob on top of the receiver.

Below: The M1 looked similar to the M1928, but was much simpler internally. Note the lack of compensator, and the cocking handle which has been moved to the side of the receiver.

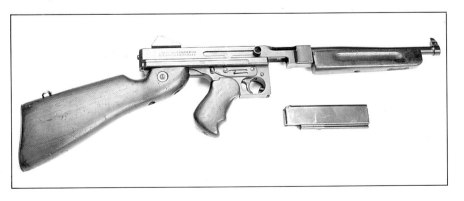

After the end of World War II, Thompsons found their way into many Third World armies. This example is carried by a South Vietnamese soldier aboard a US Army helicopter in the early 1960s.

cially when compared with the contemporary M3 'Grease Gun'. How much of this was due to the Thompson's Hollywood image is now impossible to determine, but it must have played a part. The Thompson was heavy, and even in its simplified form it was harder to strip and maintain than the M3. The Grease Gun fired the same ammunition as the Thompson, it performed as well in combat as the Thompson and it was far cheaper to manufacture. Nevertheless, it was ugly, and given the choice most soldiers would have taken the M1.

The Thompson remained in production until 1945, and although officially replaced in US service by later models of the M3, it remained in military armouries for many years. It re-emerged to be used in the Korean War, and large numbers were being exported by the US government under the 'Offshore Program' as late as 1960.

In the early days of the Vietnam War, American Special Forces units used the Thompson in preference to their issue weapons, claiming that its large-calibre, low-velocity bullets offered more penetration in the jungle. It was also widely copied in backyard workshops throughout the Far East, and could be found in both South Vietnamese and Viet Cong hands.

The Tommy Gun can still be found being used by militias and guerrillas in out-of-the-way parts of the world.

Closer to home, it was until recently a favourite weapon of IRA terrorists, and some original M1928s could be found in US police armouries right into the 1980s. More than 1,400,000 were made during a quarter century of production, but it will be almost impossible to find spares for any encountered in the late 1990s, and most of these weapons will be so worn that they would be dangerous. That has not stopped its most recent appearance in the vicious civil war in the former Yugoslavia. The USA supplied thousands of Thompsons to anti-German partisans during World War II, and after the war they went into store. They have re-emerged in the hands of Croatian forces, so 70 years after its appearance the Thompson is still in the front line.

In spite of its age, the Thompson's sturdy reliability made it a favourite weapon of many Americans in South East Asia. This M1A1-armed US Navy advisor keeps watch as VC suspects are removed from a sampan off the Vietnamese coast.

Tokarev SVT-40

An SVT-armed German soldier waves his section forwards early in the war. Captured examples of the Soviet rifle were popular with the invaders, and may have provided some inspiration for late-war German developments.

The Tokarev series of self-loading and selective-fire rifles was the result of 30 years of experimentation in Russia to develop an effective weapon, firing a full-power rifle cartridge at a much higher rate of fire, and intended to replace the bolt-action rifles which had been in general use since the late 1880s. In this the Tokarev was not entirely successful, since it never supplanted the Mosin-Nagant series, but during the Great Patriotic War from 1941 to 1945, they were an important part of the Soviet armoury.

Fyedor Vasilyevich Tokarev was born in 1871 into a poor Cossack family in the village of Yegorlykskaya, on the River Don. In 1885 he was tutored by a Tula gunsmith named Chernolikhov, who had been responsible for the design of the six-line (15.24-mm) Cossack rifle. Tokarev was trained as an armourer in 1891 at the Novocherkassk Military School, and was then assigned to the 12th Cossack Regiment, being appointed Chief Armourer in 1900. Still holding this position in 1907, while attending the Officer's Firing School at Orianenbaum, he produced a prototype self-loading rifle. This first attempt was, not surprisingly, based on a conversion of the Mosin-Nagant.

From 1908-14 Tokarev worked at the Sestroretsk Weapons Factory. At the outbreak of war he served at the

Naval infantrymen set out on an amphibious raid in the Baltic. Two of them are armed with SVT-40s. The Tokarev was a complex weapon, best suited for use by well-trained troops like these.

Inside the Tokarev SVT-40

7.62-mm calibre barrel   **Gas cylinder**

The *Samozariadnaya Vintovka Tokareva obr* 38g, or SVT-38, was one of the earliest self-loading rifles issued to the Soviet Army. The SVT-40 was basically the same rifle, modified for ease of construction. A most influential weapon, it was to lend features to both the German MP 43 Sturmgewehr and to the Kalashnikov AK-47, and as such could be said to be one of the grandfathers of the modern assault rifle.

Gas operation: Propellant gas is tapped after a round is fired, and is used to force back a piston mounted above the barrel.

front for 18 months and then returned to the factory to continue his research.

For many years a number of conditions were imposed upon designer's working on self-loading rifle prototypes: the rifles had to chamber the existing full-power rimmed cartridge; shoot as far and as accurately as a bolt-action rifle; operate under adverse conditions; and weigh no more than a standard infantry rifle in spite of the extra complexity of the mechanism.

Impossible specification

The difficulties faced by the various designers were eventually recognised by those in authority. As early as 1922, specifications were issued for a self-loading rifle, which had to be chambered for the M1891 round; should have selective fire, with a 50-round magazine; and should be fitted with a knife bayonet and weigh no more more than four kilograms (just under nine pounds). The magazine capacity requirement was later reduced to 25 rounds, but not surprisingly this specification proved impossible to meet.

Tokarev continued his work on self-loading rifles until at last one of his designs was accepted. This was the SVT-38 (*Samozariadnaya Vintovka Tokareva*, or the Self-Loading Rifle Tokarev Model 1938). The first pro-

duction SVT-38 rifle was assembled on the 16 July 1939. Nine days later regular production was underway, and by the 1 October mass production had begun. The SVT-38 entered active service immediately, as the Soviet Union was by then involved in the Winter War with Finland.

As a result of combat experience in the Winter War, the SVT-38 was considerably modified. These changes were – as is often the case in these circumstances – aimed at simplifying production and improving reliability. On the 13 April 1940 the Defence Committee approved a modified version of the Tokarev, designated SVT-40.

The Tokarev Model 1940 rifle included several improvements over the Model 1938. The major alterations included the redesign of the wooden stock, which was changed from two-piece to one-piece; the relocation of the cleaning rod to below the stock rather than alongside it; and the addition of a ventilated metal guard to replace the forward portion of the SVT-38 stock.

However, a number of disadvantages which had been noted in the SVT-38 were not addressed during the change to the SVT-40. These included dispersion of the first round fired, inconvenient regulation of the gas system, sensitivity to contamination by dust or thick grease, and sensitivity to high and low temperatures. The detachable magazine was also considered a problem because it could be lost.

Nevertheless, the SVT-40 was put into production on 1 July 1940, and 3,416 were manufactured in the first month. Output increased rapidly, with 8,100 leaving the factory in August, 10,700 in September and 11,960 during the first 18 days of October.

Sniper's rifle

The SVT-40 was also employed as a sniper's rifle, although not without certain problems. The specifications for this had been agreed on the 8 April 1940 and basically consisted of fitting a telescopic sight, with an unusual curved mount, to the rear of the action, and more careful finishing of the bore. The sniper version thus produced was tested against a Mosin-Nagant sniper rifle, with somewhat disappointing results. Production of this variant was stopped by the beginning of October 1942.

On 20 May 1942, the State Committee for Defence approved the issue of Tokarev rifles modified for selective fire, due to a shortage of machine-guns and sub-machine guns. These were designated AVT-40 (*Avtomaticheskiy Vintovka Tokareva*, or Automatic Rifle Tokarev Model 1940). The difference basically lies in the selector lever. If pushed to the left the weapon will fire semi-automatically, and if it is an AVT the lever can be swung to the right to allow full-automatic fire – in this position the trigger is allowed to travel further to the rear, disengaging the sear. To tell the difference be-

The Tokarev's low bore line means that selective fire models are easier to control than other full-power, full-auto rifles.

Operation: The gas cylinder drives a long rod back against the working parts. This ejects the used round and cocks the weapon. A powerful spring then forces the working parts forward, chambering a fresh round as it does so.

Manufacture: As with most Soviet weapons, the SVT is solidly manufactured, although its woodwork might not be of the best quality. However, the Tokarev is a complex weapon, and needs care and attention to continue working.

Ammunition: The Tokarev is fed from a 10-round box magazine, and fires the full-power 7.62-mm×54R rimmed round developed for the Russian army in the 1890s.

Trigger: The SVT-40 is semi-auto only, requiring a pull of the trigger to fire a round. A later model, the AVT-40, was a selective fire weapon capable of full-auto fire.

tween the two, apart from the cut-out in the stock to allow the lever to swing, the butt of the AVT is usually stamped on the right side with a large letter 'A'.

In spite of reliability problems, the SVT/AVT remained in production and use throughout the war. In 1941 1,031,861 SVT-40s (plus 34,782 sniper versions) left the factories; and in 1942 the figures were 264,148 and 14,210 respectively. Production continued until an order from the State Committee for Defence ended it at the beginning of January 1945.

Captured examples were coveted by German troopers, who appear to have preferred the SVT to their own G43 semi-auto rifles. One should bear in mind that generally there is a feeling that another guy's weapon may be better than your own – witness the preference by some soldiers in Vietnam for the AK-47 rather than their M16.

The SVT is easy to use. The 10-

Tokarev-armed naval infantrymen pause while on patrol somewhere near the border with German-occupied Norway. It is summer, which is fortunate, since the Tokarev is prone to jam in extreme cold weather. The man with the shorter-ranged, less accurate PPSh can at least rely on his SMG in any conditions.

bination of good stock design together with a low bore-line. The system of operation is essentially the same as that of the later FN FAL. The bolt carrier is propelled rearwards by a blow from the gas-piston rod, unlocking the bolt which extracts and ejects the fired case; the recoil spring forces the carrier and bolt forward, chambering a fresh round from the magazine. The breech is locked by the bolt being cammed down into a recess in the receiver. The SVT has a fluted chamber (like the G3 – so what's new!), to ease extraction, and fired cases are, therefore, easily identifiable.

Short-lived weapon

It would appear that Tokarev's rifle did not survive in Soviet service beyond the end of the war, although other armies (such as Finland) kept it in at least second-line service for some time afterwards. In spite of its relatively short life, it remains one of the more interesting developments in the history of modern small arms.

round magazine is inserted into the magazine well in the usual fashion, and the cocking handle pulled back and released to chamber a round. The magazine latch folds up out of the way.

Even on full-automatic the Tokarev is very controllable, in spite of the use of a full-power cartridge. Recoil tends to come straight back into the shoulder rather than cause the weapon to climb. This is due to a com-

Although the sniper variant of the Tokarev was considered a failure, Hero of the Soviet Union, Nikolai Ilyin, used one on the 2nd Ukrainian Front to make over three hundred confirmed kills.

On Target with the Tokarev

The Tokarev 7.62-mm pistol was the first handgun to be designed and produced in the USSR, and many hundreds of thousands have been made in several countries.

From the Smith & Wesson .44 Russian to the gas-seal Nagant of 1895, all Russian army pistols were of foreign design — but in the early 1920s the new Soviet army demanded a locally-designed, modern, automatic pistol instead of an archaic revolver. As a result of this demand two designs were put forward, both in 7.65-mm ACP calibre; then, the Artillery Commission (responsible for small arms design) demanded that the 7.63-mm Mauser cartridge should be the future standard pistol round. The power of this cartridge was such that it wiped out both the contestants on the spot, since neither could be adapted to take the new cartridge.

Cossack to the rescue

In 1929 a new designer appeared, Fedor Tokarev. He had spent his apprenticeship with a village blacksmith in the 1880s, then went to a Military Trade School to qualify as an armourer. He became an NCO in the Cossacks, returned to the Trade School as instructor, and by the time the 1914-18 war began was an officer, working on designs for an automatic rifle. In spite of his commissioned rank he survived the bloodier aspects of the Revolution to become Assistant Director for Inspection and Manufacture at the Sestoresk arms factory.

Now he stepped forward with a design for a 7.62-mm service automatic, one based on John Moses Browning's 'swinging link' method of breech locking used in the US Army's Colt M1911 pistol. In this system the barrel is attached to the pistol frame by link hinges at both ends. The top of the barrel carries ribs that engage in grooves in the underside of the slide. With the slide forward and the breech closed, the lugs and grooves are engaged.

When the pistol is fired, the slide moves rearwards due to the recoil and, because of the engaged lugs, takes the barrel with it. But the moving barrel is made to pivot, because the lower end of the link is pinned to the frame. As a result, after a short period of locked recoil, the barrel comes free of the slide, which continues rearwards while the barrel is stopped. The slide goes back, compressing a return spring and cocking the hammer, then goes forward under spring pressure to load a fresh round into the chamber and push the barrel forward, lifting it above the link pivot

A child in an Afghan refugee camp shows off a Tokarev pistol acquired from the Afghan army. Remember Kipling's 'arithmetic on the frontier': a 10-rupee rifle or an old Russian pistol in the hands of a boy can kill you as surely as the latest rifle. The Soviet withdrawal has left Afghanistan with one of the most heavily-armed populations outside the Middle East.

so that the lugs engage once more into the slide.

So far so good, but not very original. (And remember that by this time the Browning GP35 had been perfected, and had gone beyond the swinging link to use a fixed lug.) But Tokarev had aimed his design at the practical soldier.

For example, he designed the hammer and lockwork in a single removable module, so that the entire mechanism could be slipped out of the frame very easily for cleaning or repair. He appreciated that the weakest spot on any automatic weapon is the feed system, and particularly the magazine lips. So, the lips on his magazine were rudimentary, and the actual feed guide was machined into the steel of the frame, where it was unlikely to wear or be damaged. Minor damage to the actual magazine lips didn't matter much, and rough repair was quite sufficient to allow the weapon to work well.

No safety

Another feature was the complete absence of any sort of safety catch or grip safety. Tokarev appears to have argued that revolvers did not usually have safety catches, and that proper training would ensure the weapons were used properly. Moreover, when pistols are needed, they are usually needed in a hurry, with no time to think about safety catches. It is interesting to see that similar thinking in the 1970s led to a number of modern designs without manual safety devices, though in these some fairly complex automatic safeties were incorporated.

It would be as well here to explain why the Artillery Commission's demand for a 7.63-mm Mauser chambered pistol became translated into a 7.62-mm design. In fact there was no difference; 7.62-mm was the standard Soviet rifle calibre, and the 7.63-mm Mauser bullet worked perfectly adequately in the Soviet 7.62-mm rifling. So the cartridge was re-christened 7.62-mm to avoid problems over nomenclature and as the '7.62-mm Patron Obrazets 1930g' remained the Soviet pistol and submachine gun round until the 1960s. And having 7.62-mm as the common pistol, rifle, sub-machine gun and machine-gun calibre certainly reduced manufacturing problems in the barrel-making factories.

Tokarev's design sailed through the usual tests with flying colours, and in December 1930 manufacture of 1,000 Tula-Tokarev 30 (TT-30) pistols was authorised for troop trials. These took place in 1931/32 and approval was given for adoption into service. At the same time, however, some sugges-

Inside the Tokarev

The Tokarev is based on the Browning automatic pistol design with modifications to the lock mechanism and the magazine. There is no safety catch or grip safety, the designer apparently believing that the Soviet army did not need any since the revolvers the Tokarev replaced had no safety either. Compare this cutaway with that of the Colt M1911.

Foresight

The accuracy of the Tokarev depends largely on your choice of ammunition. Shooting the Soviet 7.62-mm M30 cartridge, it comes back into the aim quite quickly. Tokarevs can usually accept 7.63-mm Mauser, but this tends to produce too much recoil for an accurate double-tap.

tions for modifications to simplify manufacture were put forward.

The TT-30 had a removable backstrap on the butt, to simplify fitting and repairing the trigger spring; this was changed so that the entire butt formed a solid portion of the frame, the trigger spring problem being considered less important than solid design. The most significant change suggested was to do away with milling out the two lugs on top of the barrel

Field stripping the Tokarev

1 Press the magazine catch on the left-hand side of the butt and remove the magazine.

2 Rack back the slide and check the chamber is clear.

6 Remove the recoil spring and guide from the front of the slide.

7 Then turn the barrel bushing to the right to unlock the barrel.

Slide
Cock the Tokarev by pulling back the slide with your left hand. The vertical grooves help give you a grip.

Barrel link
As on the Colt M1911, the link allows the barrel to drop out of the slot in the slide, unlocking the action after firing.

Firing pin

Firing pin spring

Firing pin stop

Rear sight

Hammer spring

Disconnector

Hammer pin

Hammer and sear housing
The hammer mechanism comes out of the Tokarev as one piece.

Trigger spring

8-round box magazine

...ling
...r grooves, right-hand
...st.

Recoil spring

Recoil spring guide

Barrel link pin

Slide stop

Magazine catch

7.62-mm × 25 cartridge
The 7.63-mm Mauser bullet fitted Soviet 7.62-mm rifling, so the Soviet M30 pistol cartridge was a hybrid design. This suited the Red Army, as its rifles and SMGs were all 7.62-mm calibre.

Magazine
The magazine guide lips are machined into the pistol itself, which removes a common source of malfunctions in automatic pistols.

3 The slide stop barrel locking pin is located on the right side of the receiver.

4 Remove the locking pin from the left.

5 Now pull the barrel assembly and slide forward out of the guides in the receiver.

8 Remove the barrel and barrel bushing from the slide forwards.

9 Lift the hammer mechanism out of the receiver.

10 Completed field strip.

One of the most famous Soviet wartime photographs shows a Red Army officer leading the way with a Tokarev. The Nagant gas-seal revolvers it replaced could have most of their problems cured by a hammer, and the TT-33 was similarly built for strength and reliability.

and, instead, machine two complete rings around the barrel, the top sections of which acted as the lugs. This made no difference to the pistol's operation, but made manufacture much quicker, since the rings could be machined on the lathe as the exterior of the barrel was being turned, instead of being cut by a separate machine in a separate manufacturing step.

These changes were adopted and the design now became the TT-33 pistol; it went into production in 1936. It has been estimated that about 93,000 TT-30s were made before the TT-33 went into service. It is believed to have stayed in production in Russia until 1954.

The TT-33's variants

As is usual with their weapons, the Soviets exported countless thousands of Tokarev pistols and authorised manufacture by the satellites, so that there are several minor variations on the TT-33 design. There are the Chinese Type 54, the Polish TT, the Hungarian M48, the North Korean Type 68 and the Yugoslavian M57, all of which are simply locally-made Tokarevs. Distinguishing them is largely a matter of examining the markings, though there are some points of note. The Chinese Type 54 has grooves on the rear of the slide (in order to grip it for cocking) that are entirely narrow, whereas the original Soviet model, and the Polish copies, use alternate broad and narrow grooves. The Hungarian M48 also has narrow grooves and can be further identified by the badge moulded into the grips – a star, wheatsheaf and hammer surrounded by a wreath. The Korean Type 68 has slide grooves that are narrow but sloping forward; internally, the swinging link has been abandoned and replaced by a fixed lug with a cam path, similar to that used in the Browning GP35, and it has the magazine release positioned at the heel of the butt instead of using a push-button behind the trigger guard as do all the others. The Yugoslavian M57 also has forward-sloping grooves on the slide.

The only major variations, and perhaps the most practical designs of all, were the Hungarian-made 'Tokagypt' and the Yugoslavian M70(d), both of which were the TT-33 redesigned into 9-mm Parabellum calibre. The Tokagypt was developed for the Egyptian army, but strangely it did not go down well with them, and most of these sen-

sible pistols finished in the hands of Egyptian police and security forces.

The Yugoslavian M70(d) appears to have been developed for the export market but, again, nobody seems to have taken it up in any numbers. It is likely that countries outside the Soviet Bloc, to which these pistols may have been offered for sale, preferred to adopt more modern 9-mm

South African forces in pursuit of SWAPO guerrillas carry captured Soviet weapons. The man on the right has a Tokarev TT-33 in his holster. To his front lies an AK fitted with the 100-round drum magazine of the RPD light machine-gun.

Parabellum designs instead of the somewhat elderly Tokarev.

Elderly it may be, but as a practical combat pistol there is not much wrong with the TT-33. The 7.62-mm Mauser cartridge has a high velocity and good penetrating power, while the weight of the bullet is not such as to cause excessive recoil, so that it is possible to fire accurately and get back into the aim quite quickly. The simplicity and strength of the design you can take for granted – the Soviets would not have kept it in production for nearly 25 years unless it had those features.

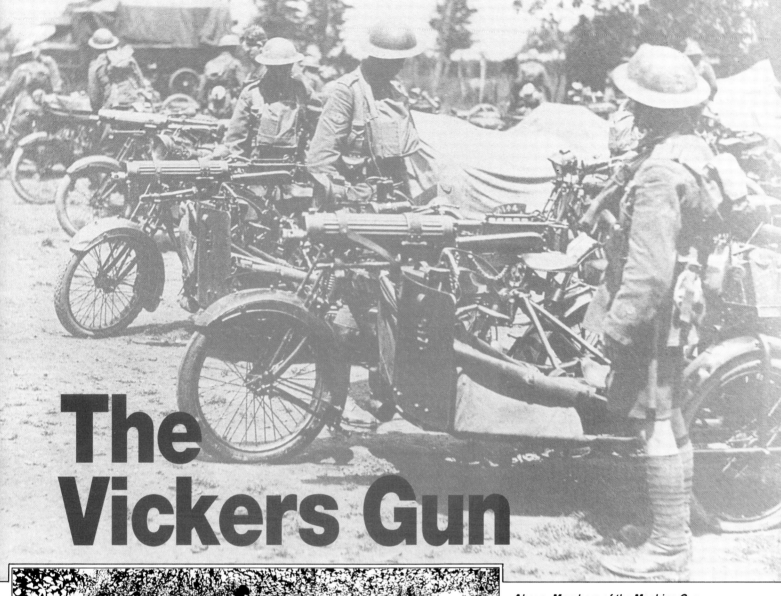

The Vickers Gun

Above: Members of the Machine Gun Corps man their motorcycle combinations in France in 1918. The Vickers gun could be fired from the side-car, but was more often dismounted and used on a tripod.

Sixty years later, the Vickers gun was still being used in combat. This South African gun is covering one of the crossings between South West Africa (now Namibia) and Angola.

Hiram Maxim has some claim to having produced the most successful of early machine-gun designs. The British Army was one of the first to adopt the Maxim gun following a demonstration in 1887. A joint company was set up with Vickers in Kent, and from this factory Maxim guns went out to serve with the British Army the length and breadth of the Empire, then at its greatest extent.

In the early years of the 20th century the engineers at Vickers realised that the Maxim could be considerably improved. Careful stress studies revealed that some weight could be saved in construction and that the basic Maxim action could be simplified.

The resulting design was the Vickers gun. It was not that much lighter than contemporary unmodified Maxims, but it was considerably more reliable. It was approved for British Army service in 1912. Issued at a rate of two guns per infantry battalion, it was looked upon as a new-fangled invention, and was not really trusted.

Once British troops reached France in 1914, however, it soon became clear that the machine-gun had changed the face of warfare. Among the first to suffer were the cavalry who had refused to issue the weapon. They soon realised that a single machine-gun firing from a hidden position on the

Inside the Vickers

It may appear somewhat archaic, and indeed it was based on one of the earliest successful machine-gun designs, but the modified Maxim gun produced by Vickers was one of the finest weapons of the 20th century. Entering service in 1912, the Vickers was supplied to many armies, and it remained in combat use into the 1980s

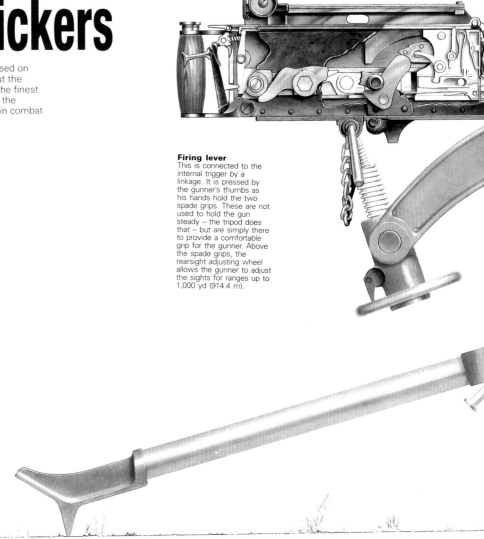

Firing lever
This is connected to the internal trigger by a linkage. It is pressed by the gunner's thumbs as his hands hold the two spade grips. These are not used to hold the gun steady – the tripod does that – but are simply there to provide a comfortable grip for the gunner. Above the spade grips, the rearsight adjusting wheel allows the gunner to adjust the sights for ranges up to 1,000 yd (914.4 m).

horizon could keep an entire cavalry battalion immobilised. As a result, the issue of Vickers guns increased dramatically. New production lines opened, many at Royal Ordnance factories.

Water-cooling system

Prolonged firing of any machine-gun raises the barrel temperature to red heat, causing it to lose rigidity and thus accuracy. The Vickers avoided that problem by encasing the barrel in a cooling jacket, filled with water. The jacket held just under four litres of water, which would boil after three minutes of sustained fire. In the early stages of the process this boiling helped to cool the barrel, as the minute bubbles of water vapour carried heat away, but once all the water turned to steam, the barrel temperature could again rise unchecked.

In the early days, the vapour was allowed to escape as fresh cooling water was added, but the cloud of steam gave the gun position away to the enemy and invited retaliatory fire.

A heavily-used Vickers gun emits a plume of steam from its cooling system, giving away its position to enemy observers. The use of a condenser prevented such tell-tale signs.

The economical solution to the problem was to divert the steam via a flexible pipe into a condensing can, from where the water could be re-used in the machine-gun's cooling jacket.

Despite the water-cooling system, the Vickers barrels needed changing every 10,000 rounds. As it was possible to fire 10,000 rounds in an hour, it became common practice to change a Vickers barrel every hour, on the hour. A well-trained crew could accomplish the task in about two minutes, with little or no loss of cooling water.

Like most machine-guns of the period the Vickers gun was prone to jamming, mainly induced by poor quality ammunition. A series of drills was devised to clear the weapon rapidly, and it was this specialist requirement, along with the need for regular skilled barrel-changing, which led to the establishment of the Machine Gun Corps. The new corps was manned by specialists who could get the best out of their weapons, and who could pass on their skills and experience more easily than if machine-gunners were spread out among all of the corps and regiments of the British

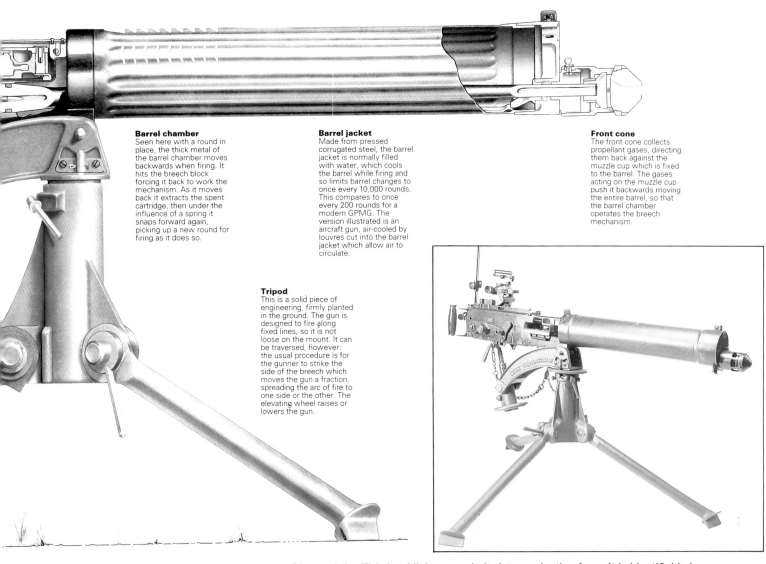

Barrel chamber
Seen here with a round in place, the thick metal of the barrel chamber moves backwards when firing. It hits the breech block forcing it back to work the mechanism. As it moves back it extracts the spent cartridge, then under the influence of a spring it snaps forward again, picking up a new round for firing as it does so.

Barrel jacket
Made from pressed corrugated steel, the barrel jacket is normally filled with water, which cools the barrel while firing and so limits barrel changes to once every 10,000 rounds. This compares to once every 200 rounds for a modern GPMG. The version illustrated is an aircraft gun, air-cooled by louvres cut into the barrel jacket which allow air to circulate.

Front cone
The front cone collects propellant gases, directing them back against the muzzle cup which is fixed to the barrel. The gases acting on the muzzle cup push it backwards moving the entire barrel, so that the barrel chamber operates the breech mechanism.

Tripod
This is a solid piece of engineering, firmly planted in the ground. The gun is designed to fire along fixed lines, so it is not loose on the mount. It can be traversed, however: the usual procedure is for the gunner to strike the side of the breech which moves the gun a fraction, spreading the arc of fire to one side or the other. The elevating wheel raises or lowers the gun.

Above, right: This is a Vickers gun in its late production form. It is identifiable by the lack of corrugation on the barrel jacket and the final form of muzzle booster. This particular weapon is fitted with an indirect fire sight adapted from that used on mortars.

Army. Gradually, the heavy machine-guns assigned to the various divisions were re-allocated to companies of the new corps. By the end of the war, the Machine Gun Corps could boast 6,432 officers and 124,920 other ranks.

In action, a Vickers gun could be kept firing as long as ammunition was fed into it and the cooling water was topped up. It was usually mounted on a heavy tripod, firing along fixed lines. There are records of Vickers guns providing support fire for days at a time, although such intensive use required equally intensive support. The gun could devour ammunition at a prodigious rate, and a considerable supply had to be kept on hand at all times.

Ammunition preparation

Once on site, the rounds could not simply be loaded into the gun. The ammunition cases were multi-purpose, the rounds being intended for use in a variety of weapons ranging

Vickers gunners provide supporting fire on a gas-covered battlefield. A good crew could change a barrel in a couple of minutes; a task which needed completing every 10,000 rounds or so, or about once an hour in sustained fire.

from Lee-Enfield rifles through Lewis guns to the Vickers. They came in 100-round cardboard cartons, and before use they had to be loaded into the fabric belts used by the Vickers. This was an extremely time-consuming process which was often done by hand, although a special loading machine was eventually produced.

The success of the Vickers during World War I ensured that after 1918 it would remain the standard sustained fire machine-gun of the British Army and of British Empire forces. During the inter-war years a number of variants on the same basic design were produced, both in the original .303-in calibre and in .50-in calibre, primarily for use in tanks. The Royal Navy also used the larger calibre, often in multiple mounts as an anti-aircraft weapon.

Large number of Vickers guns remained in service at the outbreak of

The machine-gun seen here, being used from a Chevrolet truck of the Long Range Desert Group, is not the usual .303 Vickers, but a heavier .50-calibre version originally produced for use on light tanks.

World War II, and by 1940 huge numbers of older weapons had been taken from storage and were pressed into use for home defence and as anti-aircraft weapons. The loss of much of the British Army's front-line equipment at Dunkirk increased demand, and production of the Vickers was stepped up.

The most obvious production short-cut was the introduction of a smooth barrel jacket, which used less metal than the earlier corrugated jackets. A new muzzle booster was introduced later in the war, and in 1943 the Mk 8Z boat-tailed bullet entered widespread use to provide a useful effective range of over 4,000 m (13,120 ft) in indirect fire. Normal sights were useless at such distances, and a mortar sight was adapted for long-range operations.

Around the world

Vickers guns were used everywhere, from defending England's beaches in 1940, through arming Long Range Desert Group patrols in 1941, supporting the landings in Italy in 1943, being used from Normandy to the German border in 1944 and 1945,

to contributing to the XIVth Army's defeat of the Japanese in Burma in 1945.

After the war, the Vickers remained in British Army service until 1968, when it was declared obsolete. The Royal Marines, however, kept theirs in service well into the 1970s. Commonwealth and former Commonwealth armies also used the Vickers, their weapons seeing combat on the Indian sub-continent in the 1970s and on the South African-Angolan border in the 1980s.

It is now very unlikely to be found in front-line use, but the Vickers remains one of the finest sustained fire machine-guns ever built. Although it is still better in that role than most modern general-purpose machine-guns, its weight means that it has little or no place in modern mobile warfare, and age and lack of spares have finally put an end to a long and distinguished service life. Through all of its long history, it remained essentially unchanged. The last weapons manufactured in the 1950s differed only in minor details from the original turn-of-the-century guns.

Walther P38

A German soldier armed with a P38 pistol shepherds a column of American prisoners eastwards during the early days of the Ardennes offensive, December 1944.

The seizure of power by the National Socialists in Germany in 1933 was the signal for a rapid expansion of German military might. The Nazis swept aside the provisions of the Treaty of Versailles, and the Wehrmacht set into motion long-prepared plans for conscription and for the re-establishment of a military manufacturing industry.

One of the Wehrmacht's requirements was for a new pistol to replace the famous Pistole '08, the Luger. This was an excellent weapon to fire, if a little sensitive to hard use, but it was also expensive to produce. What the high command wanted was a pistol that could be more economically manufactured than the Luger, but which would incorporate the improvements which were coming to the fore in the 1930s. The weapon which was eventually chosen was the Walther P38, but not until a long programme of development and modification had been completed.

Carl Walther Waffenfabrik of Ulm had produced its first original semi-automatic pistol design in 1908. In 1929, the firm introduced the PP or, Polizei Pistole, in 7.65-mm calibre. One of the most influential pistol designs ever produced, it was a simple blowback weapon which for the first time had a successful double action. When the Wehrmacht called for a new service pistol, the company offered an enlarged version of the PP in 9-mm calibre, known as the Militar Pistole, or MP.

Locking breech

This was not acceptable to the army, which considered 9-mm Parabellum rounds too large to fire through a blowback pistol. They wanted a weapon with some kind of locking system. The Armee Pistole, or AP, which Walther then developed had a locked breech, but was again unacceptable to the Wehrmacht because it had a concealed hammer, and the army wanted an external hammer so that it was possible to see at a glance if the weapon was cocked.

The Heeres Pistole incorporated the German army's recommendations and, with some modifications to ease production, was taken into service as the Pistole 38. Breech-locking on the P38 occurs due to a wedge-shaped locking plate under the barrel. When the gun is fired, the barrel and slide recoil until the locking plate disengages and stops the barrel. The double-action trigger mechanism was derived from that of the PP. The slide-mounted safety catch locked the firing pin and allowed the hammer to drop safely. The only way to remove the lock was by a deliberate pull on the trigger, thus allowing the weapon to be carried safely, yet instantly ready for action.

The main recipients of the first P38s were the troops of the newly formed Panzer arm, who had their weapons for the Anschluss with Austria and the occupation of Czechoslovakia. Two thousand of the essentially similar Heeres Pistole were sold to Sweden in 1939, where it entered service as the P/39. By the time World War II started, other troops were beginning to be issued with the P38.

Popular pistol

Soldiers liked the P38. In action, they proved very reliable, were handy to hold and point, and were sufficiently accurate for most tasks. The trigger action was crisp and clean, and the working parts proved resistant to the ingress of dirt which was common under operational conditions. However, one problem emerged on the Eastern Front. It was nothing to do with the design of the pistol, but arose out of the superior training of the average German soldier. From recruit stage on, the German army taught its men to strip and clean their personal weapons every day. Before reassembly the working parts were oiled. In the extreme cold of the

Russian winter, the oil would often freeze solid, and the only solution was to leave the gun clean but free of oil. Fortunately, the P38 could stand up to such treatment, unlike many other finely-tuned German weapons, which really needed lubrication in order to function.

The P38 was never able to completely replace the Luger. One reason for this state of affairs was that troops in all of the occupied territories had to be armed when not actually on a military base. As almost every soldier was either billeted amidst the population, or had tasks which would take him

Polish volunteers who fought with the French resistance pose for the camera with a heterogenous collection of weapons, including a P38, Sten guns and Mauser rifles.

out from the security of a German military establishment, then almost every soldier had to have a personal weapon.

Unfortunately, there were insufficient numbers rolling off the production lines to meet demand. Soon after the war started the HP production line was taken over, and as the war progressed and demand showed no signs

The P38 is still made today under the designation P1. This is a silenced version intercepted by British customs en route for Libya, where it was presumably intended for one of the terrorist groups then in residence.

Above: Walther pioneered the double-action/single-action semi-automatic pistol. This has proven enduringly popular with military users despite its effect on first-round accuracy.

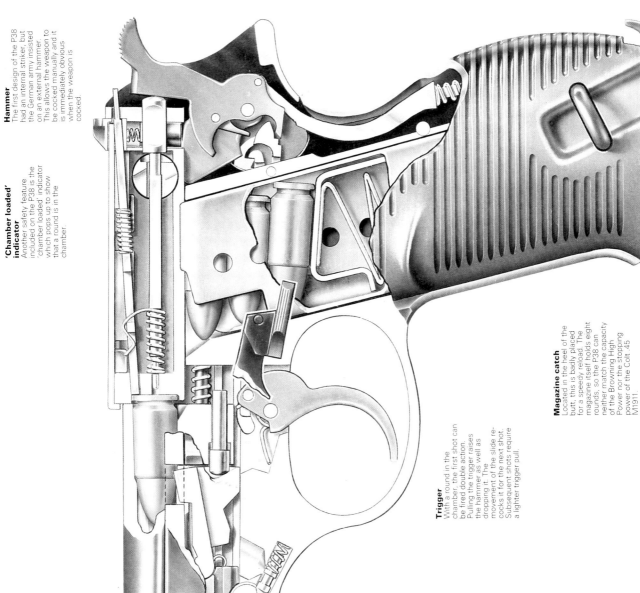

Hammer
The first design of the P38 had an internal striker, but the German army insisted on an external hammer. This allows the weapon to be cocked manually and it is immediately obvious when the weapon is cocked.

'Chamber loaded' indicator
Another safety feature included on the P38 is the 'chamber loaded' indicator which pops up to show that a round is in the chamber.

Magazine catch
Located in the heel of the butt, this is badly placed for a speedy reload. The magazine itself holds eight rounds, so the P38 can neither match the capacity of the Browning High Power nor the stopping power of the Colt .45 M1911

Trigger
With a round in the chamber, the first shot can be fired double action. Pulling the trigger raises the hammer as well as dropping it. The movement of the slide re-cocks it for the next shot. Subsequent shots require a lighter trigger pull.

Slide
The slides on late-war P38s are often poorly finished as frantic production schedules ruled out fine machine work. Slides and receivers are both stamped but were sometimes mismatched by 1944-5.

Inside the P38

Over one million Walther P38s were manufactured before the end of World War II. Production peaked during 1943-44, although the finish of wartime P38s deteriorated from 1942 onwards. Different manufacturers can be distinguished by codes stamped on the receiver. Walther-made P38s are marked 'ac'; ones manufactured by Mauser are coded 'byf' and those by Spreewerke 'cyq'.

of slackening, new production lines had been set up by Mauser at Oberndorf and by Spreewerke at Grottau. Components were manufacturerd in the occupied territories, notably at Fabrique Nationale in Belgium and at Waffenfabrik Brun, the former Brno works in Czechoslovakia. As production expanded the general standard of manufacture declined, although even in its late war form the P38 remained an excellent service pistol.

Although everybody wanted the P38 or the Luger, they had to make do with what they could get. There were vast stockpiles of captured weaponry, as well as weapons produced for the civilian market. The result must have been a quartermaster's nightmare, as troops found themselves carrying ex-Russian Nagant gas-seal revolvers, shiny little Mauser pocket pistols, imported Spanish automatics of dubious quality, and ancient French and Belgian revolvers in obsolete calibres.

Wall trophies

The end of the war was by no means the end of the P38 story. Many P38s became war trophies in 1945, and large numbers were pressed into service with countries like France, which needed to equip its forces while the native manufacturing industry got into gear again. Although French units used the P38 in Indo-China, the pistol had been replaced by the mid-1950s.

At the same time, however, the P38 got a new lease of life when it was selected to equip the new West German army. In 1957, it was once more in production at Walther. The design was slightly updated with the adoption of a dural slide, and was re-designated as the Pistole 1, or P1. Pistols manufactured for the civilian market have retained the P38 designation.

Although now rather long in the tooth and outclassed by the latest high-capacity 'super nine' pistols, the P1 and the P38 remain in production. They are effective and reliable weapons, and have been exported to a number of countries, in addition to serving the Bundeswehr.

Above: A Portuguese soldier loses his P38 during unarmed combat training. Many armies still use this famous pistol.

Below: German officers captured in Paris are on the wrong side of a Walther P38 held by a resistance fighter.

Index

Page numbers in *italics* refer to illustrations.

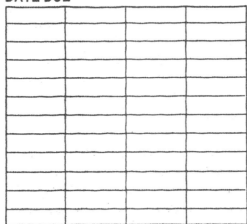